KNEELING CHRISTIAN

BY
THE UNKNOWN CHRISTIAN

INCLUDES
THE LIFE OF PRAYER
BY A.B. SIMPSON

AND

THE TRUE VINE: 31 MEDITATIONS
BY ANDREW MURRAY

Bridge-Logos
Orlando, FL 32822 USA

Bridge-Logos

Orlando, FL 32822 USA

The Kneeling Christian
by the Unknown Christian

Rewritten and updated by Harold Chadwick

Library of Congress Catalog Card Number: pending
International Standard Book Number: 978-0-88270-397-8

Scripture quotations are from the *King James Version* of the Bible.

G163.316.N.m706.352350

CONTENTS

THE KNEELING CHRISTIAN
BY AN UNKNOWN CHRISTIAN

Biography of The Unknown Christian..............................1

Preface 5

Chapter 1: God's Great Need 7

Chapter 2: Almost Incredible Promises....................15

Chapter 3: "Ask of Me and I Will Give" 25

Chapter 4: Asking for Signs.....................................37

Chapter 5: What Is Prayer? 51

Chapter 6: How Shall I Pray?...................................63

Chapter 7: Must I Agonize? 75

Chapter 8: Does God Always Answer Prayer?............91

Chapter 9: Answers to Prayer.................................101

Chapter 10: How God Answers Prayer 1-7

Chapter 11: Hindrances to Prayer 117

Chapter 12: Who May Pray?...................................129

Study Guide for The Kneeling Christian....................137

THE LIFE OF PRAYER
BY A.B. SIMPSON

Biography of A.B. Simpson 147

Photo Gallery...153

Preface 161

Chapter 1: The Pattern Prayer........................163

Chapter 2: Encouragements to Prayer........................179

Chapter 3: In His Name........................195

Chapter 4: The Prayer of Faith........................205

Chapter 5: Hindrances to Prayer........................221

Study Guide for The Life of Prayer........................237

THE TRUE VINE
MEDITATIONS ON JOHN 15:1-16
BY ANDREW MURRAY

Only a Branch........................245

Biography of Andrew Murray........................247

Photo Gallery........................253

Preface........................259

1. The Vine........................261

2. The Husbandman........................263

3. The Branch........................265

4. The Fruit........................267

5. More Fruit........................269

6. The Cleansing........................271

7. The Pruning Knife........................273

8. Abide........................275

9. Except Ye Abide........................277

10. The Vine........................279

11. Ye The Branches........................282

12. Much Fruit........................284

13. You Can Do Nothing 286

14. Withered Branches 288

15. Whatsoever Ye Will................................290

16. If Ye Abide 292

17. The Father Glorified..............................294

18. True Disciples......................................296

19. The Wonderful Love..............................298

20. Abide in My Love 300

21. Obey and Abide 302

22. Ye, Even As 304

23. Joy 306

24. Love One Another.................................308

25. Even As I Have Loved You........................310

26. Christ's Friendship: Its Origin 312

27. Christ's Friendship: Its Evidence.................314

28. Christ's Friendship: Its Intimacy.................316

29. Election 318

30. Abiding Fruit.......................................320

31. Prevailing Prayer 322

Study Guide for The True Vine.........................325

Biographical Entries 335

Index...357

BIOGRAPHY OF
THE UNKNOWN CHRISTIAN

For over 80 years, *The Kneeling Christian* has inspired, encouraged, and motivated hundreds-of-thousands to have a deeper prayer life. Only eternity will be long enough to reveal the miracles and salvations that resulted from the fervent prevailing prayers that rose to God's throne because of this book. And it will take eons of eternity for all the thanks of countless souls to be expressed to the humble author of this book who from the beginning identified himself only as an "Unknown Christian."

For years, all that readers of this book knew about the Unknown Christian was what could be determined from the book itself. He was humble, thus the pseudonym of an Unknown Christian. He was mature, probably in his fifties, because he speaks of something that happened 30 years in the past, and what happened would indicate that he was probably at least in his twenties at the time. He was extremely well-versed in the Scriptures, because he quotes them extensively. He was in a ministry of some type, and he was known by his peers for his prayer life, because he says in his Preface, "This book was written by request ..." Yet he wasn't proud of the fact, for he continues, like Paul, "and with much hesitancy." The fact that he was asked to write a book suggests that he had written other things. Last, he was obviously a student of prayer and of those who prayed, for

1

his knowledge of prayer is clearly seen, and he speaks much of many who prayed fervently and effectively and the results they obtained. A few other things can be gathered from the writing, but by and large readers have not known anything else about the author.

But now the British Library's Integrated Catalog on the Internet has identified the Unknown Christian as Albert Ernest Richardson. The catalog listing reads: "The Kneeling Christian. By the author of *How to Live a Victorious Life* [i. e., Albert E. Richardson]," and shows a publication date of 1924.

How to Live a Victorious Life is recorded by the British Library as being written "By an Unknown Christian [i.e., Albert Ernest Richardson]," and published in 1921.

An Unknown Christian [i.e., Albert Ernest Richardson], is listed as also writing two other books before 1924: *The Happy Christian* and *He Shall Come Again*. Both books were published in 1922.

From this it appears that *The Kneeling Christian*, published in 1924, was the fourth book by an Unknown Christian. The British Library currently lists in their Integrated Catalog another eight books written under the pseudonym of an Unknown Christian [i.e., Albert Ernest Richardson] that were published after 1924.

Albert Ernest Richardson was a British Anglican clergyman and missionary. The University of Birmingham Information Services, Special Collections Department, lists his date of birth on their web site, MUNDUS (Gateway to missionary collections in the United Kingdom) as being circa 1868, but they give no date for his death.

However, another web site that lists author anniversaries gives the specific dates of August 18, 1868 as his date of birth, and December 23, 1951 as his date of death. This site also identifies him as the Unknown Christian in their listing of his death: "1951: Rev. Albert Ernest RICHARDSON (ps [pseudonym]: An Unknown CHRISTIAN)."

A. E. Richardson was educated at Oxford High School, London City Technical College, and the University of Oxford. He received a Bachelor of Arts (B.A.) degree in 1894, a Masters of Arts (M.A.) degree in 1897, and a Bachelor of Divinity (B.D.) degree in 1901.

In 1895 he offered his services to the Church Missionary Society (CMS) but was not accepted. He was ordained a deacon in the Anglican Church in 1896, and a priest in 1897. From 1896 through 1898 he was curate of St. Clement's in Ipswich, England.

In 1898 Richardson applied again to the CMS for missionary service and was accepted. He was sent to Lagos in Nigeria, and from there traveled overland to Tripoli in Libya as a member of a pioneer party for the Hausaland Mission, led by Herbert Tugwell, who was the CMS Bishop of West Equatorial Africa. He returned to England in 1900.

In 1902 he applied again for service with the CMS and was again accepted. He was sent to Bombay, India, in 1903, and remained there until 1905 when he resigned and left missionary service for medical reasons.

In addition to the books he wrote under the pseudonym of an Unknown Christian, he authored *Hausaland and the Gospel* under his own name, A. E. Richardson. It was published by the Church Missionary Society in 1901.

Nothing further is recorded of his ministry or life, but the British Library's Integrated Catalog lists over a dozen books published under the pseudonym of an Unknown Christian, starting with *How to Live a Victorious Life* in 1921.

The last book currently listed in the Integrated Catalog was published in 1937: "*God's Greatest Precious Promise*. By an Unknown Christian [i.e. Albert Ernest Richardson]."

PREFACE

A traveler in China visited a heathen temple on a great feast day. Many worshippers of the hideous idol were in its sacred shrine. The visitor noticed that most of the devotees brought with them small pieces of paper on which prayers had been written or printed. These they would wrap up in little balls of stiff mud and fling at the idol. He asked the reason for this strange proceeding, and was told that if the mud ball stuck fast to the idol, then the prayer would assuredly be answered; but if the mud fell off, the prayer was rejected by the god.

We may smile at this peculiar way of testing the acceptability of a prayer. But is it not a fact that the majority of Christian men and women who pray to a living God know very little about real prevailing prayer? Yet prayer is the key that unlocks the door of God's treasure house.

It is not too much to say that all real growth in the spiritual life—all victory over temptation, all confidence and peace in the presence of difficulties and dangers, all tranquility of spirit in times of great disappointment or loss, all habitual communion with God—depend upon the practice of secret prayer.

This book was written by request, and with much hesitancy. It goes forth with much prayer. May He who said, "Men ought always to pray, and not to faint," "teach us to pray" (Luke 18:1, 11:1).

Chapter 1

GOD'S GREAT NEED

"God wondered." This is a very striking thought. The very boldness of the idea ought surely to arrest the attention of every earnest Christian man, woman, and child. A wondering God! Why, how staggered we might well be if we knew the cause of God's wonder. Yet we find it to be, apparently, a very little thing. But if we are willing to consider the matter carefully, we shall discover it to be one of the greatest possible importance to every believer in the Lord Jesus Christ. Nothing else is so momentous—so vital—to our spiritual welfare.

God "wondered that there was no intercessor" (Isaiah 59:16). But this was in the days of long ago, before the coming of the Lord Jesus Christ "full of grace and truth" (John 1:14), before the outpouring of the Holy Spirit, full of grace and power, "helping our infirmity," "himself making intercession for us" and in us (Romans 8:26). Yes, and before the truly amazing promises of our Savior regarding prayer; before people knew very much about prayer; in the days when sacrifices for their sins loomed larger in their eyes than supplication for other sinners.

Oh, how great must be God's wonder today. For how few there are among us who know what prevailing prayer really is. Every one of us would confess that we believe in prayer, yet how many of us truly believe in the power of prayer? Now, before we go a step further, may the writer most earnestly implore you not to read hurriedly what is contained in these chapters. Much—very much—depends upon the way in which every reader receives what is here recorded. For everything depends upon prayer.

Why are many Christians so often defeated? Because they pray so little. Why are many church workers so often discouraged and disheartened? Because they pray so little.

Why do most Christians see so few brought "out of darkness into his marvelous light" by their ministry? (1 Peter 2:9). Because they pray so little.

Why are not our churches simply on fire for God? Because there is so little real prayer.

The Lord Jesus is as powerful today as ever before. The Lord Jesus is as anxious for sinners to be saved as ever before. His arm is not shortened that it cannot save: but He cannot stretch forth His arm unless we pray more—and more really pray.

We may be assured of this—the secret of all failure is our failure in secret prayer.

If God wondered in the days of Isaiah, we need not be surprised to find that in the days of His flesh our Lord marveled. He marveled at the unbelief of some—unbelief that actually prevented Him from doing any mighty work in their cities (Mark 6:6).

But we must remember that those who were guilty of this unbelief saw no beauty in Him that they should desire Him, or believe on Him. What then must His marvel be today, when He sees among us who do truly love and adore Him, so few who really "stir themselves up to take hold of God" (Isaiah 64:7). Surely there is nothing so absolutely astonishing as a practically prayerless Christian? These are eventful and ominous days. In fact, there are many evidences that these are the last days in which God promised to pour out His Spirit—the Spirit of supplication—upon all flesh (Joel 2:28). Yet the vast majority of professing Christians scarcely know what supplication means; and very many of our churches not only have no prayer meeting, but sometimes unblushingly condemn such meetings, and even ridicule them.

The Church of England, recognizing the importance of worship and prayer, expects her clergy to read prayers in church every morning and evening.

But when this is done, is it not often in an empty church? And are not the prayers frequently raced through at a pace that precludes real worship? "Common prayer," too, often must necessarily be rather vague and indefinite.

And what of those churches where the old-fashioned weekly prayer meeting is retained? Would not weakly be the more appropriate word? C. H. Spurgeon had the joy of being able to say that he conducted a prayer meeting every Monday night "which scarcely ever numbers less than from a thousand to twelve hundred attendants."

My brothers and sisters, have we ceased to believe in prayer? If you still hold your weekly gathering for prayer, is it not a fact that the very great majority of your church members never come near it? Yes, and never even think of coming near it. Why is this? Whose fault is it?

"Only a prayer meeting"—how often we have heard the utterance. How many of those reading these words really enjoy a prayer meeting? Is it a joy or just a duty? Please forgive me for asking so many questions and for pointing out what appears to be a perilous weakness and a lamentable shortcoming in our churches. We are not out to criticize—far less to condemn. Anybody can do that. Our yearning desire is to stir up Christians to take hold of God as never before. We wish to encourage, to hearten, to uplift.

We are never so high as when we are on our knees.

Criticize? Who dare criticize another? When we look back upon the past and remember how much prayerlessness there has been in one's own life, words of criticism of others wither away on the lips.

But we believe the time has come when a clarion call to the individual and to the Church is needed—a call to prayer.

Now, dare we face this question of prayer? It seems a foolish question, for is not prayer a part and parcel of all religions? Yet we venture to ask you to look at this matter fairly and squarely. Do I really believe that prayer is a power? Is prayer the greatest power on earth, or is it not? Does prayer indeed "move the hand that moves the world?"

Do God's prayer-commands really concern Me? Do the promises of God concerning prayer still hold good? We have all been muttering yes, yes, yes as we read these questions. We dare not say no to any one of them. And yet... Has it ever occurred to you that our Lord never gave an unnecessary or an optional command? Do we really believe that our Lord never made a promise that He could not, or would not, fulfill? Our Savior's three great commands for definite action were: Pray ye, Do this, Go ye.

Are we obeying Him? How often His command, "Do this," is reiterated by our preachers today. One might almost think it was His only command. How seldom we are reminded of His bidding to pray and to go. Yet, without obedience to the "Pray ye," it is of little or no use at all either to "Do this" or to "Go."

In fact, it can easily be shown that all lack of success, and all failure in the spiritual life and in Christian work, is due to defective or insufficient prayer. Unless we pray correctly we cannot live correctly or serve correctly. This may appear, at first sight, to be gross exaggeration, but the more we think it over in the light Scripture throws upon it, the more convinced we will be of the truth of this statement.

Now, as we begin once more to see what the Bible has to say about this mysterious and wonderful subject, let us endeavor to read some of our Lord's promises as though we had never heard them before—and see what the effect will be.

Some twenty years ago the writer was studying in a Theological College. One morning early, a fellow-student— who is today one of England's foremost missionaries—burst into the room holding an open Bible in his hands. Although he was preparing for Holy Orders, he was at that time only a young convert to Christ.

He had gone up to the University caring for none of these things. Popular, clever, athletic—he had already won a place among the smart set of his college, when Christ claimed him. He accepted the Lord Jesus as his personal Savior, and became a very keen follower of his Master. The Bible was, comparatively, a new book to him, and as a result he was constantly making discoveries. On that memorable day on which he bolted into my room he cried excitedly—his face all aglow with mingled joy and surprise, "Do you believe this? Is it really true?"

"Believe what?" I asked, glancing at the open Bible with some astonishment.

"Why, this, " and he read in eager tones Matthew 21:21-22: "'If ye have faith and doubt not ... all things whatsoever ye shall ask in prayer, believing, ye shall receive.' Do you believe it? Is it true?"

"Yes," I replied, with much surprise at his excitement, "of course it's true—of course I believe it. Yet, through my mind there flashed all manner of thoughts.

"Well, that's a very wonderful promise," said he. "It seems to me to be absolutely limitless. Why don't we pray more?" And he went away, leaving me thinking hard. I had never looked at those verses quite in that way. As the door closed upon that eager young follower of the Master, I had a vision of my Savior and His love and His power such as I never had before. I had a vision of a life of prayer—yes, and limitless power, which I saw depended upon two things only—faith and prayer. For the moment I was thrilled. I fell on my knees, and as I bowed before my Lord what thoughts surged through my mind—what hopes and aspirations flooded my soul. God was speaking to me in an extraordinary way. This was a great call to prayer. But—to my shame be it said—I did not heed that call.

Where did I fail? True, I prayed a little more than before, but nothing much seemed to happen. Why? Was it because I did not see what a high standard the Savior requires in the inner life of those who would pray successfully?

Was it because I had failed to measure up my life to the perfect love standard so beautifully described in the thirteenth chapter of the first Epistle to the Corinthians?

For, after all, prayer is not just putting into action good resolutions to pray. Like David, we need to cry, "Create in me a clean heart, O God" (Psalm 51:10) before we can pray correctly. And the inspired words of the Apostle of love need to be heeded today as much as ever before: "Beloved, if our heart condemn us not, we have boldness toward God; and [then] whatsoever we ask, we receive of him" (1 John 3:21).

That is true, and I believe it. It is a limitless promise, and yet how little we realize it, how little we claim from Christ. And our Lord marvels at our unbelief. But if we could only read the Gospels for the first time, what an amazing book it would seem. Should not we marvel and wonder? And today I pass on that great call to you. Will you give heed to it? Will you profit by it? Or shall it fall on deaf ears and leave you prayerless?

Fellow Christians, let us awake! The devil is blinding our eyes. He is endeavoring to prevent us from facing this question of prayer. These pages are written by special request. But it is many months since that request came.

Every attempt to begin to write has been frustrated, and even now one is conscious of a strange reluctance to do so. There seems to be some mysterious power restraining the hand. Do we realize that there is nothing the devil dreads so much as prayer? His great concern is to keep us from praying. He loves to see us up to our eyes in work—provided we do not pray. He does not fear because we are eager and earnest Bible students—provided we are little in prayer. Someone has wisely said, "Satan laughs at our toiling, mocks at our wisdom, but trembles when we pray." All this is so familiar to us—but do we really pray? If not, then failure must dog our footsteps, whatever signs of apparent success there may be.

Let us never forget that the greatest thing we can do for God or for humanity is to pray. For we can accomplish far more by our prayers than by our work. Prayer is omnipotent; it can do anything that God can do. When we pray God works. All fruitfulness in service is the outcome of prayer—of the worker's prayers, or of those who are holding up holy hands on his behalf. We all know how to pray but perhaps many of us need to cry as the disciple of old did, "Lord teach us to pray." (Luke ll:1)

> Lord, by whom ye come to God,
> The life, the truth, the way,
> The path of prayer thyself hast trod;
> Lord, teach us now to pray.

Chapter 2

ALMOST INCREDIBLE PROMISES

"When we stand with Christ in glory, looking o'er life's finished story," the most amazing feature of that life as it is looked back upon will be its prayerlessness.

We will be almost beside ourselves with astonishment that we spent so little time in real intercession. It will be our turn to wonder.

In our Lord's last discourse to His loved ones, just before the most wonderful of all prayers, the Master again and again held out His kingly golden scepter and said, as it were, "What is your request? It shall be granted unto you, even unto the whole of my kingdom."

Do we believe this? We must do so if we believe our Bibles. Shall we just read over very quietly and thoughtfully one of our Lord's promises, reiterated so many times? If we had never read them before, we should open our eyes in bewilderment, for these promises are almost incredible. From the lips of any mere man they would be quite unbelievable. But it is the Lord of heaven and earth who speaks, and He is speaking at the most solemn moment of His life. It is the eve of His death and passion. It is a farewell message. Now listen.

"Verily, verily, I say unto you, he that believeth on me, the works that I do shall he do also; and greater works than these shall he do; because I go unto my Father. And whatsoever ye shall ask in my name, that will I do, that the Father may be glorified in the Son. If ye shall ask any thing in my name, I will do it." (John 14:13-14). Now, could any words be plainer or clearer than these? Could any promise be greater or grander? Has anyone else, anywhere, at any time, ever offered so much?

How staggered those disciples must have been. Surely they could scarcely believe their own ears. But that promise is made also to you and to me.

And, lest there should be any mistake on their part, or on ours, our Lord repeats himself a few moments afterwards. Yes, and the Holy Spirit bids John record those words again. "If ye abide in me, and my words abide in you, ye shall ask what ye will, and it shall be done unto you. Herein is my Father glorified, that ye bear much fruit; so shall ye be my disciples" (John 15: 7-8).

These words are of such grave importance, and so momentous, that the Savior of the world is not content even with a threefold utterance of them. He urges His disciples to obey His command to ask. In fact, He tells them that one sign of their being His friends will be their obedience to His commands in all things (verse 14). Then He once more repeats His wishes: "Ye have not chosen me, but I have chosen you, and ordained you, that ye should go and bring forth fruit, and that your fruit should remain: that whatsoever ye shall ask of the Father in my name, he may give it you" (John 15:16).

One would think that our Lord had now made it plain enough that He wanted them to pray, that He needed their prayers, and that without prayer they could accomplish nothing. But to our intense surprise He returns again to the same subject, saying very much the same words.

"In that day ye shall ask me nothing" (i.e., "ask me no question"). "Verily, verily, I say unto you, Whatsoever ye shall ask the Father in my name, he will give it you. Hitherto have ye asked nothing in my name: ask, and ye shall receive, that your joy may be full" (John 16:23-24).

Never before had our Lord laid such stress on any promise or command—never. This truly marvelous promise is given us six times over. Six times, almost in the same breath, our Savior commands us to ask whatsoever we will. This is the greatest—the most wonderful—promise ever made to man. Yet most people—Christian people—practically ignore it. Is it not so?

The exceeding greatness of the promise seems to overwhelm us. Yet we know that He is "able to do exceeding abundantly above all that we ask or think" (Ephesians 3:20).

So our blessed Master gives the final exhortation, before He is seized, and bound, and scourged, before His gracious lips are silenced on the Cross, "Ye shall ask in My name ... for the Father himself loveth you" (John 16:26-27). We have often spent much time in reflecting upon our Lord's seven words from the Cross. And it is well we should do so. Have we ever spent one hour in meditating upon our Savior's sevenfold invitation to pray?

Today He sits on the throne of His Majesty on High, and He holds out to us the scepter of His power. Shall we touch it and tell Him our desires? He bids us take of His treasures. He yearns to grant us "according to the riches of His ," that we may "be strengthened with might by his Spirit in the inner man" (Ephesians 3:16). He tells us that our strength and our fruitfulness depend upon our prayers. He reminds us that the fullness of our joy depends upon answered prayer (John 16:24).

And yet we allow the devil to persuade us to neglect prayer. He makes us believe that we can do more by our own efforts than by our prayers—by our intercourse with people than by our intercession with God. It passes one's comprehension that so little heed should be given to our Lord's sevenfold invitation—command—promise. How dare we work for Christ without being much on our knees? Quite recently an earnest Christian worker—a Sunday school teacher and communicant—wrote me, saying, "I have never had an answer to prayer in all my life." But why? Is God a liar? Is not God trustworthy? Do His promises count for nothing. Does He not mean what He says? And doubtless there are many reading these words who in their hearts are saying the same thing as that Christian worker. Payson is right—is Scriptural—when he says, "If we would do much for God, we must ask much of God: we must be people of prayer." If our prayers are not answered—always answered, but not necessarily granted—the fault must be entirely in ourselves, and not in God. God delights to answer prayer, and He has given us His word that He will answer.

Fellow laborers in His vineyard, it is quite evident that our Master desires us to ask, and to ask much. He tells us we glorify God by doing so. Nothing is beyond the scope of prayer that is not beyond the will of God—and we do not desire to go beyond His will.

We dare not say that our Lord's words are not true. Yet somehow or other few Christians really seem to believe them. What holds us back? What seals our lips? What keeps us from making much of prayer? Do we doubt His love? Never! He gave His life for us and to us. Do we doubt the Father's love? No. "The Father himself loveth you," said Jesus when urging His disciples to pray.

Do we doubt His power? Not for a moment. Hath He not said, "All power is given unto me in heaven and in earth. Go ye ... and lo, I am with you alway ..."? (Matthew 28:18-20). Do we doubt His wisdom? Do we mistrust His choice for us? Not for a moment. And yet so very few of His followers consider prayer really worth while. Of course, they would deny this—but actions speak louder than words. Are we afraid to put God to the test? He has said we may do so. "Bring ye all the tithes into the storehouse,..., and prove me now herewith, saith the LORD of hosts, if I will not open you the windows of heaven, and pour you out a blessing, that there shall not be room enough to receive it. " (Malachi 3:10). Whenever God makes us a promise, let us boldly say, as did the apostle Paul, "I believe God" (Acts 27:25), and trust Him to keep His word.

Shall we begin today to be people of prayer, if we have never done so before? Let us not put it off until a more convenient season. God wants me to pray. The dear Savior wants me to pray. He needs my prayers. So much—in fact, everything—depends upon prayer. How dare we hold back? Let every one of us ask on our knees this question: "If no one on earth prayed for the salvation of sinners more fervently or more frequently than I do, how many of them would be converted to God through prayer?"

Do we spend ten minutes a day in prayer? Do we consider it important enough for that?

Ten minutes a day on our knees in prayer—when the kingdom of Heaven can be had for the asking.

Ten minutes? It seems a very inadequate portion of our time to spend in taking hold of God (Isaiah 64:7).

And is it prayer when we do *say* our prayers, or are we just repeating daily a few phrases that have become practically meaningless, while our thoughts are wandering here and there?

If God were to answer the words we repeated on our knees this morning would we know it? Would we recognize the answer? Do we even remember what we asked for? He does answer. He has given us His word for it. He always answers every real prayer of faith.

But we shall see what the Bible has to say on this point in a later chapter. We are now thinking of the amount of time we spend in prayer.

"How often do you pray?" was the question put to a Christian woman. "Three times a day, and all the day beside," was the quick reply. But how many are there like that? Is prayer to me just a duty, or is it a privilege, a pleasure, a real joy, a necessity?

Let us get a fresh vision of Christ in all His glory; and a fresh glimpse of all the "riches of His glory" that He places at our disposal, and of all the mighty power given to Him. Then let us get a fresh vision of the world and all its needs. (And the world was never so needy as it is today.)

Why, the wonder is not that we pray so little, but that we can ever get up from our knees if we realize our own needs, the needs of our home and our loved ones, the needs of our pastor and the Church, the needs of our city and country, and the needs of the heathen and Mohammedan world. All these needs can be met by the riches of God in Christ Jesus. The apostle Paul had no doubt about this—nor have we. Yes! "My God shall supply all your need according to his riches in glory by Christ Jesus" (Philippians 4:19). But to share His riches we must pray, for "the same Lord over all is rich unto all that call upon him" (Romans 10:12).

So great is the importance of prayer that God has taken care to anticipate all the excuses or objections we may be likely to make.

People plead their weakness or infirmity—or they declare they do not know how to pray.

God foresaw this inability long ages ago. Did He not inspire the apostle Paul to say: "likewise the Spirit also helpeth our infirmities: for we know not what we should pray for as we ought: but the Spirit itself maketh intercession for us with groanings which cannot be uttered. And he that searcheth the hearts knoweth what is the mind of the Spirit, because he maketh intercession for the saints according to the will of God" (Romans 8:26-27).

Yes. Every provision is made for us. But only the Holy Spirit can stir us up to take hold of God. And if we will but yield ourselves to the Spirit's promptings, we will most assuredly follow the example of the apostles of old who said, "we will give ourselves continually to prayer" (Acts 6:4).

We may rest fully assured of this—a person's influence in the world can be gauged not by eloquence, or zeal, or orthodox, or energy, but by prayers. Yes, and we will go further and maintain that no one can live correctly who does not pray correctly.

We may work for Christ from morning until night. We may spend much time in Bible study. We may be most earnest and faithful and acceptable in our preaching and in our individual dealing. But none of these things can be truly effective unless we are much in prayer. We will only be full of good works, but not "being fruitful in every good work" (Colossians 1:10). To be little with God in prayer is to be little for God in service. Much secret prayer means much public power. Yet is it not a fact that while our organizing is well near perfect, our agonizing in prayer is well near lost?

Christians are wondering why the revival delays its coming. There is only one thing that can delay it, and that is lack of prayer. All revivals have been the outcome of prayer. One sometimes longs for the voice of an archangel, but what would that avail if the voice of Christ himself does not stir us up to pray? It seems almost impertinence for any Christian to take up the cry when our Savior has put forth His limitless promises. Yet we feel that something should be done, and we believe that the Holy Spirit is prompting Christians to remind themselves and others of Christ's words and power. No words of mine can impress anyone with the value of prayer, the need of prayer, and the omnipotence of prayer.

But these utterances go forth steeped in prayer that God the Holy Spirit will himself convict Christian men and women of the sin of prayerlessness, and drive them to their knees, to call upon God day and night in burning, believing, prevailing intercession. The Lord Jesus, now in the eternal heaven, beckons to us to fall upon our knees and claim the riches of His grace.

No one dare prescribe for another how long a time they ought to spend in prayer, nor do we suggest that you should make a vow to pray so many minutes or hours a day. Of course, the Bible command is to "Pray without ceasing" (1 Thessalonians 5:17). This is evidently an attitude of prayer, which should be the attitude of one's life.

Here we are speaking of definite acts of prayer. Have you ever timed your prayers? We believe that most of our readers would be amazed and confounded if they did time themselves.

Some years ago the writer faced this prayer question. He felt that for himself at least one hour a day was the minimum time that he should spend in prayer. Every day he carefully noted down a record of his prayer life. As time went on he met a workingman who was being much used of God.

When asked to what he chiefly attributed his success, this man quietly replied, "Well, I could not get on without two hours a day of private prayer."

Then there came across my path a Spirit-filled missionary from overseas, who told very humbly of the wonderful things God was doing through his ministry. (One could see all along that God was given all the praise and all the glory.) "I find it necessary, oftentimes, to spend four hours a day in prayer," said this missionary.

And we remember how the greatest missionary of all sometimes spent whole nights in prayer. Why? Our blessed Lord did not pray simply as an example to us. He never did things merely as an example. He prayed because He needed to pray. If as perfect man, prayer was necessary to Him, then how much more is it necessary to you and me?

"Four hours a day in prayer?" exclaimed a man who is giving his whole life to Christian work as a medical missionary. "Four hours? Give me ten minutes and I'm done." That was an honest and a brave confession—even if a sad one. Yet, if some of us were to speak out as honestly ...?

Now, it was not by accident that these men crossed my path. God was speaking through them. It was just another call to prayer from the "God of patience" (Romans 15:5), who is also "the God of all comfort" (2 Corinthians 1:3). When their quiet message had sunk into my soul, a book came into my hands, by chance as people say. It told briefly and simply the story of John Hyde—*Praying Hyde*, as he came to be called. Just as God sent John the Baptist to prepare the way of our Lord at His first coming, so He sent in these last days John the Pray-er to make straight paths for His coming again. Praying Hyde—what a name! As one read of his marvelous life of prayer, one began to ask, "Have I ever prayed?"

I found others were asking the same question. One lady, who is noted for her wonderful intercession, wrote me, saying, "When I laid down this book, I began to think I had never in all my life really prayed."

But here we must leave the matter. Shall we get on our knees before God and allow His Holy Spirit to search us through and through? Are we sincere? Do we really desire to do God's will? Do we really believe His promises? If so, will it not lead us to spend more time on our knees before God? Do not vow to pray *so many minutes or hours* a day. Resolve to pray much, but prayer, to be of value, must be spontaneous, and not from constraint.

But we must bear in mind that mere resolutions to take more time for prayer, and to conquer reluctance to pray, will not prove lastingly effective unless there is a wholehearted and absolute surrender to the Lord Jesus Christ. If we have never taken this step, we must take it now if we desire to be people of prayer.

I am quite certain of this fact: God wants me to pray, and wants you to pray. The question is, are we willing to pray?

Gracious Savior, pour out upon us the fullness of the Holy Spirit, that we may indeed become *Kneeling Christians*.

> *To God your every need*
> *In instant prayer display.*
> *Pray always; pray and never faint;*
> *Pray! Without ceasing, pray.*

Chapter 3

"ASK OF ME AND I WILL GIVE"

God wants me to pray, to be much in prayer—because all success in spiritual work is dependent on prayer.

A preacher who prays little may see some results of his labors. But if he does, it will be because someone, somewhere, is praying for him. The fruit is the pray-er's—not the preacher's. How surprised some of us preachers will be on that day when the Lord shall "reward every man according to his works" (Matthew 16:27).

"Lord! Those were my converts! It was I who conducted that mission at which so many were brought into the fold." Ah, yes—I did the preaching, the pleading, the persuading; but was it I who did the praying?

Every convert is the result of the Holy Spirit's pleading in answer to the prayers of some believer. O God, grant that such surprise may not be ours. O Lord, teach us to pray.

We have had a vision of a God pleadingly calling for prayer from His children. How am I treating that call? Can I say with the apostle Paul, "I was not disobedient to the heavenly vision"? (Acts 26:19). Again we repeat, if there are any regrets in heaven, the greatest will be that we spent so little time in real intercession while we were on earth.

Think of the wide sweep of prayer. "Ask of me, and I will give thee the heathen for thine inheritance, and the uttermost parts of the earth for thy possession" (Psalm 2:8). Yet many people do not trouble to bring even the little details of their own lives to God in prayer, and nine out of ten Christian people never think of praying for the heathen.

One is staggered at the unwillingness of Christians to pray. Perhaps it is because they have never experienced, or even heard of, convincing answers to prayer.

In this chapter we are setting out to do the impossible. What is that? We long to bring home to the heart and conscience of every reader the power of prayer. We venture to describe this as impossible. For if Christians will not believe and act upon our Lord's promises and commands, how can we expect them to be persuaded by any mere human exhortations?

But do you remember that when our Lord was speaking to His disciples, He asked them to believe that He was in the Father and the Father in Him? Then He added, in effect, "If you cannot believe my bare word about this, believe me for the very works' sake" (John 14:11). It was as if He said, "If my person, my sanctified life, and my wonderful words do not elicit belief in me, then look at my works. Surely they are sufficient to compel belief? Believe me because of what I do."

Then He went on to promise that if they would believe, they should do greater works than these. It was after this utterance that He gave the first of those six wonderful promises in regard to prayer. The inference surely is that those greater works are to be done only as the outcome of prayer.

May the disciple therefore follow the Master's method? Fellow worker, if you fail to grasp, fail to trust our Lord's astounding promises regarding prayer, will you not believe them "for the very works' sake"? That is, because of those

26

greater works than men and women are performing today—
or, rather, the works that the Lord Jesus is doing through
their prayerful cooperation?

What are we looking for? What is our real aim in life?
Surely we desire most of all to be abundantly fruitful in the
Master's service. We do not seek position, or prominence, or
power. But we do long to be fruitful servants. Then we must
be much in prayer. God can do more through our prayers
than through our preaching. A. J. Gordon once said, "You
can do more than pray after you have prayed, but you can
never do more than pray until you have prayed." If only we
would believe this.

A lady in India was cast down through the failure of her
life and work. She was a devoted missionary, but somehow
or other conversions never resulted from her ministry.

The Holy Spirit seemed to say to her, "Pray more." But
she resisted the promptings of the Spirit for some time. "At
length," said she, "I set apart much of my time for prayer.
I did it in fear and trembling lest my fellow-workers should
complain that I was shirking my work. After a few weeks I
began to see men and women accepting Christ as their Savior.
Moreover, the whole district was soon awakened, and the
work of all the other missionaries was blessed as never before.
God did more in six months than I had succeeded in doing
in six years. And," she added, "no one ever accused me of
shirking my duty."

Another lady missionary in India felt the same call to pray.
She began to give much time to prayer. No opposition came
from without, but it did come from within. But she persisted,
and in two years the baptized converts increased sixfold.

God promised that He would pour out the Spirit of grace
and supplication upon all flesh (Joel 2:28). How much of
that Spirit of supplication is ours? Surely we must get that
Spirit at all costs? Yet if we are not willing to spend time in
supplication, God must by necessity withhold His Spirit, and

we become numbered among those who are resisting the Spirit, and possibly quenching the Spirit (1 Thessalonians 5:19). Has not our Father promised the Holy Spirit to them that ask Him? (Luke 11:13).

Are not the very converts from heathendom putting some of us to shame?

A few years ago, when in India, I had the great joy of seeing something of Pandita Ramabai's work. She had a boarding-school of 1,500 Hindu girls. One day some of these girls came with their Bibles and asked a lady missionary what Luke 12:49 meant—"I am come to send fire on the earth; and what will I, if it be already kindled?" The missionary tried to put them off with an evasive answer, not being very sure herself what those words meant. But they were not satisfied, so they determined to pray for this fire. And as they prayed—and because they prayed—the very fire of heaven came into their souls. A very Pentecost from above was granted them. No wonder they continued to pray.

A party of these girls upon whom God had poured the spirit of supplication came to a mission house where I spent some weeks. "May we stay here in your town and pray for your work?" they asked. The missionary did not entertain the idea with any great enthusiasm. He felt that they ought to be at school, and not gadding about the country. But they only asked for a hall or barn where they could pray, and we all value prayers on our behalf. So their request was granted, and the good man sat down to his evening meal, thinking about the praying that was taking place. As the evening wore on, a native pastor came round. He broke down completely. He explained, with tears running down his face, that God's Holy Spirit had convicted him of sin, and that he felt compelled to come and openly confess his wrongdoing. He was quickly followed by one Christian after another, all under deep conviction of sin.

There was a remarkable time of blessing. Backsliders were restored, believers were sanctified, and heathen brought into the fold—all because a few mere children were praying.

God is no respecter of persons. If anyone is willing to conform to His conditions, He for His part will assuredly fulfill His promises. Does not our heart burn within us as we hear of God's wonderful power? And that power is ours for the asking. I know there are conditions. But you and I can fulfill them all through Christ. And those of us who cannot, have the privilege of serving God in India or any other overseas mission, may yet take our part in bringing down a like blessing. When the revival in Wales was at its height, a Welsh missionary wrote home begging the people to pray that India might be moved in like manner. So the coal miners met daily at the mouth of the mine half an hour before dawn to pray for their comrade overseas. In a few weeks' time the welcome message was sent home: "The blessing has come."

Isn't it just splendid to know that by our prayers we can bring down showers of blessing upon India, or Africa, or China, just as readily as we can get the few drops needed for our own little plot?

Many of us will recall the wonderful things that God did for Korea a few years ago (1907), entirely in answer to prayer. A few missionaries decided to meet together to pray daily at noon. At the end of the month one brother proposed that, "as nothing had happened," the prayer meeting should be discontinued. "Let us each pray at home as we find it convenient," said he. The others, however, protested that they ought rather to spend even more time in prayer each day. So they continued the daily prayer meeting for four months. Then suddenly the blessing began to be poured out. Church services here and there were broken up by weeping and confessing of sins. At length a mighty revival broke out.

At one place during a Sunday evening service the leading man in the church stood up and confessed that he had stolen one hundred dollars in administering a widow's legacy. Immediately conviction of sin swept the audience. That service did not end until 2 o'clock on Monday morning. God's wondrous power was felt as never before. And when the Church was purified, many sinners found salvation.

Multitudes flocked to the churches out of curiosity. Some came to mock, but fear laid hold of them, and they stayed to pray. Among the curious was a brigand chief, the leader of a robber band. He was convicted and converted. He went straight off to the magistrate and gave himself up. "You have no accuser," said the astonished official, "yet you accuse yourself! We have no law in Korea to meet your case." So he dismissed him.

One of the missionaries declared, "It paid well to have spent several months in prayer, for when God gave the Holy Spirit, He accomplished more in half a day than all the missionaries together could have accomplished in half a year."

In less than two months, more than 2,000 heathen were converted. The burning zeal of those converts has become a byword. Some of them gave all they had to build a church, and wept because they could not give more. Needless to say, they realized the power of prayer. Those converts were themselves baptized with the spirit of supplication. In one church it was announced that a daily prayer meeting would be held at 4:30 every morning. The very first day 400 people arrived long before the stated hour—eager to pray. The number rapidly increased to 600 as days went on. In Seoul, the average attendance is 1,100 at the weekly prayer meeting.

Heathen people came—to see what was happening. They exclaimed in astonishment, "The living God is among you." Those poor heathen saw what many Christians fail to see. Did not Christ say, "Where two or three are gathered together in my name, there am I in the midst of them"? (Matthew 18:20). What is possible in Korea is possible here. God is no respecter of nations. He is longing to bless us, longing to pour His Spirit upon us.

Now, if we—here in this so-called Christian country—really believed in prayer, i.e., in our Lord's own gracious promises, should we avoid prayer meetings? If we had any genuine concern for the lost condition of thousands in our own land and tens of thousands in heathen lands, should we withhold our prayers? Surely we do not think, or we should pray more. "Ask of me—I will give," says an almighty, all-loving God, and we scarcely heed His words.

Verily, converts from heathendom put us to shame. In my travels I came to Rawal Pindi, in N.W. India. What do you think happened there? Some of Pandita Ramabai's girls went there to camp. But a little while before this, Pandita Ramabai had said to her girls, "If there is any blessing in India, we may have it. Let us ask God to tell us what we must do in order to have the blessing."

As she read her Bible she paused over the verse, "Wait for the promise of the Father ... ye shall receive power, after that the Holy Ghost is come upon you" (Acts 1:4-8). "*Wait!*" she exclaimed, "Why, we have never done this. We have prayed, but we have never expected any greater blessing today than we had yesterday." Oh, how they prayed. One prayer meeting lasted six hours. And what a marvelous blessing God poured out in answer to their prayers.

While some of these girls were at Rawal Pindi, a lady missionary, looking out of her tent about midnight, was surprised to see a light burning in one of the girls' tents—a thing quite contrary to rules. She went to express her disapproval, but found the youngest of those ten girls—a child of fifteen—kneeling in the farthest corner of the tent, holding a little tallow candle in one hand and a list of

31

names for intercession in the other. She had 500 names on her list—500 out of the 1,500 girls in Pandita Ramabai's school. Hour after hour she was naming them before God. No wonder God's blessing fell wherever those girls went, and upon whomsoever those girls prayed for.

Pastor Ding Li Mei of China has the names of 1,100 students on his prayer list. Many hundreds have been won to Christ through his prayers. And so enthusiastic are his converts that many scores of them have entered the Christian ministry.

It would be an easy matter to add to these amazing and inspiring stories of blessing through prayer. But there is no need to do so. I know that God wants me to pray. I know that God wants you to pray.

"If there is any blessing in England we may have it." No, more—if there is any blessing in Christ we may have it. "Blessed be the God and Father of our Lord Jesus Christ, who hath blessed us with all spiritual blessing in heavenly places in Christ" (Ephesians 1:3). God's great storehouse is full of blessings. Only prayer can unlock that storehouse. Prayer is the key, and faith turns the key, opens the door, and claims the blessing. "Blessed are the pure in heart: for they shall see God" (Matthew 5:8). And to see Him is to pray correctly.

Listen! We have come—you and I—once more to the parting of the ways. All our past failure, all our past inefficiency and insufficiency, all our past unfruitfulness in service, can be banished now, once and for all, if we will only give prayer its proper place. Do it today. Do not wait for a more convenient time.

Everything worth having depends upon the decision we make. Truly God is a wonderful God! And one of the most wonderful things about Him is that He puts His all at the disposal of the prayer of faith. Believing prayer from a wholly cleansed heart never fails. God has given us His word for it. Yet vastly more wonderful is the amazing fact that Christian men and women should either not believe God's word, or should fail to put it to the test.

When Christ is all in all—when He is savior and Lord and king of our whole being, then it is really He who prays our prayers. We can then truthfully alter one word of a well-known verse and say that the Lord Jesus ever lives to make intercession in us. Oh, that we might make the Lord Jesus marvel not at our unbelief but at our faith. When our Lord shall again marvel, and say of us, "Verily ... I have not found so great faith, no, not in Israel" (Matthew 8:10), then indeed will palsy—paralysis—be transformed into power.

Has not our Lord come to cast fire upon us? Are we already kindled? Can He not use us as much as He used those mere children of Khedgaon? God is no respecter of persons. If we can humbly and truthfully say, "For me to live is Christ" (Philippians 1:21), will He not manifest forth His mighty power in us?

Some of us have been reading about Praying Hyde. Truly, his intercession changed things. People tell us that they were thrilled when John Hyde prayed. They were stirred to their inmost being when he just pleaded the name "Jesus—Jesus—Jesus," and a baptism of love and power came upon them.

But it was not John Hyde, it was the Holy Spirit of God whom one consecrated man, filled with that Spirit, brought down upon all around him. May we not all become Praying Hydes? Do you say, "No! He had a special gift of prayer"? Very well—how did he get it? He was once just an ordinary Christian man—just like any of us.

Have you noticed that, humanly speaking, he owed his prayer life to the prayers of his father's friend? Now get hold of this point. It is one of greatest importance, and one that may profoundly affect your whole life. Perhaps I may be allowed to tell the story fully, for so much depends upon it. Shall we quote John Hyde himself?

33

He was on board a ship sailing for India, where he was going as a missionary. He says, "My father had a friend who greatly desired to be a foreign missionary, but was not permitted to go. This friend wrote me a letter directed in care of the ship. I received it a few hours out of New York harbor. The words were not many, but the purport of them was this: 'I shall not cease praying for you, dear John, until you are filled with the Holy Spirit.' When I had read the letter I crumpled it up in anger and threw it on the deck. Did this friend think I had not received the baptism of the Spirit, or that I would think of going to India without this equipment? I was angry. But by and by better judgment prevailed, and I picked up the letter, and read it again. Possibly I did need something which I had not yet received. I paced up and down the deck, a battle raging within. I felt uncomfortable: I loved the writer; I knew the holy life he lived, and down in my heart there was a conviction that he was right, and that I was not fit to be a missionary.... This went on for two, or three days, until I felt perfectly miserable.... At last, in a kind of despair, I asked the Lord to fill me with the Holy Spirit; and the moment I did this ... I began to see myself, and what a selfish ambition I had."

But he did not yet receive the blessing he sought. He landed in India and went with a fellow missionary to an open-air service. This is what he said about it.

The missionary spoke, and I was told that he was speaking about Jesus Christ as the real Savior from sin. When he had finished his address, a respectable-looking man, speaking good English, asked the missionary whether he himself had been thus saved? The question went home to my heart; for if it had been asked me, I would have had to confess that Christ had not fully saved me, because I knew there was a sin in my life which had not been taken away. I realized what a dishonor it would be on the name of Christ to have to confess that I was preaching a Christ that had not delivered me from sin, though I was proclaiming to others that He was a perfect Savior. I went back to my room and shut myself in, and told the Lord that it must be one of two things: either He must give me victory over all my sins, and especially over the sin that so easily beset me, or I must return to America and seek there for some other work. I said I could not stand up to preach the Gospel until I could testify of its power in my own life. I ... realized how reasonable this was, and the Lord assured me that He was able and willing to deliver me from all sin. He did deliver me, and I have not had a doubt of this since.

It was then, and then only, that John Hyde became Praying Hyde. And it is only by such a full surrender and such a definite claiming to be delivered from the power of sin in our lives that you and I can be people of prevailing prayer. The point we wish to emphasize, however, is the one already mentioned. A comparatively unknown man prays for John Hyde, who was then unknown to the world, and by his prayers brings down such a blessing upon him that everyone knows of John Hyde now as *Praying Hyde.*

Did you say in your heart, dear reader, a little while ago, that you could not hope to be a Praying Hyde? Of course we cannot all give so much time to prayer. For physical or other reasons we may be hindered from constant praying. But we may all have his spirit of prayer. And may we not all do for others what the unnamed friend did for John Hyde?

Can we not pray the blessing down upon others—upon your pastor or priest? Upon your friend? Upon your family? What a ministry is ours, if we will but enter it. But to do so, we must make the full surrender that John Hyde made. Have we done it? Failure in prayer is due to fault in the heart. Only the "pure in heart" can see God (Matthew 5:8). And only those who "call on the Lord out of a pure heart" (2 Timothy 2:22) can confidently claim answers to their prayers.

What a revival would break out, what a mighty blessing would come down if only everyone who read these words would claim the fullness of the Holy Spirit now.

Do you not see why it is that God wants us to pray? Do you now see why everything worth having depends upon prayer? There are several reasons, but one stands out very clearly and vividly before us after reading this chapter. It is just this: if we ask and God does not give, then the fault is with us. Every unanswered prayer is a clarion call to search the heart to see what is wrong there; for the promise is unmistakable in its clearness: "If ye shall ask any thing in my name, I will do it" (John 14:14).

Truly, when you pray you put not God but your own spiritual life to the test.

> *Let me come closer to Thee, Jesus,*
> *Oh, closer every day;*
> *Let me lean harder on Thee, Jesus,*
> *Yes, harder all the way.*

Chapter 4

ASKING FOR SIGNS

"Does God indeed answer prayer?" is a question often on the lips of people, and oftener still in their inmost hearts. "Is prayer of any real use?" Somehow or other we cannot help praying; but then even pagan savages cry out to someone or something to aid them in times of danger and disaster and distress.

And those of us who really do believe in prayer are soon faced with another question: "Is it right to put God to the test?" Moreover, a further thought flashes into our minds: "Dare we put God to the test?" For there is little doubt failure in the prayer-life is often—always?—due to failure in the spiritual life. So many people harbor much unbelief in the heart regarding the value and effectiveness of prayer; and without faith, prayer is vain.

Asking for signs? Putting God to the test? Would to God we could persuade Christian men and women to do so. Why, what a test this would be of our own faith in God, and of our own holiness of life. Prayer is the touchstone of true godliness. God asks our prayers, values our prayers, needs our prayers. And if those prayers fail, we have only ourselves to blame. We do not mean by this that effective prayer always gets just what it asks for. Now, the Bible teaches us that we are allowed to put God to the test. The example of Gideon in Old Testament days is sufficient to show us that God honors our faith even when that faith is faltering. He allows us to prove Him even after He gives us a definite promise. This is a very great comfort to us.

Gideon said unto God, "If thou wilt save Israel by mine hand, as thou hast said, Behold, I will put a fleece of wool in the floor; and if the dew be on the fleece only, and it be dry upon all the earth beside, then shall I know that thou wilt save Israel by mine hand, as thou hast said" (Judges 6:36-37). Yet, although there was a "bowl full of water" in the fleece the next morning, this did not satisfy Gideon. He dares to put God to the test the second time, and to ask that the fleece should be dry instead of wet the following night. "And God did so that night" (Judges 6:38-40).

It is all very wonderful, the Almighty God just doing what a hesitating man asks Him to do. We catch our breath and stand amazed, scarcely knowing which startles us the more—the daring of the man, or the condescension of God. Of course, there is more in the story than meets the eye. No doubt Gideon thought that the fleece represented himself, Gideon.

If God would indeed fill him with His Spirit, why, salvation was assured. But as he wrung the fleece out, he began to compare himself with the saturated wool. "How unlike this fleece am I. God promises deliverance, but I do not feel full of the Spirit of God. No inflow of the mighty power of God seems to have come into me. Am I indeed fit for this great feat?" No! But then, it is not I but God. "O God, let the fleece be dry. Canst thou still work? Even if I do not feel any superhuman power, any fullness of spiritual blessing within me: even if I feel as dry as this fleece, canst thou still deliver Israel by my arm?" (Little wonder that he prefaced his prayer with the words, "Let not thine anger be hot against me.") "And God did so that night: for it was dry upon the fleece only, and there was dew on all the ground" (verse 40).

Yes, there is more in the story than can be seen at a glance. And is it not so in our own case? The devil so often assures us that our prayers cannot claim an answer because of the dryness of our souls. Answers to prayer, however, do not depend upon our feelings, but upon the trustworthiness of the one who promised.

Now, we are not urging that Gideon's way of procedure is for us, or for anyone, the normal course of action. It seems to reveal much hesitation to believe God's word. In fact, it looks gravely like doubting God. And surely it grieves God when we show a faith in Him which is but partial.

The higher and better and safer way is to *ask, nothing doubting.* But it is very comforting and assuring to us to know that God allowed Gideon to put Him to the test. Nor is this the only such case mentioned in Scripture.

The most surprising instance of proving God happened on the Sea of Galilee. Peter put our Lord himself to the test. "If it be thou." Yet our Savior had already said, "It is I." "If it be thou, bid me come unto thee on the water." And our Lord said, "Come," and Peter "walked on the water" (Matthew 14:27-29). But Peter's faith soon failed him. "Little faith" so often and so quickly becomes doubt. Remember that Christ did not reprove him for coming. Our Lord did not say, "Wherefore didst thou come?" but "Wherefore didst thou doubt?" (v. 31).

To put God to the test is, after all, not the best method. He has given us so many promises contingent on believing prayer, and has so often proved His power and His willingness to answer prayer, that we ought, as a rule, to hesitate a long time before we ask Him for signs as well as for wonders.

But, someone may be thinking, does not the Lord God Almighty himself bid us to put Him to the test? Did He not say, "Bring ye all the tithes into the storehouse, . . . , and prove me now herewith, saith the LORD of hosts, if I will not open you the windows of heaven, and pour you out a blessing, that there shall not be room enough to receive it"? (Malachi 3:10).

Yes that is true: God does say, "Prove me, test me." But it is really we ourselves who are thus tested. If the windows of heaven are not opened when we pray, and this blessing of fullness-to-overflowing is not bestowed upon us, it can only be because we are not whole-tithers. When we are indeed wholly yielded to God—when we have brought the whole tithe into the storehouse for God—we shall find such a blessing that we shall not need to put God to any test. This is a thing we shall have to speak about when we come to the question of unanswered prayer.

Meanwhile we want every Christian to ask, "Have I ever fairly tested prayer?" How long is it since you last offered up a definite prayer? People pray for a blessing upon an address, or a meeting, or a mission; and some blessing is certain to come, for others are also pleading with God about the matter. You ask for relief from pain or healing of sickness, but Godless people, for whom no one appears to be praying, often recover, and sometimes in a seemingly miraculous way. And we may feel that we might have gotten better even if no prayer had been offered on our behalf. It seems to me that so many people cannot put their finger upon any really definite and conclusive answer to prayer in their own experience. Most Christians do not give God a chance to show His delight in granting His children's petitions, for their requests are so vague and indefinite. If this is so, it is not surprising that prayer is so often a mere form—an almost mechanical repetition, day by day, of certain phrases. A few minutes of spiritual exercise morning and evening.

Then there is another point. Have you, when in prayer, ever had the witness borne in upon you that your request was granted? Those who know something of the private life of people of prayer are often amazed at the complete assurance that comes over them at times that their prayers are answered, long before the boon they seek is actually in their possession. One prayer-warrior would say, "A peace came over my soul. I was confident my request was granted me." He then just thanked God for what he was quite sure God had done for him. And his assurance would prove to be absolutely well founded.

Our Lord Himself always had this assurance, and we should ever bear in mind that, although He was God, He lived His earthly life as a perfect man, depending upon the Holy Spirit of God.

When He stood before the opened tomb of Lazarus, before He had actually called upon the dead body to come forth, He said, "Father, I thank thee that thou hast heard me. And I knew that thou hearest me always" (John 11:41-42). Why, then, did He utter His thanks? "Because of the people which stand by I said it, that they may believe that thou hast sent me." If Christ is dwelling in our hearts by faith; if the Holy Spirit is breathing into us our petitions, and we are "praying in the Holy Ghost," ought we not to know that the Father hears us? (Jude 20). And will not those who stand by begin to recognize that we, too, are sent by God?

Men of prayer and women of prayer will agonize before God for something which they know is according to His will, because of some definite promise on the page of Scripture. They may pray for hours, or even for days, when suddenly the Holy Spirit reveals to them in no uncertain way that God has granted their request; and they are confident that they need no longer send up any more petitions to God about the matter. It is as if God said in clear tones: "Thy prayer is heard and I have granted thee the desire of thy heart." This is not the experience of only one person, but most Christians to whom prayer is the basis of their life will bear witness to the same fact. Nor is it a solitary experience in their lives, it occurs again and again.

Then prayer must give place to action. God taught Moses this: "Wherefore criest thou unto me? speak unto the children of Israel, that they go forward" (Exodus 14:15).

We are not surprised to find that Jonathan Goforth, a much used missionary in China, often has this assurance given him that his petitions are granted. He said this about a certain prayer, "I knew that God had answered. I received definite assurance that He would open the way." For why should anyone be surprised at this? The Lord Jesus said, "Ye are my friends, if ye do whatsoever I command you. Henceforth I call you not servants; for the servant knoweth not what his lord doeth; but I have called you friends" (John 15:14-15). Do you think it surprising, then, if the Lord lets us, His friends, know something of His plans and purposes?

The question at once arises, does God mean this to be the experience of only a few chosen saints, or does He wish all believers to exercise a like faith, and to have a like assurance that their prayers are answered?

We know that God is no respecter of persons, and therefore we know that any true believer in Him may share His mind and will. We are His friends if we do the things He commands us. One of those things is prayer. Our Savior begged His disciples to "have faith in God" (the literal translation is "Have the *faith of God*"). Then, He declares, you can say to a mountain, "Be thou removed, and be thou cast into the sea," and if you believe and doubt not in your heart, it will come to pass. Then He gives this promise: "What things soever ye desire, when ye pray, believe that ye receive them, [literally: believe that ye *have received them*] (in heaven), and ye shall have them (on earth)" (Mark 11:23-24).

Now, this is exactly the experience we have been talking about. This is just what real people of prayer do. Such things naturally pass the comprehension of unbelievers. Such things are perplexing to the half-believers. Our Lord, however, desires that we should know that we are His disciples, sent as He was sent (John 8:18 and 20:21). They will know this if we love one another (John 13:35). But another proof is provided, and it is this: if we know and they see that God hears us always (John 11:42).

Some of us at once recall to mind George Muller's wonderful prayer life. On one occasion, when crossing from Quebec to Liverpool, he had prayed very definitely that a chair he had written to New York for should arrive in time to catch the steamer, and he was quite confident that God had granted his petition. About half an hour before the tender was timed to take the passengers to the ship, the agents informed him that no chair had arrived, and that it could not possibly come in time for the steamer. Now, Mrs. Muller suffered much from seasickness, and it was absolutely essential that she should have the chair. Yet nothing would induce Mr. Muller to buy another one from a shop near by. "We have made special prayer that our heavenly Father would be pleased to provide it for us, and we will trust Him to do so," was his reply, and he went on board absolutely sure that his trust was not misplaced, and would not miscarry. Just before the tender left, a van drove up, and on the top of the load it carried was Mr. Muller's chair. It was hurried on board and placed into the hands of the very man who had urged George Muller to buy another one. When he handed it to Mr. Muller, the latter expressed no surprise, but quietly removed his hat and thanked his heavenly Father. To this man of God such an answer to prayer was not wonderful, but natural. And do you not think that God allowed the chair to be held back until the very last minute as a lesson to Mr. Muller's friends—and to us? We should never have heard of that incident but for that delay.

God does all He can to induce us to pray and to trust, and yet how slow we are to do so. Oh, what we miss through lack of faith and want of prayer. No one can have very real and deep communion with God who does not know how to pray so as to get answers to prayer.

If one has any doubt as to God's willingness to be put to the test, let him read a little book called *Nor Scrip* (Marshall, Morgan and Scott, Ltd. [out of print]). Miss Amy Wilson Carmichael tells us in its pages how again and again she proved God. One gets the impression from the book that it was no accident that led her to do so. Surely God's hand was in it? For instance, in order to rescue a Hindu child from a life of religious shame, it was necessary to spend a hundred rupees. Was she justified in doing so? She could help many girls for such a sum: ought she to spend it on just one? Miss Carmichael felt led to pray that God would send her the round sum of a hundred rupees—no more, no less—if it was His will that the money should be spent in this way. The money came—the exact amount—and the sender of it explained that she had sat down to write a check for a broken sum, but had been impelled to make it just a hundred rupees.

That happened over fifteen years ago, and since that time this same missionary has put God to the test over and over again, and He has never failed her. This is what she says:

Never once in fifteen years has a bill been left unpaid; never once has a man or woman been told when we were in need of help; but never once have we lacked any good thing. Once, as if to show what could be done if it were required, twenty-five pounds came by telegram. Sometimes a man would emerge from the clamoring crowd at a railway station, and slip some indispensable gift of money into the hand, and be lost in the crowd again before the giver could be identified.

Is it wonderful? Wonderful! Why, what does the apostle John say, speaking by the Spirit of God? "And this is the confidence that we have in him, that, if we ask any thing according to his will, he heareth us: And if we know that he hear us, whatsoever we ask, we know that we have the petitions that we desired of him." (1 John 5:14-15). Have you and I such confidence? If not, why not?

To call it wonderful is to show our lack of faith. It is natural to God to answer prayer. It is normal, not extraordinary.

The fact is—let us be quite honest and straightforward about it—the fact is so many of us do not believe God. We may just as well be quite candid about it. If we love God we ought to pray, because He wants us to pray, and commands us to pray. If we believe God we will pray because we cannot help doing so, okay we cannot get on without it. Christian, you believe in God, and you believe in Christ (John 3:16), but have you advanced far enough in the Christian life to *believe* Him; that is, to believe *what* He says and *all* He says? Does it not sound blasphemous to ask such a thing of a Christian? Yet how few believers really believe God. God forgive us!

Has it ever struck you that we trust the word of others more easily than we trust God's Word? And yet, when we do believe God, what miracles of grace God works in and through us. No person ever lived who has been revered and respected by so many peoples and tongues as that man of whom we are told three times over in the New Testament that *he believed God* (Romans 4:3; Galatians 3:6; James 2:23). Yes, "Abraham believed God, and it was counted unto him for righteousness." And today, Christian and Jew and Moslem vie with each other in honoring Abraham's name. We implore you who believe in Christ Jesus never to rest until you can say, "I believe God, and will act on that belief" (Acts 27:25).

But before we leave the question of testing God, we should like to point out that sometimes God leads us on *to prove Him.* Sometimes God has put it into the heart of Miss

Amy Carmichael to ask for things she saw no need for. Yet she felt impelled by the Holy Spirit to ask. Not only were they granted her, but they also proved an inestimable boon. Yes, God knows what things we have need of, whether we want them or not, before we ask (Matthew 6:8). Has not God said to us, as well as to Joshua, "I will not fail thee"? (Joshua 1:5).

Oftentimes the temptation would come to Amy Carmichael to let others know of some special need. But always the inner assurance would come, as in the very voice of God, "I know, and that is enough," she would say. And, of course, God was glorified. During the trying days of the war [World War I], even the heathen used to say, "Their God feeds them." "Is it not known all the country round," said a worldly heathen, "that your God hears prayer?"

Oh, what glory to God was brought about by their simple faith. Why do not we believe God? Why do we not take God at His word? Do believers or unbelievers ever say of us, "We know your prayers are answered"? You missionaries the wide world over, listen! (Oh, that these words might reach every ear, and stir every heart.) It is the yearning desire of God—of our loving Savior Jesus Christ—that every one of us should have the same strong faith as that devoted lady missionary we are speaking about.

Our loving Father does not wish any child of His to have one moment's anxiety or one unsatisfied need. No matter how great our need may be, no matter how numerous our requirements, if we only prove Him in the manner He bids us, we shall never have room enough to receive all the blessing He will give (Malachi 3:10).

> *Oh, what peace we often forfeit,*
> *Oh, what needless pain we bear;*
> *All because we do not carry*
> *Everything to God in prayer;*

Or all because when we do carry it, we do not believe God's Word. Why is it we find it so hard to trust Him? Has He ever failed us? Has He not said over and over and over again that He will grant all petitions offered out of a pure heart? "Ask of Me," "Pray ye," "Prove Me." Did not our Lord say that whatever we ask in His name He will do? (John 14:13-14), and whatsoever we ask the Father in His name, the Father will give us? (John 16:23). The Bible is full of answers to prayer—wonderful answers, miraculous answers—and yet somehow our faith fails us, and we dishonor God by distrusting Him.

> *If our faith were but more simple*
> *We should take Him at His word,*
> *And our lives would be all sunshine*
> *In the bounties of our Lord.*

But our eye must be "single" if our faith is to be simple and our "whole body ... full of light" (Matthew 6:22). Christ must be the sole Master. We cannot expect to be free from anxiety if we are trying to serve God and mammon (Matthew 6:24-25). Again we are led back to the victorious life. When we indeed present our bodies "a living sacrifice, holy, acceptable unto God" (Romans 12:1); when we present our members "servants to righteousness unto holiness" (Romans 6:19); then He presents himself to us and fills us with all the fullness of God (Ephesians 3:19).

Let us ever bear in mind that real faith not only believes that God can, but that He does answer prayer. We may be slothful in prayer, but "The Lord is not slack concerning His promise" (2 Peter 3:9). Is not that a striking expression?

Perhaps the most extraordinary testing of God which that Dohnavur missionary, Amy Carmichael, tells us of is the following. The question arose of purchasing a rest house in the hills near by. Was it the right thing to do? Only God could decide. Much prayer was made. Eventually the petition was offered up that if it was God's will that the house should be purchased, the exact sum of 100 pounds should be received. That amount came at once. Yet they still hesitated. Two months later they asked God to give them again the same sign of His approval of the purchase. That same day another check for 100 pounds came. Even now they scarcely liked to proceed in the matter. In a few days' time, however, another round sum of 100 pounds was received, earmarked for the purchase of such a house.

Does it not flood our hearts with joy to remember that our gracious Savior is so kind? It is Luke the physician who tells us that God is kind (Luke 6:35). Love is always kind (1 Corinthians 13:4); and God is love. Think over it when you pray. Our God is kind. It will help us in our intercessions. He bears so patiently with us when our faith would falter. "How excellent is Thy lovingkindness, O God" (Psalm 36:7); "Thy lovingkindness is better than life" (Psalm 63:3).

The danger is that we read of such simple faith in prayer and explain, "How wonderful!" and forget that God desires every one of us to have such faith and such prayer. God has no favorites. He wants me to pray. He wants you to pray. He allows such things to happen as we have described above, and allows them to come to our knowledge, not to surprise us, but to stimulate us. One sometimes wishes that Christian people would forget all the man-made rules with which we have hedged prayer about. Let us be simple. Let us be natural. Take God at His word. Let us remember that "the kindness and love of God our Savior toward man" has appeared (Titus 3:4). God sometimes leads us into a prayer life. And sometimes God has to drive us into such a life.

As some of us look back over our comparatively prayerless life, what a thrill of wonder and of joy comes over us that God is not only kind He is also patient (Romans 15:5). Where should we have been without that? We fail Him, but, blessed be His name, He has never failed us, and He never will do so. We doubt Him, we mistrust His love and His providence and His guidance; we become "much discouraged because of the way" (Numbers 21:4); we murmur because of the way; yet all the time He is there blessing us, and waiting to pour out upon us a blessing so great that there shall not be room to receive it (Malachi 3:10).

The promise of Christ still holds good: "Whatsoever ye shall ask in my name, that will I do, that the Father may be glorified in the Son" (John 14:13).

> *Prayer changes things—and yet how blind*
> *And slow we are to taste and see,*
> *The blessedness that comes to those*
> *Who trust in Thee.*
> *But henceforth we will just believe God.*

49

Chapter 5

WHAT IS PRAYER?

Dwight Moody was once addressing a crowded meeting of children in Edinburgh. In order to get their attention he began with a question: "What is prayer?" He was not looking for a reply, and expected to give the answer himself.

To his amazement scores of little hands shot up all over the hall. He asked one lad to reply; and the answer came at once, clear and correct, "Prayer is an offering up of our desires onto God for things agreeable to His will, in the name of Christ, with confession of our sins and thankful acknowledgment of His mercies." Mr. Moody's delighted comment was, "Thank God, my boy, that you were born in Scotland." But that was half a century ago. What sort of answer would he get today? How many English children could give a definition of prayer? Think for a moment and decide what answer you yourself would give.

What do we mean by prayer? I believe the vast majority of Christians would say, "Prayer is asking things from God." But surely prayer is much more than merely "getting God to run our errands for us," as someone put it. It is a higher thing than the beggar knocking at the rich man's door.

The word *prayer* really means "a wish directed toward," that is, toward God. All that true prayer seeks is God himself, for with Him we get all we need. Prayer is simply the turning of the soul to God. David describes it as the lifting up of the living soul to the living God. "Unto Thee, O LORD, do I lift up my soul" (Psalm 25:1). What a beautiful description of prayer that is. When we desire the Lord Jesus Christ to behold our souls, we also desire that the beauty of holiness may be upon us.

When we lift up our souls to God in prayer, it gives God an opportunity to do what He will in us and with us. It is putting ourselves at God's disposal. God is always on our side. When man prays, it is God's opportunity. The poet says:

> *Prayer is the soul's sincere desire,*
> *Uttered or unexpressed,*
> *The motion of a hidden fire*
> *That trembles in the breast.*

"Prayer," says an old Jewish mystic, "is the moment when heaven and earth kiss each other."

Prayer, then, is certainly not persuading God to do what we want God to do. It is not bending the will of a reluctant God to our will. It does not change His purpose, although it may release His power. "We must not conceive of prayer as overcoming God's reluctance," says Archbishop Trench, "but as laying hold of His highest willingness."

For God always purposes our greatest good. Even the prayer offered in ignorance and blindness cannot swerve Him from that, although, when we persistently pray for some harmful thing, our willfulness may bring it about, and we suffer accordingly. "He gave them their request," says the Psalmist, "but sent leanness into their soul" (Psalm 106:15). They brought this leanness upon themselves. They were cursed with the burden of a granted prayer that was not God's will for them.

Prayer, in the minds of some people, is only for emergencies. Danger threatens, sickness comes, things are lacking, difficulties arise—then they pray. Like the infidel down a coal mine. When the roof began to fall he began to pray. An old Christian standing by quietly remarked, "Aye, there's nothing like lumps of coal to make a heathen pray."

Prayer is, however, much more than merely asking God for something, although that is a very valuable part of prayer if only because it reminds us of our utter dependence upon God. It is also communion with God—**communicating and** sharing with God—talking with (not only *to*) God. We get to know people by talking with them. We get to know God in like manner. The highest result of prayer is not deliverance from evil, or the securing of some coveted thing, but knowledge of God. "And this is life eternal, that they might know thee the only true God" (John 17:3). Yes, prayer discovers more of God, and that is the soul's greatest discovery. People still cry out, "O that I knew where I might find him! that I might come even to his seat" (Job 23:3).

The kneeling Christian always finds Him, and is found of Him. The heavenly vision of the Lord Jesus blinded the eyes of Saul of Tarsus on his downward course, but he tells us later that when he was praying in the temple at Jerusalem he fell into a trance and saw Jesus. "I was in a trance ... and saw him" (Acts 22:17-18). Then it was that Christ gave him His great commission to go to the Gentiles. Vision is always a precursor of vocation and venture. It was so with Isaiah. "I saw also the Lord sitting upon a throne, high and lifted up, and his train filled the temple" (Isaiah 6:1). This vision also was a prelude to a call to service, "Go ..." (Isaiah 6:9). Now, we cannot get a vision of God unless we pray. And where there is no vision the soul perishes [the people perish] (Proverbs 29:18).

A vision of God, how precious it is. Brother Lawrence once said, "Prayer is nothing else than a sense of God's presence"—and that is just the practice of the presence of God.

A friend of Horace Bushnell was present when that man of God prayed. There came over him a wonderful sense of God's nearness. He says: "When Horace Bushnell buried his face in his hands and prayed, I was afraid to stretch out my hand in the darkness, lest I should touch God."

Was the Psalmist of old conscious of such a thought when he cried, "My soul, wait thou only upon God"? (Psalm 62:5.) I believe that much of our failure in prayer is due to the fact that we have not looked into this question, "What is prayer?" It is good to be conscious that we are always in the presence of God. It is better to gaze upon Him in adoration. But it is best of all to commune with Him as a friend—and that is prayer.

Real prayer at its highest and best reveals a soul thirsty for God—just for God alone. Real prayer comes from the lips of those whose affection is set on things above. What a man of prayer Zinzendorf was. Why? He sought the giver rather than His gifts. He said: "I have one passion: it is He, He alone."

Of course, we know that God bids us to *ask of Him*. We all obey Him that far, and we may rest well assured that prayer both pleases God and supplies all our need. But it would be a strange child who only sought his father's presence when he desired some gift from him. And do we not all yearn to rise to a higher level of prayer than mere petition? How is it to be done?

It seems to me that only two steps are necessary—or shall we say two thoughts? First of all, there must be a realization of God's glory, and then of God's grace. We sometimes sing:

> *Grace and glory flow from Thee;*
> *Shower, O shower them, Lord, on me.*

That is not just a fanciful desire, although some may ask what God's glory has to do with prayer. But should we not remind ourselves who He is to whom we pray? There is logic in the couplet:

> *Thou art coming to a King;*
> *Large petitions with thee bring.*

Do you think that any one of us spends enough time in pondering over—yes, and marveling over—God's exceeding great glory? And do you suppose that any one of us has grasped the full meaning of the word *grace*? Are not our prayers so often ineffective and powerless—and sometimes even prayerless—because we rush unthinkingly and unpreparedly into God's presence, without realizing the majesty and glory of the God whom we are approaching, and without reflecting upon the exceeding great riches of His glory in Christ Jesus, which we hope to draw upon? We must think magnificently of God.

May we then suggest that before we lay our petitions before God we first dwell in meditation upon His glory and then upon His grace—for He offers us both. We must lift up our soul to God. Let us place ourselves, as it were, in the presence of God and direct our prayer to "the King of kings, and Lord of lords; Who only hath immortality, dwelling in the light which no man can approach unto; whom no man hath seen, nor can see: to whom be honor and power everlasting" (1 Timothy 6:16). Let us then give Him adoration and praise because of His exceeding great glory. Consecration is not enough. There must be adoration.

"Holy, holy, holy, is the LORD of hosts," cry the seraphim; "the whole earth is full of his glory" (Isaiah 6:3). A "multitude of the heavenly host" cries "Glory to God in the highest" (Luke 2: 13-14). Yet some of us try to commune with God without stopping to "put off our shoes from off our feet" (Exodus 3:5).

> *Lips cry "God be merciful"*
> *That ne'er cry "God be praised."*
> *O come let us adore Him!*

And we may approach His glory with boldness. Did not our Lord pray that His disciples might behold His glory? (John 17:24). Why? And why is "the whole earth full of His glory"? The telescope reveals His infinite glory. The microscope reveals His uttermost glory. Even the unaided eye sees surpassing glory in landscape, sunshine, sea, and sky. What does it all mean? These things are but a partial revelation of God's glory. It was not a desire for self-display that led our Lord to pray, "Father, glorify thy Son" ... "O Father, glorify thou me" (John 17:1, 5). Our dear Lord wants us to realize His infinite trustworthiness and unlimited power, so that we can approach Him in simple faith and trust.

In heralding the coming of Christ the prophet declared that the "glory of the LORD shall be revealed, and all flesh shall see it together" (Isaiah 40:5). Now we must get a glimpse of that glory before we can pray correctly. So our Lord said, "When ye pray, say our Father, who art in heaven [the realm of glory], hallowed be thy name" (Matthew 6:9). There is nothing like a glimpse of glory to banish fear and doubt. Before we offer up our petitions, may it not help us to offer up our adoration in the words of praise used by some of the saints of old? Some devout souls may not need such help. We are told that Francis of Assisi would frequently spend an hour or two in prayer on the top of Mount Averno, while the only word that escaped his lips would be "God" repeated at intervals. He began with adoration—and often stopped there.

But most of us need some help to realize the glory of the invisible God before we can adequately praise and adore Him. Old William Law said, "When you begin to pray, use such expressions of the attributes of God as will make you sensible of His greatness and power."

This point is of such tremendous importance that we venture to remind you of helpful words. Some of us begin every day with a glance heavenwards while saying, "Glory be to the Father, and to the Son, and to the Holy Ghost." The prayer, "O Lord God most holy, O Lord most mighty, O holy and merciful Savior!" is often enough to bring a solemn awe and a spirit of holy adoration upon the soul. The *Gloria in Excelsis* of the Communion service is most uplifting: "Glory be to God on high and in earth peace. ... We praise thee; we bless thee; we worship thee; we glorify thee; we give thanks to thee for thy great glory, O Lord God, heavenly king, God the Father almighty." Which of us can from the heart utter praise like that and remain unmoved, unconscious of the very presence and wondrous majesty of the Lord God almighty? A verse of a hymn may serve the same purpose.

> *My God, how wonderful thou art!*
> *Thy majesty how bright.*
> *How beautiful thy mercy-seat*
> *In depths of burning light!*
> *How wonderful, how beautiful*
> *The sight of thee must be;*
> *Thine endless wisdom, boundless power*
> *And awful purity.*

This carries us into the very heavens, as also do the words:

> *Holy, holy, holy, Lord God almighty,*
> *All thy works shall praise thy name*
> *In earth, and sky, and sea.*

57

We need to cry out, and to cry often, "My soul doth magnify the Lord, And my spirit hath rejoiced in God my Savior" (Luke 1:46-47). Can we catch the spirit of the Psalmist and sing, "Bless the LORD, O my soul: and all that is within me, bless his holy name"? (Psalm 103:1). " Bless the LORD, O my soul. O LORD my God, thou art very great; thou art clothed with honor and majesty" (Psalm 104:1). When shall we learn that "in his temple doth every one speak of His glory"? (Psalm 29:9). Let us, too, cry, *Glory!*

Such worship of God, such adoration and praise and thanksgiving, not only put us into the spirit of prayer, but in some mysterious way they help God to work on our behalf. Praise and thanksgiving not only open the gates of heaven for me to approach God, but also prepare a way for God to bless me. Paul cries, "Rejoice evermore" before he says, "Pray without ceasing" (1 Thessalonians 5:16-17). So then our praise, as well as our prayers, is to be without ceasing.

At the raising of Lazarus, our Lord's prayer had as its first utterance a note of thanksgiving. "Father, I thank thee that thou has heard me" (John 11:41). He said it for those around to hear. Yes, and for us to hear.

You may perhaps be wondering why it is that we should specially give thanks to God for His great glory when we kneel in prayer, and why we should spend any time in thinking of and gazing upon that glory. But is He not the King of Glory? All He is and all He does is glory. His holiness is glorious (Exodus 15:11). His name is glorious (Deuteronomy 28:58). His work is glorious (Psalm 111:3). His power is glorious (Colossians 1:11). His voice is glorious (Isaiah 30:30).

All things bright and beautiful,
All creatures great and small.
All things wise and wonderful,
The Lord God made them all ... for His glory.

"For of him, and through him, and to him, are all things: to whom be glory for ever" (Romans 11:36). And this is the God who bids us come to Him in prayer. This God is our God, and He has "gifts for men" (Psalm 68:18). God says that everyone that is called by His name has been created for His glory (Isaiah 43:7). His Church is to be a glorious Church—holy and without blemish (Ephesians 5:27).

Have you ever fully realized that the Lord Jesus desires to share with us the glory we see in Him? This is His great gift to you and me, His redeemed ones. Believe me, the more we have of God's glory, the less shall we seek His gifts. Not only in that day "when he shall come to be glorified in his saints" (2 Thessalonians 1:10) is there glory for us, but here and now—today. He wishes us to be partakers of His glory. The Lord himself said so. "The glory which thou gavest me I have given them" (John 17:22). What is God's command? "Arise, shine; for thy light is come, and the glory of the LORD is risen upon thee." Nay, more than this: "His glory shall be seen upon thee," says the inspired prophet (Isaiah 60:1-2).

God would have people say of us as the apostle Peter said of the disciples of old: "the Spirit of glory and of God resteth upon you" (1 Peter 4:14). Would not that be an answer to most of our prayers? Could we ask for anything better? How can we get this glory? How are we to reflect it? Only as the result of prayer. It is when we pray, that the Holy Spirit takes of the things of Christ and reveals them to us (John 16:15).

It was when Moses prayed, "And he said, I beseech thee, show me thy glory," that he not only saw somewhat of it, but shared something of that glory, and his own face shone with the light of it (Exodus 33:18, 34:29). And when we, too, gaze upon "the glory of God in the face of Jesus Christ" (2 Corinthians 4:6), we shall see not only a glimpse of that glory, but we shall gain something of it ourselves.

Now, that is prayer, and the highest result of prayer. Nor is there any other way of securing that glory, that God may be glorified in us (Isaiah 60:21).

Let us often meditate upon Christ's glory—gaze upon it and so reflect it and receive it. This is what happened to our Lord's first disciples. They said in awed tones, "We beheld his glory" (John 1:14). Yes, but what followed? A few plain, unlettered, obscure fishermen fellowshipped with Christ a little while, seeing His glory; and behold! they themselves caught something of that glory. And then others marveled and "took knowledge of them, that they had been with Jesus" (Acts 4:13). And when we can declare with the apostle John, "and truly our fellowship is with the Father, and with his Son Jesus Christ" (1 John 1:3), people will say the same of us: "They have been with Jesus."

As we lift up our soul in prayer to the living God, we gain the beauty of holiness as surely as a flower becomes beautiful by living in the sunlight. Was not our Lord himself transfigured when He prayed? (Matthew 17:1-2). And the very fashion of our countenance will change (Luke 9:29), and we shall have our Mount of Transfiguration when prayer has its rightful place in our lives. People will then see in our faces, as someone has put it, "the outward and visible sign of an inward and spiritual grace." Our value to God and to others is in exact proportion to the extent in which we reveal the glory of God to them.

What is prayer? It is a sign of spiritual life. I should as soon expect life in a dead person as spiritual life in a prayerless soul. Our spirituality and our fruitfulness are always in proportion to the reality of our prayers. If, then, we have at all wandered away from home in the matter of prayer, let us today resolve, "I will arise and go to my Father, and say unto him, Father ..." (Luke 15:18).

At this point I laid down my pen, and on the page of the first paper I picked up were these words: "The secret of failure is that we see men rather than God. Romanism trembled when Martin Luther saw God. The 'great awakening' sprang into being when Jonathan Edwards saw God. The world became the parish of one man when John Wesley saw God. Multitudes were saved when George Whitefield saw God. Thousands of orphans were fed when George Muller saw God. And He is 'the same yesterday, and today, and forever'" (Hebrews 13:8).

Is it not time that we got a new vision of God—of God in all His glory? Who can say what will happen when the Church sees God? But let us not wait for others. Let us, each one of us, with unveiled face and undefiled heart, get this vision of the glory of the Lord.

"Blessed are the pure in heart: for they shall see God" (Matthew 5:8). No missioner whom it has been my joy to meet ever impressed me quite as much as Dr. Wilbur Chapman. He wrote to a friend:

I have learned some great lessons concerning prayer. At one of our missions in England the audiences were exceedingly small. But I received a note saying that an American missionary ... was going to pray God's blessing down upon our work. He was known as Praying Hyde. Almost instantly the tide turned. The hall became packed, and at my first invitation fifty men accepted Christ as their Savior. As we were leaving I said, "Mr. Hyde, I want you to pray for me." He came to my room, turned the key in the door, and dropped on his knees, and waited five minutes without a single syllable coming from his lips. I could hear my own heart thumping and his beating. I felt the hot tears running down my face. I knew I was with God. Then, with upturned face, down which the tears were streaming, he said "O God!" Then for five minutes at least he was still again; and then, when he knew that he was talking with God ... there came up from the depth of his heart such petitions for men as I had never heard before. I rose from my knees to know what real prayer was. We believe that prayer is mighty, and we believe it as we never did before.

Dr. Chapman used to say, "It was a season of prayer with John Hyde that made me realize what real prayer was. I owe to him more than I owe to any man for showing me what a prayer life is, and what a real consecrated life is ... Jesus Christ became a new ideal to me, and I had a glimpse of His prayer life; and I had a longing that has remained to this day to be a real praying man." And God the Holy Spirit can so teach us.

> *Oh, ye who sigh and languish*
> *And mourn your lack of power,*
> *Hear ye this gentle whisper:*
> *"Could ye not watch one hour?"*
> *For fruitfulness and blessing*
> *There is no royal road;*
> *The power for holy service*
> *Is intercourse with God.*

Chapter 6

HOW SHALL I PRAY?

How shall I pray? Could there be a more important question for a Christian to ask? How shall I approach the King of Glory?

When we read Christ's promises regarding prayer we are apt to think that He puts far too great a power into our hands—unless, indeed, we hastily conclude that it is impossible for Him to act as He promises. He says, ask "anything," "whatsoever," "what ye will," and "it shall be done" (John 14:13-14, 15:7).

But then He puts in a qualifying phrase. He says that we are to ask *in His name*. That is the condition, and the only one, although, as we shall remind ourselves later on, it is sometimes phrased in different words.

If, therefore, we ask and do not receive, it can only be that we are not fulfilling this condition. If then, we are true disciples of His—if we are sincere—we shall take pains (infinite pains, if need be) to discover just what it means to ask in His name; and we shall not rest content until we have fulfilled that condition. Let us read the promise again to be quite sure about it. "Whatsoever ye shall ask in my name, that will I do, that the Father may be glorified in the

Son. If ye shall ask anything in my name, I will do it" (John 14:13-14).

This was something quite new, for our Lord said so. "Hitherto have ye asked nothing in my name," but now, "ask, and ye shall receive, that your joy may be full" (John 16:24).

Five times over our Lord repeats this simple condition, "In my name" (John 14:13-14, 15:16, 16:23-24, 26). Evidently something very important is here implied. It is more than a condition—it is also a promise, an encouragement, for our Lord's bidding is always His enabling. What, then, does it mean to ask in His name? We must know this at all costs, for it is the secret of all power in prayer. And it is possible to make a wrong use of those words. Our Lord said, "Many shall come in my name, saying, I am Christ; and shall deceive many" (Matthew 24:5). He might well have said, "And many shall think they are praying to the Father in my name, while deceiving themselves."

Does it mean just adding the words, "and all this we ask in the name of Jesus Christ," at the end of our prayers?

Many people apparently think that it does. But have you never heard—or offered—prayers full of self-will and selfishness that ended up in that way, "for Christ's sake. Amen"?

God could not answer the prayers James refers to in his epistle just because those who offered them added, "we ask these things in the name of our Lord Jesus Christ." Those Christians were asking "amiss" (James 4:3). A wrong prayer cannot be made right by the addition of some mystic phrase, and a right prayer does not fail if some such words are omitted.

No! It is more than a question of words. Our Lord is thinking about faith and facts more than about some formula. The chief object of prayer is to glorify the Lord Jesus. We are to ask in Christ's name "that the Father may be glorified in the Son" (John 14:13). Listen! We are not to seek wealth or health, prosperity or success, ease or comfort, spirituality or fruitfulness in service simply for our own enjoyment or advancement or popularity, but only for Christ's sake—for His glory. Let us take three steps to a right understanding of those important words, "in my name."

1. There is a sense in which some things are done only "for Christ's sake"—because of His atoning death. Those who do not believe in the atoning death of Christ cannot pray "in His name." They may use the words, but without effect. For we are "justified by his blood" (Romans 5:9), and "we have redemption through his blood, the forgiveness of sins" (Ephesians 1:7, Colossians 1:14). In these days when Unitarianism under its guileful name of Modernism has invaded all sects, it is most important to remember the place and work of the shed blood of Christ, or prayer—so-called—becomes a delusion and a snare.

Let us illustrate this point by an experience that happened quite early in Mr. Moody's ministry. The wife of an infidel judge—a man of great intellectual gifts—begged Dwight Moody to speak to her husband. Moody, however, hesitated at arguing with such a man, and told him so quite frankly. "But," he added, "if ever you are converted will you promise to let me know?" The judge laughed cynically, and replied, "Oh, yes, I'll let you know quick enough if I am ever converted!" Moody went his way, relying upon prayer. That judge was converted, and within a year. He kept his promise and told Moody just how it came about.

I began to grow very uneasy and miserable one night when my wife was at a prayer meeting. I went to bed before she came home. I could not sleep all that night. Getting up early the next morning, I told my wife I should not need any breakfast, and went off to my office. Telling the clerks they could take a holiday, I shut myself up in my private room.

65

But I became more and more wretched. Finally, I fell on my knees and asked God to forgive me my sins, but I would not say "for Jesus' sake," for I was Unitarian, and I did not believe in the atonement. In an agony of mind I kept praying, "O God, forgive me my sins," but no answer came. At last, in desperation, I cried, "O God, for Christ's sake forgive my sins." Then I found peace at once.

That judge had no access to the presence of God until he sought it in the name of Jesus Christ. When he came in Christ's name he was at once heard and forgiven. Yes, to pray in the name of the Lord Jesus is to ask for things that the blood of Christ has secured—purchased—for us. We have "boldness to enter into the holiest by the blood of Jesus" (Hebrews 10:19). There is entrance by no other way.

But this is not all that those words *in my name* mean.

2. The most familiar illustration of coming in the name of Christ is that of drawing money from a bank by means of a check. I can draw from my bank account only up to the amount of my deposit there. In my own name, I can go no further. In the Bank of England I have no money whatsoever, and can therefore draw nothing from there. But suppose a very wealthy man who has a big account in that bank gives me a blank check bearing his signature, and bids me fill it in to any amount I choose. He is my friend. What shall I do? Shall I just satisfy my present need, or shall I draw as much as I dare? I shall certainly do nothing to offend my friend, or to lower myself in his esteem.

Well, we are told by some that heaven is our bank. God is the great banker, for "every good gift and every perfect gift is from above, and cometh down from the Father" (James 1:17). We need a check with which we can draw upon this boundless store. The Lord Jesus gives us a blank check in prayer. "Fill it in," says He, "to any amount; ask anything, what you will, and you shall have it. Present your check in my name, and your request will be honored."

Let me put this in the words of a well-known evangelist of today.

That is what happens when I go to the bank of heaven—when I go to God in prayer. I have nothing deposited there; I have no credit there; and if I go in my own name I will get absolutely nothing. But Jesus Christ has unlimited credit in heaven, and He has granted me the privilege of going with His name on my checks. And when I thus go, my prayers will be honored to any extent. To pray, then, in the name of Christ is to pray, not on the ground of my credit, but His.

This is all very delightful, and, in a sense, very true.

If the check were drawn on a Government account, or upon some wealthy corporation, one might be tempted to get all one could. But remember, we are coming to a loving Father to whom we owe all, and whom we love with all our heart, and to whom we may come repeatedly. In cashing our checks at the bank of heaven, we desire chiefly His honor and His glory. We wish to do only that which is pleasing in His sight. To cash some of our checks—to answer some of our prayers—would only bring dishonor to His name, and discredit and discomfort to us. True, His resources are unlimited, but His honor is assailable.

Experience, however, makes argument unnecessary. Dear reader, have we not—all of us—often tried this method only to fail?

How many of us dare say we have never come away from the bank of heaven without getting what we asked for, although we have apparently asked "in Christ's name"? Wherein do we fail? Is it because we do not seek to learn God's will for us? We must not try to exceed His will.

May I give a personal experience of my own that has never been told in public, and that is probably quite unique? It happened over thirty years ago, and now I see why. It makes such a splendid illustration of what we are now trying to learn about prayer.

A well-to-do friend, and an exceedingly busy one, wished to give me one pound toward a certain object. He invited me to his office, and hastily wrote out a check for the amount. He folded the check and handed it to me, saying, "Will you kindly cash this at the bank?"

On arriving at the bank I glanced at my name on the check without troubling to verify the amount, endorsed it, and handed it to a clerk. "This is rather a big sum to cash over the counter," he said, eyeing me narrowly.

"Yes, I replied laughingly, "one pound."

"No," said the clerk: "this is made out for one thousand pounds.'"

And so it was. My friend was, no doubt, accustomed to writing big checks; and he had actually written 1000 pounds instead of 1 pound. Now, what was my position legally? The check was truly in his name. The signature was all right. My endorsement was all right. Could I not demand the 1000 pounds, provided there was sufficient money in his account? The check was written deliberately, if hurriedly, and freely to me—why should I not take the gift? Why not?

But I was dealing with a friend—a generous friend to whom I owed many deeds of loving kindness. He had revealed his mind to me. I knew his wishes and desires.

He meant to give me one pound, and no more. I knew his intention, his mind, and at once took back the all-too-generous check, and in due time I received just one pound, according to his will. Had that donor given me a blank check the result would have been exactly the same. He would have expected me to write in one pound, and my honor would have been at stake in my doing so.

Need we draw the lesson? God has His will for each one of us, and unless we seek to know that will we are likely to ask for a *thousand*, when He knows that *one* will be best for us. In our prayers we are coming to a friend—a loving Father. We owe everything to Him. He bids us come to Him whenever we like for all we need. His resources are infinite.

But He bids us to remember that we should ask only for those things that are according to His will—only for that which will bring glory to His name. John says, "If we ask anything according to His will, He heareth us" (1 John 5:14). So then our friend gives us a blank check, and leaves us to fill in anything we desire. But He knows that if we truly love Him we will never put down—never ask for—things He is not willing to give us, because they would be harmful to us.

Perhaps with most of us the fault lies in the other direction. God gives us a blank check and says, "Ask for a thousand"—and we ask for a hundred! Are we not insulting God for treating Him thus? Do we ask enough? Do we dare to ask "according to his riches in glory"? (Philippians 4:19).

The point we are dwelling upon, however, is this—we cannot be sure that we are praying in His name unless we learn His will for us.

3. But even now we have not exhausted the meaning of those words *in my name*. We all know what it is to ask for a thing in the name of another. But we are very careful not to allow anyone to use our name who is not to be trusted, or they might abuse our trust and discredit our name. Gehazi, the trusted servant, dishonestly used Elisha's name when he ran after Naaman. In Elisha's name he secured riches, but also inherited a curse for his wickedness.

A trusted clerk often uses his employer's name and handles great sums of money as if they were his own. But this he does only so long as he is thought to be worthy of such confidence in him. And he uses the money for his master, and not for himself. All our money belongs to our Master, Christ Jesus. We can go to God for supplies in His name if we use all we get for His glory.

When I go to cash a check payable to me, the banker is quite satisfied if the signature of his client is genuine and that I am the person authorized to receive the money. He does not ask for references to my character. He has no right whatever to enquire whether I am worthy to receive the money or to be trusted to use it correctly. It is not so with the bank of Heaven. Now, this is a point of greatest importance. Do not hurry over what is now to be said.

When I go to heaven's bank in the name of the Lord Jesus, with a check drawn upon the unsearchable riches of Christ, God demands that I be a worthy recipient. Not worthy in the sense that I merit or deserve anything from a holy God—but worthy in the sense that I am seeking the gift not for my glory or self-interest, but for the glory of God.

Otherwise I may pray and not get. "Ye ask, and receive not, because ye ask amiss, that ye may consume it upon your lusts" (James 4:3).

The great heavenly banker will not cash checks for us if our motives are not right. Is not this why so many fail in prayer? Christ's name is the revelation of His character.

To pray in His name is to pray in His character, as His representative sent by Him. It is to pray by His Spirit and according to His will. It is to have His approval in our asking, to seek what He seeks, to ask help to do what He himself would wish to be done, and to desire to do it not for our own glorification, but for His glory alone. To pray in His name we must have identity of interests and purpose. Self and its aims and desires must be entirely controlled by God's Holy Spirit, so that our wills are in complete harmony with Christ's will.

We must reach the attitude of St. Augustine when he, cried, "O Lord, grant that I may do thy will as if it were my will, so that thou mayest do my will as if it were thy will."

Child of God, does this seem to make prayer in His name quite beyond us? That was not our Lord's intention. He is not mocking us. Speaking of the Holy Spirit our Lord used these words: "The Comforter ... whom the Father will send in my name" (John 14:26). Now, our Savior wants us to be so controlled by the Holy Spirit that we may act in Christ's name. "As many as are led by the Spirit of God, they are the sons of God" (Romans 8:14). And only sons can say, "Our Father."

Our Lord said of Saul of Tarsus, "He is a chosen vessel unto me, to bear my name before the Gentiles, and kings, and the children of Israel" (Acts 9:15). Not to them, but before them. So Paul says, "It pleased God ... to reveal his Son in me" (Galatians 1:15-16). We cannot pray in Christ's name unless we bear that name before people. And this is only possible so long as we abide in Him and His words abide in us. So we come to this—unless the heart is right the prayer must be wrong.

Christ said, "If ye abide in me, and my words abide in you, ye shall ask what ye will, and it shall be done unto you" (John 15:7).

Those three promises are really identical—they express the same thought in different words. Look at them.

Ask any thing in my name, I will do it (John 14:13-14).

Ask what ye will (if ye abide in me and my words abide in you), and it shall be done unto you (John 15:7).

Ask any thing according to His will,... we have the petitions we desired of Him (1 John 5:14-15).

We could sum them all up in the words of the apostle John, "'Whatsoever we ask, we receive of him, because we keep his commandments, and do those things that are pleasing in his sight" (1 John 3:22). When we do what He bids, He does what we ask. Listen to God and God will listen to you. Thus our Lord gives us power of attorney over His kingdom, the kingdom of Heaven, but only if we fulfill the condition of abiding in Him.

71

Oh, what a wonder is this. How eagerly and earnestly we should seek to know His mind, His wish, His will. How amazing it is that any one of us should by our own self-seeking miss such unsearchable riches. We know that God's will is the best for us. We know that He longs to bless us and make us a blessing. We know that to follow our own inclination is absolutely certain to harm us and to hurt us and those whom we love. We know that to turn away from His will for us is to court disaster. O child of God, why do we not trust Him fully and wholly? Here we are, then, once again brought face to face with a life of holiness. We see with the utmost clearness that our Savior's call to prayer is simply a clarion call to holiness. "Be ye holy," for without holiness "no man shall see the Lord," and prayer cannot be efficacious (1 Peter 1:16, Hebrews 12:14).

When we confess that we never get answers to our prayers, we are condemning not God, or His promises, or the power of prayer, but ourselves. There is no greater test of spirituality than prayer. Christians who try to pray quickly discover just where they stand in God's sight.

Unless we are living the victorious life we cannot truly pray in the name of Christ, and our prayer life must of necessity be feeble, fitful, and often unfruitful.

In His name must be according to His will But can we know His will? Assuredly we can. Paul not only says, "Let this mind be in you, which was also in Christ Jesus" (Philippians 2:5). He also boldly declares, "we have the mind of Christ" (1 Corinthians 2:16). How, then, can we get to know God's will?

We shall remember that "the secret of the LORD is with them that fear him" (Psalm 25:14).

In the first place, we must not expect God to reveal His will to us unless we desire to know that will and intend to do that will. Knowledge of God's will and the performance of that will go together. We are apt to desire to know God's will so that we may decide whether we will obey or not. Such an attitude is disastrous. "If any man will do his will, he shall know of the doctrine, whether it be of God" (John 7:17).

God's will is revealed in His Word in holy Scriptures. What He promises in His Word I may know to be according to His will.

For example, I may confidently ask for wisdom, because His Word says, "If any ... lack wisdom, let him ask of God, ... and it shall be given him" (James 1:5). We cannot be people of prevailing prayer unless we study God's Word to find out His will for us.

But it is the Holy Spirit of God who is prayer's great helper. Read again those wonderful words of Paul: "In the same way the Spirit also helps us in our weakness; for we do not know what prayers to offer nor in what way to offer them, but the Spirit himself pleads for us in yearnings that can find no words, and the Searcher of hearts knows what the Spirit's meaning is, because His intercessions for God's people are in harmony with God's will" (Romans 8:26-28, Weymouth).

What comforting words. Ignorance and helplessness in prayer are indeed blessed things if they cast us upon the Holy Spirit. Blessed be the name of the Lord Jesus. We are left without excuse. Pray we must, pray we can.

Remember our heavenly Father is pledged to "give the Holy Spirit to them that ask him" (Luke 11:13), and any other "good things," too (Matthew 7:11).

Child of God, you have often prayed. You have, no doubt, often bewailed your feebleness and slackness in prayer. But have you really prayed in His name?

It is when we have failed and know not what prayers to offer or in what way, that the Holy Spirit is promised as our helper.

Is it not worthwhile to be wholly and wholeheartedly yielded to Christ? The half-and-half Christian is of very little

73

use either to God or humanity. God cannot use him, and humanity has no use for him, but considers him a hypocrite. One sin allowed in the life wrecks at once our usefulness and our joy, and robs prayer of its power.

Beloved, we have caught a fresh glimpse of the grace and the glory of our Lord Jesus Christ. He is willing and waiting to share with us both His glory and His grace. He is willing to make us channels of blessing. Shall we not worship God in sincerity and truth, and cry eagerly and earnestly, "What shall I do, Lord?" (Acts 22:10) and then, in the power of His might, do it?

Paul once shot up that prayer to Heaven: "What shall I do?" What answer did he get? Listen! He tells us in his counsel to believers everywhere just what it meant to him, and should mean to us.

Put on therefore, as the elect of God, holy and beloved, bowels of mercies, kindness, humbleness of mind, meekness, longsuffering; Forbearing one another, and forgiving one another, if any man have a quarrel against any: even as Christ forgave you, so also do ye. And above all these things put on charity, which is the bond of perfectness. And let the peace of God rule in your hearts, to the which also ye are called in one body; and be ye thankful. Let the word of Christ dwell in you richly in all wisdom; teaching and admonishing one another in psalms and hymns and spiritual songs, singing with grace in your hearts to the Lord. And whatsoever ye do in word or deed, do all in the name of the Lord Jesus, giving thanks to God and the Father by him (Colossians 3:12-17).

It is only when whatever we do is done in His name that He will do whatever we ask in His name.

Chapter 7

MUST I AGONIZE?

Prayer is measured, not by time, but by intensity. Earnest souls who read of Christians like Praying Hyde are today anxiously asking, "Am I expected to pray like that?"

They hear of others who sometimes remain on their knees before God all day or all night, refusing food and scorning sleep, while they pray and pray and pray. They naturally wonder, "Are we to do the same? Must all of us follow their examples?" We must remember that those men of prayer did not pray by time. They continued so long in prayer because they could not stop praying.

Some have ventured to think that in what has been said in earlier chapters I have hinted that we must all follow in their train. Child of God, do not let any such thought—such fear?—distress you. Just be willing to do what He will have you do—what He leads you to do. Think about it, pray about it. We are bidden by the Lord Jesus to pray to our loving heavenly Father. We sometimes sing, "Oh, how He loves." And no one can fathom that love.

Prayer is not given us as a burden to be borne, or an irksome duty to fulfill, but to be a joy and power to which there is no limit. It is given us that we "may obtain mercy, and find grace to help in time of need" (Hebrews 4:16). And every time is a time of need. "Pray ye" is an invitation to be accepted rather than a command to be obeyed (Matthew 6:9). Is it a burden for a child to come to his father to ask for some boon? How a father loves his child, and seeks its highest good. How he shields that little one from any sorrow or pain or suffering. Our heavenly Father loves us infinitely more than any earthly father. The Lord Jesus loves us infinitely more than any earthly friend. God forgive me if any words of mine, on such a precious theme as prayer, have wounded the hearts or consciences of those who are yearning to know more about prayer. "Your Father knoweth," said our Lord (Matthew 6:8), and if He knows, we can but trust and not be afraid.

A schoolmaster may blame a boy for neglected homework, or unpunctual attendance, or frequent absence, but the loving father in the home knows all about it. He knows all about the devoted service of the little lad in the home circle, where sickness or poverty throws so many loving tasks in his way. Our dear loving Father knows all about us. He sees, and He knows how little leisure some of us have for prolonged periods of prayer.

For some of us God makes leisure. He makes us lie down (Psalm 23:2) that He may make us look up. Even then, weakness of body often prevents prolonged prayer. Yet I question if any of us, however great and reasonable our excuses, spend enough thought over our prayers. Some of us are bound to be much in prayer. Our very work demands it. We may be looked upon as spiritual leaders; we may have the spiritual welfare or training of others. God forbid that we should sin against the Lord in ceasing to pray enough for them (1 Samuel 12:23). Yes, with some it is our very business—almost our life's work—to pray. Others:

> *Have friends who give them pain,*
> *Yet have not sought a friend in Him.*

For them they cannot help praying. If we have the burden of souls upon us we will never ask, "How long need I pray?"

But how well we know the difficulties that surround the prayer life of many. A little pile of letters lies before me as I write. They are full of excuses, and kindly protests, and reasoning about why they cannot pray. But is that why they are written? No! No! Far from it. In every one of them there is an undercurrent of deep yearning to know God's will, and how to obey the call to prayer amid all the countless claims of life.

Those letters tell of many who cannot get away from others for times of secret prayer, of those who share bedrooms and have no proper place to pray. They tell of busy mothers, and maids, and wives who scarcely know how to get through the endless washing and cooking, mending and cleaning, shopping and visiting. Tired workers write and say they are too weary to pray when the day's work is done.

Child of God, our heavenly Father knows all about it. He is not a taskmaster. He is our Father. if you have no time for prayer, or no chance of secret prayer, why, just tell Him all about it—and you will discover that you are praying.

To those who seem unable to get any solitude at all, or even the opportunity of stealing into a quiet church for a few moments, may we point to the wonderful prayer life of the apostle Paul. Did it ever occur to you that he was in prison when he wrote most of those marvelous prayers of his that we possess? Picture him. He was chained to a Roman soldier day and night, and was never alone for a moment. Epaphras was there part of the time, and caught something of his Master's passion for prayer. Luke may have been there. What prayer meetings! No opportunity for secret prayer. No! But how much we owe to the uplifting of those chained hands. You and I may be never, or rarely ever, alone, but at least our hands are not fettered with chains, and our hearts are not fettered, nor our lips.

Can we make time for prayer? I may be wrong, but my own belief is that it is not God's will for most of us—and perhaps not for any of us—to spend so much time in prayer as to injure our physical health through getting insufficient food or sleep. With very many it is a physical impossibility, because of bodily weakness, to remain long in the spirit of intense prayer.

The posture in which we pray is immaterial. God will listen whether we kneel, stand, sit, walk, or work.

I am quite aware that many have testified to the fact that God sometimes gives special strength to those who curtail their hours of rest in order to pray more. At one time the writer tried getting up very early in the morning—and every morning—for prayer and communion with God. After a time he found that his daily work was suffering in intensity and effectiveness, and that it was difficult to keep awake during the early evening hours. But do we pray as much as we might do? It is a lasting regret to me that I allowed the days of youth and vigor to pass by without laying more stress upon those early hours of prayer.

Now, the inspired command is clear enough: "Pray without ceasing" (1 Thessalonians 5:17). Our dear Lord said, "Men ought always to pray, and not to faint" [and never lose heart, Weymouth] (Luke 18:1).

This, of course, cannot mean that we are to be always on our knees. I am convinced that God does not wish us to neglect rightful work in order to pray. But it is equally certain that we might work better and do more work if we gave less time to work and more to prayer.

Let us work well. We are to be "Not slothful in business" (Romans 12:11). Paul says, "We beseech you, brethren, that ye increase more and more; and that ye ... do your own business, and to work with your hands, ... that ye may walk honestly ... and have lack of nothing" (1 Thessalonians 4:10-12). "If any would not work, neither should he eat" (2 Thessalonians 3:10).

But are there not endless opportunities during every day of "lifting up holy hands" (1 Timothy 2:8), or at least holy hearts, in prayer to our Father? Do we seize the opportunity, as we open our eyes upon each new day, of praising and blessing our Redeemer? Every day is an Easter day to the Christian. We can pray as we dress. Without a reminder we might often forget. Stick a piece of paper in the corner of your mirror, with the words, "Pray without ceasing." Try it. We can pray as we go from one duty to another. We can often pray at our work. The washing and the writing, the mending and the minding, the cooking and the cleaning will be done all the better for it.

Do not children, both young and old, work better and play better when some loved one is watching? Will it not help us ever to remember that the Lord Jesus is always with us, watching? Aye, and helping. The very consciousness of His eye upon us will be the consciousness of His power within us.

Do you not think that Paul had in his mind this habitual praying rather than fixed seasons of prayer when he said, "The Lord is at hand [i.e., is near, Weymouth]. Be careful for nothing [In nothing be anxious]; but in everything by prayer and supplication with thanksgiving let your requests be made known unto God"? (Philippians 4:5-6). Does not "in everything" suggest that as thing after thing befalls us moment by moment, we should then and there make it an object of prayer and praise to the Lord who is near?

What a blessed thought: prayer is to a God who is near. When our Lord sent His disciples forth to work, He said, "lo, I am with you alway" (Matthew 28:20).

Sir Thomas Browne, the celebrated physician, had caught this spirit. He made a vow:

79

To pray in all places where quietness inviteth; in any house, highway or street; and to know no street in this city that may not witness that I have not forgotten God and my Savior in it; and that no town or parish where I have been may not say the like. To take occasion of praying upon the sight of any church which I see as I ride about. To pray daily and particularly for my sick patients, and for all sick people, under whose care soever. And at the entrance into the house of the sick to say, "The peace and the mercy of God be upon this house." After a sermon to make a prayer and desire a blessing, and to pray for the minister.

But we question if this habitual communion with our blessed Lord is possible unless we have times of definite prayer, whether long or brief. And what of these prayer seasons? We have said earlier that prayer is as simple as a little child asking something of its father. Nor would such a remark need any further comment were it not for the existence of the evil one.

There is no doubt whatever that the devil opposes our approach to God in prayer, and does all he can to prevent the prayer of faith. His chief way of hindering us is to try to fill our minds with the thought of our needs, so that they shall not be occupied with thoughts of God, our loving Father, to whom we pray. He wants us to think more of the gift than of the Giver. The Holy Spirit leads us to pray for a brother. We get as far as "O God, bless my brother," and away go our thoughts to the brother and his affairs, difficulties, hopes, and fears. Away goes prayer.

How hard the devil makes it for us to concentrate our thoughts upon God. This is why we urge people to get a realization of the glory, power, and presence of God before offering up any petition. If there were no devil, there would be no difficulty in prayer, but it is the evil one's chief aim to make prayer impossible. That is why most of us find it hard to sympathize with those who profess to condemn what they call "vain repetitions" and "much speaking" in prayer—quoting our Lord's words in His sermon on the mount (Matthew 6:7).

A prominent London minister said quite recently, "God does not wish us to waste either His time or ours with long prayers. We must be businesslike in our dealings with God, and just tell Him plainly and briefly what we want, and leave the matter there." But does our friend think that prayer is merely making God acquainted with our needs? If that is all there is in it, then there is no need of prayer. "For your Father knoweth what things ye have need of, before ye ask Him," said our Lord when urging the disciples to pray (Matthew 6:8).

We are aware that Christ Himself condemned some long prayers (Matthew 23:14). But they were long prayers made for a pretense, for a show (Luke 20:47). Dear praying Christian, believe me, the Lord would equally condemn many of the long prayers made every week in some of our prayer meetings. Those long prayers that kill the prayer meeting, and that finish up with a plea that God would hear these feeble breathings or unworthy words.

But He never condemns long prayers that are sincere. Let us not forget that our Lord sometimes spent long nights in prayer. We are told of one of these—we do not know how frequently they were (Luke 6:12). He would sometimes rise a "great while before day" and depart to a solitary place for prayer (Mark 1:35). The perfect man spent more time in prayer than we do. It would seem an undoubted fact that with God's saints in all ages, nights of prayer with God have been followed by days of power with people.

Nor did our Lord excuse Himself from prayer—as we, in our ignorance, might think He could have done—because of the pressing calls to service and boundless opportunities of usefulness. After one of His busiest days, at a time when His popularity was at its highest, just when everyone sought His company and His counsel, He turned His back upon them all and retired to a mountain to pray (Matthew 14:23).

We are told that once "great multitudes came together to hear, and to be healed by him of their infirmities" (Luke 5:15). Then comes the remark, "But Jesus himself constantly withdrew into the desert, and there prayed" (Luke 5:16, Weymouth). Why? Because He knew that constant prayer was then far more potent than constant service.

We say we are too busy to pray. But the busier our Lord was, the more He prayed. Sometimes He had no leisure so much as to eat (Mark 3:20); and sometimes He had no leisure for needed rest and sleep (Mark 6:31). Yet He always took time to pray. If frequent prayer, and at times long hours of prayer, were necessary for our Savior, are they less necessary for us?

I do not write to persuade people to agree with me, that is a very small matter. We only want to know the truth. Charles Spurgeon once said:

There is no need for us to go beating about the bush, and not telling the Lord distinctly what it is that we crave at His hands. Nor will it be seemly for us to make any attempt to use fine language; but let us ask God in the simplest and most direct manner for just the things we want. ... I believe in business prayers. I mean prayers in which you take to God one of the many promises which He has given us in His Word, and expect it to be fulfilled as certainly as we look for the money to be given us when we go to the bank to cash a check. We should not think of going there, lolling over the counter chattering with the clerks on every conceivable subject except the one thing for which we had gone to the bank, and then coming away without the coin we needed; but we should lay before the clerk the promise to pay the bearer a certain sum, tell him in what form we wished to take the amount, count the cash after him, and then go on our way to attend to other business. That is just an illustration of the method in which we should draw supplies from the bank of Heaven.

Now that is splendid!

So by all means let us be definite in prayer, let us put eloquence aside if we have any, let us avoid needless chatter, and let us come in faith expecting to receive.

But would the bank clerk pass me the money over the counter so readily if there stood by my side a powerful, evil-faced, well-armed thief whom he recognized to be a desperate criminal waiting to snatch the money before my weak hands could grasp it? Would he not wait until the thief had gone? This is no fanciful picture. The Bible teaches us that, in some way or other, Satan can hinder our prayers and delay the answer. Does not Peter urge certain things upon Christians, that their "prayers be not hindered"? (1 Peter 3:7). Our prayers can be hindered. "Then cometh the wicked one, and catcheth away that which was sown in his heart" (Matthew 13:19).

Scripture gives us one instance—probably only one out of many—where the evil one delayed for three weeks an answer to prayer. We only mention this to show the need of repeated prayer, persistence in prayer, and also to call attention to the extraordinary power that Satan possesses. We refer to Daniel 10:12-13: "Fear not, Daniel: for from the first day that thou didst set thine heart to understand, and to chasten thyself before thy God, thy words were heard, and I am come for thy words. But the prince of the kingdom of Persia withstood me one and twenty days: but lo, Michael, one of the chief princes, came to help me."

We must not overlook this Satanic opposition and hindrance to our prayers. If we were to be content to ask God only once for some promised thing or one we deemed necessary, these chapters would never have been written. Are we never to ask again? For instance, I know that God wills

83

not the death of a sinner. So I come boldly in prayer: "O God, save my friend." Am I never to ask for his conversion again? George Muller prayed daily and often for sixty years for the conversion of a friend. But what light does the Bible throw upon businesslike prayers? Our Lord gave two parables to teach persistence and continuance in prayer. The man who asked three loaves from his friend at midnight received as many as he needed "because of his importunity" or persistency; i.e., his *shamelessness*, as the word literally means (Luke 11:8). The widow who "troubled" the unjust judge with her "continual coming" at last secured the results she desired. Our Lord adds "And shall not God avenge his own elect, which cry day and night unto him, though he bear long with them?" (Luke 18:7).

How delighted our Lord was with the poor Syro-Phoenician woman who would not take refusals or rebuffs for an answer. Because of her continual request He said: "O woman, great is thy faith: be it unto thee even as thou wilt" (Matthew 15:28). Our dear Lord, in His agony in Gethsemane, found it necessary to repeat even His prayer. "And he left them, and went away again, and prayed the third time, saying the same words" (Matthew 26:44). And we find Paul, the apostle of prayer, asking God time after time to remove his thorn in the flesh. "For this thing," says he, "I besought the Lord thrice, that it might depart from me" (2 Corinthians 12:8).

God does not always grant our petitions immediately. Sometimes we are not spiritually fit to receive the gift. Sometimes He says no in order to give us something far better. Think, too, of the days when Peter was in prison. If your boy was unjustly imprisoned, expecting death at any moment, would you, could you, be content to pray just once, a businesslike prayer: "O God, deliver my son from the hands of these men"? Would you not be very much in prayer and very much in earnest?

This is how the Church prayed for Peter. "Long and fervent prayer was offered to God by the Church on his behalf" (Acts 12:5, Weymouth). Bible students will have noticed that the King James Version rendering, "without ceasing," reads "earnestly" in the Revised Version. R. A. Torrey points out that neither translation gives the full force of the Greek. The word means literally "stretched-out-ed-ly." It represents the soul on the stretch of earnest and intense desire. Intense prayer was made for the apostle Peter. The very same word is used of our Lord in Gethsemane: "And being in an agony he prayed more earnestly: and his sweat became as it were great drops of blood falling down to the ground" (Luke 22:44).

Ah! there was earnestness, even agony in prayer. Now, what about our prayers? Are we called upon to agonize in prayer? Many of God's dear saints say no. They think such agonizing in us would reveal great lack of faith. Yet most of the experiences that befell our Lord are to be ours. We have been crucified with Christ, and we are risen with Him. Shall there be no travailing for souls with us?

Come back to human experience. Can we refrain from agonizing in prayer over dearly beloved children who are living in sin? I question if any Christians can have the burden of souls upon them, a passion for souls, and not agonize in prayer.

Can we help crying out like John Knox, "O God, give me Scotland or I die"? Here again the Bible helps us. Was there no travail of soul and agonizing in prayer when Moses cried out to God, "Oh, this people have sinned a great sin, and have made them gods of gold. Yet now, if thou wilt forgive their sin—; and if not, blot me, I pray thee, out of thy book which thou hast written"? (Exodus 32:32).

Was there no agonizing in prayer when Paul said, "I could wish [pray] that I myself were cursed from Christ for my brethren"? (Romans 9:3).

85

We may, at all events, be quite sure that our Lord, who wept over Jerusalem, and who "offered up prayers and supplications with strong crying and tears" (Hebrews 5:7), will not be grieved if He sees us weeping over erring ones. Will it not rather gladden His heart to see us agonizing over the sin that grieves Him? In fact, may not the scarcity of conversions in so many ministries be due to lack of agonizing in prayer?

We are told that "as soon as Zion travailed, she brought forth her children" (Isaiah 66:8). Was Paul thinking of this passage when he wrote to the Galatians, "My little children, of whom I travail in birth again until Christ be formed in you"? (Galatians 4:19). And will not this be true of spiritual children? Oh, how cold our hearts often are! How little we grieve over the lost. And shall we dare to criticize those who agonize over the perishing? God forbid! There is such a thing as wrestling in prayer. Not because God is unwilling to answer, but because of the opposition of the "rulers of the darkness of this world" (Ephesians 6:12).

The very word used for *striving* in prayer means *a contest*. The contest is not between God and ourselves. He is at one with us in our desires. The contest is with the evil one, although he is a conquered foe (1 John 3:8). He desires to impede our prayers.

"We wrestle not against flesh and blood, but against principalities, against powers, against the rulers of the darkness of this world, against spiritual wickedness in high places." (Ephesians 6:12). We, too, are in the "heavenly places in Christ" (Ephesians 1:3); and it is only in Christ that we can be victorious. Our wrestling may be a wrestling of our thoughts from thinking Satan's suggestions, and keeping them fixed on Christ our Savior—that is, watching as well as praying: "watching thereunto" (Ephesians 6:18).

We are comforted by the fact that "the Spirit helpeth our infirmities: for we know not what we should pray for as we ought" (Romans 8:26) How does the Spirit help us, teach us, if not by example as well as by precept? How does the Spirit pray? "The Spirit itself maketh intercession for us with groanings which cannot be uttered" (Romans 8:26). Does the Spirit agonize in prayer as the Son did in Gethsemane?

If the Spirit prays in us, shall we not share His groanings in prayer? And if our agonizing in prayer weakens our body at the time, will an angel come to strengthen us, as it did our Lord? (Luke 22:43). We may, perhaps, like Nehemiah, weep, and mourn, and fast when we pray before God (Nehemiah 1:4). "But," one asks, "may not a godly sorrow for sin, and a yearning desire for the salvation of others, induce in us an agonizing that is unnecessary and dishonoring to God?"

May it not reveal a lack of faith in God's promises? Perhaps it may do so. But there is little doubt that Paul regarded prayer—at least sometimes—as a conflict (see Romans 15:30). In writing to the Colossian Christians he says, "I would have ye know what great conflict I have for you ... and for as many as have not seen my face in the flesh; That their hearts might be comforted" (Colossians 2:1-2). Undoubtedly he refers to his prayers for them.

Again, he speaks of Epaphras as one who is "always labouring [striving] fervently for you in prayers, that ye may stand perfect and complete in all the will of God." (Colossians 4:12).

The word for *strive* is our word *agonize*, the very word used of our Lord "being in an agony" when praying Himself (Luke 22:44).

The apostle says again, "Epaphras ... hath a great zeal for you"—that is, in his prayers (Colossians 4:12-13). Paul saw him praying there in prison, and witnessed his intense striving as he engaged in a long, untiring, effort on behalf of the Colossians. How the Praetorian guard to whom Paul was chained must have wondered—yes, and have been deeply touched—to see these men at their prayers. Their agitation, their tears, their earnest supplications as they lifted up chained hands in prayer must have been a revelation to him. *What would they think of our prayers?*

No doubt Paul was speaking of his own custom when he urged the Ephesian Christians and others "Stand therefore, ... Praying always with all prayer and supplication in the Spirit, and watching thereunto with all perseverance and supplication for all saints; And for me ... an ambassador in bonds" (Ephesians 6:14,18-20). That is a picture of his own prayer life, we may be sure.

So then prayer meets with obstacles that must be prayed away. That is what Christians mean when they talk about praying through. We must wrestle with the workings of Satan. It may be bodily weariness or pain, or the insistent claims of other thoughts, or doubt, or the direct assaults of spiritual hosts of wickedness. With us, as with Paul, prayer is something of a conflict, a wrestle, at least sometimes, which compels us to stir ourselves up to take hold of God (Isaiah 64:7). Should we be wrong if we ventured to suggest that very few people ever wrestle in prayer? Do we? But let us never doubt our Lord's power and the riches of His grace.

The author of *The Christian's Secret of a Happy Life*, Hannah Whitall-Smith, told a little circle of friends, just before her death, of an incident in her own life. Perhaps I may be allowed to tell it abroad. A lady friend who occasionally paid her a visit for two or three days was always a great trial, a veritable tax upon her temper and her patience. Every such visit demanded much prayer preparation. The time came when this critical Christian planned a visit for a whole week. Hannah felt that nothing but a whole night of prayer could fortify her for this great testing. So, providing herself with a little plate of biscuits, she retired in good time to her bedroom, to spend the night on her knees before God, to beseech Him to give her grace to keep sweet and loving during the impending visit. No sooner had she knelt beside her bed than there flashed into her mind the words of Philippians 4:19: "God shall supply all your need according to His riches in glory by Christ Jesus." Her fears vanished. She said, "When I realized that, I gave Him thanks and praised Him for His goodness. Then I jumped into bed and slept the night through. My guest arrived the next day, and I quite enjoyed her visit."

No one can lay down hard and fast rules of prayer, even for himself. God's gracious Holy Spirit alone can direct us moment by moment. There we must leave the matter. God is our judge and our guide. But let us remember that prayer is a many-sided thing. As Bishop H. C. Moule says, "True prayer can be uttered under innumerable circumstances." Very often ...

> *Prayer is the burden of a sigh*
> *The falling of a tear,*
> *The upward glancing of an eye*
> *When none but God is near.*

It may be just letting your request be made known unto God (Philippians 4:6). We cannot think that prayer need always be a conflict and a wrestle. For if it were, many of us would soon become physical wrecks, suffering from nervous breakdown, and coming to an early grave.

Also with many it is a physical impossibility to stay any length of time in a posture of prayer. Dr. Moule says: "Prayer, genuine and victorious, is continually offered without the least physical effort or disturbance. It is often in the deepest stillness of soul and body that it wins its longest way. But there is another side of the matter. Prayer is never meant to be indolently easy, however simple and reliant it may be. It is meant to be an infinitely important transaction between man and God. And therefore, very often ... it has to be viewed

89

involving labor, persistence, conflict, if it would prayer indeed."

No one can prescribe for another. But be persuaded in your own mind how to pray, and the Holy Spirit will inspire you and guide you in how long to pray. And let us all be so full of the love of God our Savior that prayer, at all times and in all places, may be a joy as well as a means of grace.

> *Shepherd divine, our wants relieve*
> *In this and every day;*
> *To all thy tempted followers give*
> *The power, to watch and pray.*
> *The spirit of interceding grace*
> *Give us the faith to claim;*
> *To wrestle until we see thy face*
> *And know thy hidden name.*

Chapter 8

DOES GOD ALWAYS
ANSWER PRAYER?

We now come to one of the most important questions that any one can ask. Very much depends upon the answer we are led to give. Let us not shrink from facing the question fairly and honestly. Does God always answer prayer? Of course, we all grant that He does answer prayer—some prayers, and sometimes. But does He always answer true prayer? Some so-called prayers He does not answer, because He does not hear them. When His people were rebellious, He said, "When ye make many prayers, I will not hear" (Isaiah 1:15).

But a child of God ought to expect answers to prayer. God means every prayer to have an answer; and not a single real prayer can fail of its effect in heaven.

Yet that wonderful declaration of the apostle Paul: "All things are yours ... and ye are Christ's" (1 Corinthians 3:21, 23), seems so plainly and so tragically untrue for most Christians. Yet it is not so. They are ours, but so many of us do not possess our possessions. The owners of Mount Morgan, in Queensland, toiled arduously for years on its barren slopes, eking out a miserable existence, never knowing that under their feet was one of the richest sources of gold the world has ever known. There was wealth, vast, undreamt of, yet unimagined and unrealized. It was theirs and yet not theirs.

The Christian, however, knows of the riches of God in glory in Christ Jesus, but does not seem to know how to get them.

Now, our Lord tells us that they are to be had for the asking. May He indeed give us all a right judgment in prayer-things. When we say that no true prayer goes unanswered we are not claiming that God always gives just what we ask for. Have you ever met a parent so foolish as to treat his child like that? We do not give our child a red-hot poker because he clamors for it. Wealthy people are the most careful not to allow their children much pocket money.

Why, if God gave us all we prayed for, we should rule the world, and not He. And surely we would all confess that we are not capable of doing that. Moreover, more than one ruler of the world is an absolute impossibility.

God's answer to prayer may be yes, or it may be no. It may be wait, for it may be that He plans a much larger blessing than we imagined, and one which involves other lives as well as our own.

God's answer is sometimes no. But this is not necessarily a proof of known and willful sin in the life of the petitioner, although there may be sins of ignorance. He said no to Paul sometimes (2 Corinthians 12:8-9). More often than not the refusal is due to our ignorance or selfishness in asking. "For we know not what we should pray for as we ought" (Romans 8:26). That was what was wrong with the mother of Zebedee's children. She came and worshipped our Lord and prayed to Him. He quickly replied, "Ye know not what ye ask" (Matthew 20:22). Elijah, a great man of prayer, sometimes had no for an answer. But when he was swept up to glory in a chariot of fire, did he regret that God said no when he cried out "O LORD, take away my life"? (1 Kings 19:4).

God's answer is sometimes wait. He may delay the answer because we are not yet fit to receive the gift we crave—as with wrestling Jacob. Do you remember the famous prayer of Augustine: "O God, make me pure, but not now"? Are not our prayers sometimes like that? Are we always really willing to drink the cup; that is, pay the price of answered prayer? Sometimes He delays so that greater glory may be brought to himself.

God's delays are not denials. We do not know why He sometimes delays the answer and at other times answers before we call (Isaiah 65:24). George Muller, one of the greatest men of prayer of all time, had to pray over a period of more than sixty-three years for the conversion of a friend. Who can tell why? "The great point is never to give up until the answer comes," said Muller. "I have been praying for sixty-three years and eight months for one man's conversion. He is not converted yet, but he will be. How can it be otherwise? There is the unchanging promise of Jehovah, and on that I rest."

Was this delay due to some persistent hindrance from the minions of Satan? (Daniel 10:13). Was it a mighty and prolonged effort on the part of Satan to shake or break Muller's faith? For no sooner was Muller dead than his friend was converted—even before the funeral.

Yes, his prayer was granted, though the answer tarried long in coming. So many of George Muller's petitions were granted him, however, that he once exclaimed, "Oh, how good, kind, gracious and condescending is the one with whom we have to do. I am only a poor, frail, sinful man, but He has heard my prayers ten thousands of times."

Perhaps some are asking, How can I discover whether God's answer is no or wait? We may rest assured that He will not let us pray sixty-three years to get a no! Muller's prayer, so long repeated, was based upon the knowledge that God does not will the death of a sinner, but that He "will have all men to be saved" (1 Timothy 2:4).

Even as I write, the postman brings me an illustration of this. A letter comes from one who very rarely writes me, and did not even know my address—one whose name is known to every Christian worker in England. A loved one was stricken down with illness. Is he to continue to pray for her recovery? Is God's answer no, or is it wait but go on praying?

My friend writes, "I had distinct guidance from God regarding my beloved ... that it was the will of God she should be taken ... I retired into the rest of surrender and submission to His will. I have much to praise God for." A few hours later God took that loved one to be with Him in glory.

Again may we urge our readers to hold on to this truth: *true prayer never goes unanswered.*

If we only gave more thought to our prayers we would pray more intelligently. That sounds like a truism. But we say it because some dear Christian people seem to lay their common sense and reason aside before they pray. A little reflection would show that God cannot grant some prayers. During the war every nation prayed for victory. Yet it is perfectly obvious that all countries could not be victorious. Two men living together might pray, the one for rain and the other for fine weather. God cannot give both these things at the same time in the same place.

But the truthfulness of God is at stake in this matter of prayer. We have all been reading again those marvelous prayer promises of our Lord, and have almost staggered at them—the wideness of their scope, the fullness of their intent, the largeness of that one word *whatsoever.* Very well. "Let God be true" (Romans 3:4), and true He will always be.

Do not stop to ask the writer if God has granted all his prayers. He has not. To have said yes to some of them would have spelled curse instead of blessing. To have answered others was, alas!, a spiritual impossibility—he was not worthy of the gifts he sought. The granting of some of them would but have fostered spiritual pride and self-satisfaction. How plain all these things seem now in the fuller light of God's Holy Spirit.

As one looks back and compares one's eager, earnest, prayers with one's poor, unworthy service and lack of true spirituality, one sees how impossible it was for God to grant the very things He longed to impart. It was often like asking God to put the ocean of His love into a heart the size of a thimble. And yet, how God yearns to bless us with every spiritual blessing. How the dear Savior cries again and again, "how often would I have ... and ye would not!" (Matthew 23:37).

The sadness of it all is that we often ask and do not receive because of our unworthiness—and then we complain because God does not answer our prayers. The Lord Jesus declares that God gives the Holy Spirit, who teaches us how to pray, just as readily as a father gives good gifts to his children. But no gift is a good gift if the child is not fit to use that gift. God never gives us something that we cannot, or will not, use for His glory (I am not referring to talents, for we may abuse or bury those, but to spiritual gifts).

Did you ever see a father give his baby boy a razor when he asked for it, because he hoped the boy would grow into a man and then find the razor useful? Does a father never say to his child, "Wait until you are older, or bigger, or wiser, or better, or stronger"? May not our loving heavenly Father also say to us, *wait*? In our ignorance and blindness we must surely sometimes say:

> *In very love refuse*
> *Whatever thou seest*
> *Our weakness would abuse.*

Rest assured that God never bestows tomorrow's gift today. It is not unwillingness on His part to give. It is not that God is ever restricted by something in Himself. His resources are infinite, and His ways are past finding out. It was after bidding His disciples to ask, that our Lord goes on to hint not only at His providence, but at His resources. "Behold the fowls of the air: ... your heavenly Father feedeth them" (Matthew 6:26). How simple it sounds. Yet have you ever reflected that not a single millionaire the wide world over is wealthy enough to feed all the birds of the air even for one day? Your heavenly Father feeds them every day, and is none the poorer for it. Shall He not much more feed you, clothe you, take care of you?

Oh, let us rely more upon prayer. Do we not know that "he is a rewarder of them that diligently seek him"? (Hebrews 11:6). The oil of the Holy Spirit will never cease to flow so long as there are empty vessels to receive it (2 Kings 4:6). It is always we who are to blame when the Spirit's work ceases. God cannot trust some Christians with the fullness of the Holy Spirit. God cannot trust some workers with definite spiritual results in their labors. They would suffer from pride and vainglory. No! we do *not* claim that God grants every Christian everything they pray for.

As we saw in an earlier chapter, there must be purity of heart, purity of motive, purity of desire, if our prayers are to be in His name. God is greater than His promises, and often gives more than either we desire or deserve, but He does not always do so. So, then, if any specific petition is not granted, we may feel sure that God is calling us to examine our hearts, for He has undertaken to grant every prayer that is truly offered in His name. Let us repeat His blessed words once more—we cannot repeat them too often: "Whatsoever ye shall ask in my name, that will I do, that the Father may be glorified in the Son. If ye shall ask any thing in my name, I will do it" (John 14:13-14).

Remember that it was impossible for Christ to offer up any prayer that was not granted. He was the Son of God—He knew the mind of God—He had the mind of the Holy Spirit.

Doesn't He once say, "Father, if it be possible, let ..." as He kneels in agony in Gethsemane's garden, pouring out strong crying and tears? (Matthew 26:39). Yes, and "He was heard in that he feared [because of his godly fear, his reverent submission]" (Hebrews 5:7). Surely not the agony but the Sonlike fear gained the answer? Our prayers are heard not so much because they are persistent but because we are children of God.

Beloved, we cannot fully understand that hallowed scene of dreadful awe and wonder. But we know that our Lord never yet made a promise that He cannot keep, or does not mean to fulfill. The Holy Spirit makes intercession for us (Romans 8:26), and God cannot say no to Him. The Lord Jesus makes intercession for us (Hebrews 7:25), and God cannot say no to Him. His prayers are worth a thousand of ours, but it is He who bids us pray.

"But was not Paul filled with the Holy Spirit?" you ask, "and did he not say, 'we have the mind of Christ?' (1 Corinthians 2:16). Yet he asked three times that the Lord remove the thorn in his flesh (2 Corinthians 12:7-8), and the Lord distinctly told him He would not do so."

It is a very striking thing, too, that the only petition recorded of the apostle Paul seeking something for himself was refused. The difficulty, however, is this: why did Paul, who had the mind of Christ, ask for something that he soon discovered was contrary to God's wishes? There are doubtless many fully-consecrated Christians reading these words who have been perplexed because God has not given some things they prayed for.

We must remember that we may be filled with the Spirit and yet be wrong in judgment or desire. We must remember,

97

too, that we are never completely filled with God's Holy Spirit once for all. The evil one is always on the watch to put his mind into us, so as to strike at God through us. At any moment we may become disobedient or unbelieving, or may be betrayed into some thought or act contrary to the Spirit of love.

We have an astonishing example of this in the life of the apostle Peter. At one moment, under the compelling influence of God's Holy Spirit, he cries, "Thou art the Christ, the Son of the living God!" Our Lord turns, and with words of high commendation says, "Blessed art thou, Simon Barjona: for flesh and blood hath not revealed it unto thee, but my Father which is in heaven." Yet, a very little while after, the devil gets his mind into Peter, and our Lord turns and says to him, "Get thee behind me, Satan!" (Matthew 16:17, 23). Peter was now speaking in the name of Satan. Satan still desires to have us.

Paul was tempted to think that he could do far better work for his beloved Master if only that thorn could be removed. But God knew that Paul would be a better man with the thorn than without it.

Is it not a comfort to us to know that we may bring more glory to God under something that we are apt to regard as a hindrance or handicap, than if that undesired thing was removed? "My grace is sufficient for thee: for my strength is made perfect in weakness" (2 Corinthians 12:9).

Paul was not infallible, nor was Peter or John; nor is the Pope or any other man. We may and do offer up mistaken prayers. The highest form of prayer is not "Your way, O God, not mine," but "My way, O God, is thine." We are taught to pray not "your will be changed," but "your will be done."

May we, in conclusion, give the testimony of two who have proved that God can be trusted?

Sir H. M. Stanley [1841-1904], the great explorer, wrote:

I for one must not dare to say that prayers are inefficacious. Where I have been in earnest, I have been answered. When I prayed for light to guide my followers wisely through the perils that beset them, a ray of light has come upon the perplexed mind, and a clear road to deliverance has been pointed out. You may know when prayer is answered, by the glow of content which fills one who has flung his cause before God, as he rises to his feet. I have evidence, satisfactory to myself, that prayers are granted.

Mary Slessor [1848-1915], the story of whose life in West Africa has surely thrilled us all, was once asked what prayer meant to her. She replied:

My life is one long, daily, hourly record of answered prayer for physical health, for mental overstrain, for guidance given marvelously, for errors and dangers averted, for enmity to the Gospel subdued, for food provided at the exact hour needed, for everything that goes to make up life and my poor service. I can testify with a full and often wonder-stricken awe that I believe God answers prayer. I know God answers prayer.

Chapter 9

ANSWERS TO PRAYER

Mere human nature would choose a more startling title to this chapter. Remarkable answers, wonderful answers, amazing answers. But we must allow God to teach us that it is as natural to Him to answer prayer as it is for us to ask. How He delights to hear our petitions, and how He loves to answer them. When we hear of some wealthy person giving a treat to poverty-stricken people, or wiping out some crushing deficit in a missionary society, we exclaim, "How nice to be able to do a thing like that." Well, if it is true that God loves us—and we know it is true—do you not think it gives Him great joy to give us what we ask? We would like, therefore, to recount one or two answers to prayer out of very many that have come to our notice, so that we may have greater boldness in coming to the throne of grace. God saves sinners for whom we pray. Try it.

In talking over this question with a man of prayer a few days ago, he suddenly asked me, "Do you know St. M-'s Church, L-?"

"Quite well—have been there several times."

"Let me tell you what happened when I lived there. We had a prayer meeting each Sunday before the 8 o'clock communion service. As we rose from our knees one Sunday a church worker said, 'Vicar, I wish you would pray for my boy. He is twenty-two years old now, and has not been to church for years.' 'We can spare five minutes now,' replied the vicar. They knelt down again and offered up earnest supplication on behalf of that man. Although nothing was said to him about this, that youth came to church that same evening. Something in the sermon convicted him of sin. He came into the vestry broken-hearted, and accepted Jesus Christ as his Savior."

On Monday morning my friend, who was working as a Church Army captain in the parish, was present at the weekly meeting of the staff. He said to the vicar, "That conversion last night is a challenge to prayer—a challenge from God. Shall we accept it?"

"What do you mean?" asked the vicar.

"Well," said he, "shall we single out the worst man in the parish and pray for him?"

By unanimous consent they fixed upon K- as the worst man they knew. So they agreed in prayer for his conversion. At the end of that week, as they were conducting a Saturday night prayer meeting in the mission hall, and while his very name was on their lips, the door swung open and in staggered K-, much the worse for liquor. He had never been in that mission hall before. Without thinking of removing his cap he sank on a chair near the door and buried his face in his hands. The prayer meeting suddenly became an inquiry-room. Drunken as he was, he sought the Lord who was seeking him. Nor did he ever go back into sin. Today he is one of the finest dockyard missioners in the land.

Oh, why do we not pray for our unconverted friends? They may not listen to us when we plead *with* them, but they cannot hold out if we pray *for* them. Let two or three agree in prayer over the salvation of the worst, and then see what God will do. Tell God and then trust God. God works in a wonderful way, as well as in a mysterious way, His wonders to perform.

Dan Crawford [unknown] told us recently that when returning to his mission field after a furlough, it was necessary to make all possible haste. But a deep stream that had to be crossed was flooded, and no usable boats were available. So he and his party camped and prayed. An infidel might well have laughed aloud. How could God get them across that river? But as they prayed, a tall tree that had battled with that river for scores of years began to totter and fall. It fell clear across the stream. As Mr. Crawford says, "The royal engineers of heaven had laid a pontoon bridge for God's servants."

Many young people will be reading these prayer stories. May we remind them that God still hears the voices of young boys and girls (Genesis 21:17). For them may we be allowed to add the following story, with the earnest desire that prayer may be their heritage, their very life, and that answered prayer may be their daily experience.

Some little time ago, a Chinese boy of twelve years old, named Ma-Na-Si, a boarder in the mission school at Chefoo, went home for the holidays. He is the son of a native pastor.

While standing on the doorstep of his father's house he saw a horseman galloping toward him. The man was a heathen and was highly disturbed. He eagerly inquired for the *Jesus man*—the pastor. The boy told him that his father was away from home. The poor man was much distressed, and hurriedly explained the cause of his visit. He had been sent from a heathen village some miles away to fetch the holy men to cast a devil out of the daughter-in-law of a heathen friend. He poured out his sad story of this young woman who was being torn by devils. She was raving and reviling, pulling out her hair, clawing her face, tearing her clothes, smashing up furniture, and dashing away dishes of food. He told of her spirit of sacrilege, outrageous impiety, and brazen blasphemy. These outbursts were followed by foaming at the mouth and great exhaustion, both physical and mental. "But my father is not at home," the boy kept reiterating.

At length the frenzied man seemed to understand. Suddenly he fell on his knees, and, stretching out his hands in desperation, cried, "You, too, are a Jesus man. Will you come ?"

Think of it—a boy of twelve. Yes, but even a lad, when fully yielded to his Savior, is not fearful of being used by that Savior. There was but one moment of surprise, and a moment of hesitation, and then the boy put himself wholly at the Lord's disposal. Like little Samuel of old he was willing to obey God in all things. He accepted the earnest entreaty as a call from God. The heathen stranger sprang into the saddle, and, swinging the Christian boy up behind him, he galloped away.

Ma-Na-Si began to think over things. He had accepted an invitation to cast out a devil in the name of Christ Jesus. But was he worthy to be used of God in this way? Was his heart pure and his faith strong? As they galloped along he carefully searched his heart for sin to be confessed and repented of. Then he prayed for guidance about what to say and how to act, and tried to recall Bible instances of demoniacal possession and how they were dealt with. Then he simply and humbly cast himself upon the God of power and of mercy, asking His help for the glory of the Lord Jesus.

On arrival at the house they found that some of the members of the family were forcibly holding down the tortured woman upon the bed. Although she had not been told that a messenger had gone for the native pastor, as soon as she heard footsteps in the court outside she cried, "All of you get out of my way quickly so that I can escape. I must flee. A Jesus man is coming. I cannot endure him. His name is Ma-Na-Si."

Ma-Na-Si entered the room, and after a ceremonial bow knelt down and began to pray. Then he sang a Christian hymn to the praise of the Lord Jesus. Then, in the name of the risen Lord, glorified and omnipotent, he commanded the demon to come out of the woman. At once she was calm, though prostrate with weakness.

From that day she was perfectly whole. She was amazed when they told her that she had uttered the name of the Christian boy, for she had never heard of it or read of it before, for the whole of that village was heathen. But that day was veritably a *beginning of days* to those people, for from it the Word of the Lord had free course and was glorified.

Beloved reader, I do not know how this little narrative affects you. It is one that moves me to the very depths of my being. It seems to me that most of us know so little of the power of God—so little of His overwhelming, irresistible love. Oh, what love is His! Now every time we pray that wonderful love envelops us in a special way.

If we really loved our blessed Savior, should we not oftener seek communion with Him in prayer? Dear Christian, is it because we pray so little that we criticize so much? Oh, let us remember that we, like our dear Savior, are not sent into the world to judge and condemn the world and, "but that the world through Him might be saved" (John 3:17).

Will any thoughtless word of criticism of anyone move anyone nearer to Christ? Will it even help the utterer of that fault-finding to be more like the Master? Oh, let us lay aside the spirit of criticism, of blaming, of fault-finding, of disparaging others or their work. Would not Paul say to us all, "And such were some of you: but ye are washed"? (1 Corinthians 6:11).

Do you see what we are aiming at? All the evil dispositions and failings we detect in others are due to the devil. It is the evil one in the heart who causes those words and deeds that we are so ready to condemn and to exaggerate. Demon

105

possession is not unknown in civilized countries, but it takes a different form, perhaps. Our very friends and acquaintances, so kindly and lovable, are often tied and bound by some besetting sin: "whom Satan hath bound, lo, these *many* years" (Luke 13:16).

We may plead with them in vain. We may warn them in vain. Courtesy and charity, and our own failings and shortcomings, forbid us standing over them like Ma-Na-Si and exercising the evil spirit. But have we tried prayer, prayer that is always backed up by love that thinks no evil and is not easily provoked? (1 Corinthians 13:5).

God answers prayer from old and young when there is a clean heart, a holy life, and a simple faith. God answers prayer. We are but frail and faulty servants at the best. Sincere as we may be, we shall sometimes ask amiss. But God is faithful to keep His promises, and He will guard us from all harm and supply every need.

> *Can I have the things I pray for?*
> *God knows best;*
> *He is wiser than His children.*
> *I can rest.*

"Beloved, if our heart condemn us not, then have we confidence toward God. And whatsoever we ask, we receive of Him, because we keep His commandments, and do those things that are pleasing in His sight." (1 John 3:21).

Chapter 10

HOW GOD ANSWERS PRAYER

For us fully to understand God and all His dealings with us is an utter impossibility. "O the depth of the riches both of the wisdom and knowledge of God! how unsearchable are His judgments, and His ways past finding out!" (Romans 11:33). True, but we need not make difficulties where none exists. If God has all power and all knowledge, surely prayer has no difficulties, though occasionally there may be perplexities. We cannot discover God's method, but we know something of His manner of answering prayer.

But at the very outset may we remind ourselves how little we know about ordinary things? Mr. Thomas Edison, whose knowledge is pretty profound, wrote in August, 1921:

> We don't know the millionth part of one per cent about anything. We don't know what water is. We don't know what light is. We don't know what gravitation is. We don't know what enables us to keep on our feet to stand up. We don't know what electricity is. We don't know what heat is. We don't know anything about magnetism. We have a lot of hypotheses, but that is all.

But we do not allow our ignorance about all these things to deprive us of their use. We do not know much about prayer, but surely this need not prevent us from praying. We do know what our Lord has taught us about prayer. And we do know that He has sent the Holy Spirit to teach us all things (John 14:26). How, then, does God answer prayer? One way is just this:

He reveals His mind to those who pray. His Holy Spirit puts fresh ideas into the minds of praying people. We are quite aware that the devil and his angels are busy enough putting bad thoughts into our minds. Surely, then, God and His Holy Spirit can give us good thoughts? Even poor, weak, sinful men and women can put good thoughts into the minds of others. That is what we try to do in writing. We do not stop to think what a wonderful thing it is that a few peculiar shaped black marks on this white paper can uplift and inspire, or depress and cast down, or even convict of sin. But, to an untutored savage, it is a stupendous miracle. Moreover, you and I can often read people's thoughts or wishes from an expression on the face or a glance of the eye. Even thought transference between person and person is a commonplace today. And God can in many ways convey His thoughts to us.

A remarkable instance of this was related by a speaker last year at Northfield. Three or four years ago, he met an old whaling captain who told him this story.

A good many years ago, I was sailing in the desolate seas off Cape Horn, hunting whales. One day we were beating directly south in the face of a hard wind. We had been tacking this way and that all the morning, and were making very little headway. About 11 o'clock, as I stood at the wheel, the idea suddenly came into my mind, 'Why batter the ship against these waves? There are probably as many whales to the north as to the south. Suppose we run with the wind instead of against it? In response to that sudden idea I changed the course of the ship, and began to sail north instead of south. One hour later, at noon, the lookout at the masthead shouted, "Boats ahead!" Presently we overtook four lifeboats in which were fourteen sailors, the only survivors of the crew of a ship that had burned to the water's edge ten days before. Those men had been adrift in their boats ever since, praying God frantically for rescue; and we arrived just in time to save them. They could not have survived another day.

Then the old whaler added:

I don't know whether you believe in religion or not, but I happen to be a Christian. I have begun every day of my life with prayer that God would use me to help someone else, and I am convinced that God that day put the idea into my mind to change the course of my ship. That idea was the means of saving fourteen lives.

God has many things to say to us. He has many thoughts to put into our minds. We are apt to be so busy doing His work that we do not stop to listen to His voice. Prayer gives God the opportunity of speaking to us and revealing His will to us. May our attitude often be: "Speak, LORD; for thy servant heareth" (1 Samuel 3:9).

God answers other prayers by putting new thoughts into the minds of those we pray for. At a series of services dealing with the victorious life, the writer one afternoon urged the congregation to make up their quarrels if they really desired a holy life. One lady went straight home, and after very earnest prayer wrote to her sister, with whom, owing to some disagreement, she had had nothing to do for twenty years.

Her sister was living thirty miles away. The very next morning the writer of that note received a letter from that same sister asking forgiveness and seeking reconciliation. The two letters had crossed in the post. While the one sister was praying to God for the other, God was speaking to that other sister, putting into her mind the desire for reconciliation.

You may say, "Why did not God put that desire there before?" It may be that He foresaw that it would be useless for the distant sister to write asking forgiveness until the other sister was also willing to forgive. The fact remains that when we pray for others, somehow or other it opens the way for God to influence those we pray for. God needs our prayers, or He would not beg us to pray.

A little time back, at the end of a weekly prayer meeting, a godly woman begged those present to pray for her husband, who would never go near a place of worship. The leader suggested that they should continue in prayer then and there. Most earnest prayers were offered up. Now, the husband was devoted to his wife, and frequently came to meet her. He did so that night, and arrived at the hall while the prayer meeting was still in progress. God put it into his mind to open the door and wait inside—a thing he had never done before. As he sat on a chair near the door, leaning his head upon his hand, he overheard those earnest petitions. During the homeward walk he said, "Wife, who was the man they were praying for tonight?"

"Oh," she replied, "it is the husband of one of our workers."

"Well, I am quite sure he will be saved," said he. "God must answer prayers like that." A little later in the evening he again asked, "Who was the man they were praying for?" She replied in similar terms as before. On retiring to rest he could not sleep. He was under deep conviction of sin. Awaking his wife, he begged her to pray for him.

How clearly this shows us that when we pray, God can work. God could have prompted that man to enter that prayer meeting any week. But had he done so it is a question whether any good at all would have come from it. When once those earnest, heartfelt petitions were being offered up on his behalf God saw that they would have a mighty influence upon that poor man.

It is when we pray that God can help us in our work and strengthen our resolves, for we can answer many of our own prayers. One bitter winter a prosperous farmer was praying that God would keep a neighbor from starving. When the family prayers were over, his little boy said, "Father, I don't think I should have troubled God about that."

"Why not?" he asked.

"Because it would be easy enough for you to see that they don't starve," the boy replied.

There is not the slightest doubt that if we pray for others we shall also try to help them.

A young convert asked his vicar to give him some Christian work. "Have you a close friend?"

"Yes," replied the boy.

"Is he a Christian?"

"No, he is as careless as I was."

"Then go and ask him to accept Christ as his Savior."

"Oh, no!" said the lad, "I could never do that. Give me anything but that."

"Well," said the vicar, "promise me two things. That you will not speak to him about his soul, and that you will pray to God twice daily for his conversion."

"Why, yes, I'll gladly do that," answered the boy. Before a fortnight was up he rushed round to the vicarage. "Will you let me off my promise? I must speak to my friend!" he cried. When he began to pray God could give him strength to witness. Communion with God is essential before we can have real communion with our fellowman. My belief is that

Christians so seldom speak to others about their spiritual condition because they pray so little for them.

The writer has never forgotten how his faith in prayer was confirmed when, as a lad of thirteen, he earnestly asked God to enable him on a certain day to secure twenty new subscribers for missions overseas. Exactly twenty new names were secured before night closed in. The consciousness that God would grant that prayer was an incentive to eager effort, and gave an unusual courage in approaching others.

A minister in England suggested to his people that they should each day pray for the worst man or woman and then go to them and tell them about Jesus. Only six agreed to do so. On arrival home he began to pray. Then he said, "I must not leave this to my people. I must take it up myself. I don't know the bad people. I'll have to go out and inquire." Approaching a rough-looking man at a street corner, he asked, "Are you the worst man in this district?"

"No, I'm not."

"Would you mind telling me who is?"

"I don't mind. You'll find him at No. 7, down that street."

He knocked at No. 7 and entered. "I'm looking for the worst man in my parish. They tell me it might be you?"

"Whoever told you that? Fetch him here, and I'll show him who's the worst man. No, there are lots worse than me."

"Well, who is the worst man you know?"

"Everybody knows him. He lives at the end house in that court. He's the worst man."

So down the court the minister went and knocked at the door. A surly voice cried, "Come in!"

There were a man and his wife. "I hope you'll excuse me, but I'm the minister of the chapel along the round. I'm looking for the worst man in my district, because I have something to tell him. Are you the worst man?"

The man turned to his wife and said, "Lass, tell him what I said to you five minutes ago."

"No, tell him yourself."

"What were you saying?" inquired the minister.

"Well, I've been drinking for twelve weeks. I've had the D.T.'s and have pawned all in the house worth pawning. And I said to my wife a few minutes ago, 'Lass, this thing has to stop, and if it doesn't, I'll stop it myself—I'll go and drown myself.' Then you knocked at the door. Yes, sir, I'm the very worst man. What have you got to say to me?"

"I'm here to tell you that Jesus Christ is the greatest Savior, and that He can make out of the worst man one of the best. He did it for me, and He will do it for you."

"D'you think He can do it even for me?"

"I'm sure He can. Kneel down and ask Him."

Not only was the poor drunkard saved from his sins, but he is today a radiant Christian man, bringing other drunken people to the Lord Jesus Christ.

Surely none of us finds it difficult to believe that God can, in answer to prayer, heal the body, send rain or fair weather, dispel fogs, or avert calamities?

We have to do with a God whose knowledge is infinite. He can put it into the mind of a doctor to prescribe a certain medicine, or diet, or method of cure. All the doctor's skill is from God. "He knoweth our frame," for He made it (Psalm 103:14). He knows it far better than the cleverest doctor or surgeon. He made, and He can restore. We believe that God desires us to use medical skill, but we also believe that God, by His wonderful knowledge, can heal, and sometimes does heal, without human cooperation. And God must be allowed to work in His own way. We are so apt to tie God down to the way we approve of. God's aim is to glorify His name in answering our prayers. Sometimes He sees that our desire is right, but our petition wrong. The apostle Paul thought he could bring more glory to God if only the thorn in the flesh could be removed. The Lord knew that he would be a better man and do better work with the thorn than without it. So the Lord said no, no, no to his prayer, and then explained why.

So it was with Monica, who prayed so many years for the conversion of Augustine, her licentious son. When he was determined to leave home and cross the seas to Rome she prayed earnestly, even passionately, that God would keep him by her side, and under her influence. She went down to a little chapel on the seashore to spend the night in prayer near where the ship her son was sailing on lay at anchor. But, when morning came, she found that the ship had sailed even while she prayed. Her petition was refused, but her real desire was granted. For it was in Rome that Augustine met the sainted Ambrose, who led him to Christ. How comforting it is to know that God knows what is best.

But we should never think it unreasonable that God should make some things dependent upon our prayers. Some people say that if God really loves us He would give us what is best for us whether we ask Him or not. Dr. Fosdick has so beautifully pointed out that God has left us many things to do for ourselves. He promises seedtime and harvest. Yet we must prepare the soil, sow, till, and reap in order to allow God to do His share. God provides us with food and drink. But He leaves us to take, eat, and drink. There are some things God cannot, or at least will not, do without our help. God cannot do some things unless we think. He never emblazons His truth upon the sky. The laws of science have always been there. But we must think, experiment, and think again if we would use those laws for our own good and God's glory.

God cannot do some things unless we work. He stores the hills with marble, but He has never built a cathedral. He fills the mountains with iron ore, but He never makes a needle or a locomotive. He leaves that to us. We must work.

If God has left many things dependent upon our thinking and working, why should He not leave some things dependent upon our praying? He has done so. "Ask, and ye shall receive" (John 16:24). And there are some things God will not give us unless we ask. Prayer is one of the three ways in which we can cooperate with God; and the greatest of these is prayer.

People of power are without exception people of prayer. God bestows His Holy Spirit in His fullness only on people of prayer. And it is through the operation of the Spirit that answers to prayer come. Every believer has the Spirit of Christ dwelling in him. For "if any man have not the Spirit of Christ, he is none of his" (Romans 8:9). But a person of prevailing prayer must be filled with the Spirit of God.

A lady missionary wrote recently that it used to be said of Praying Hyde that he never spoke to an unconverted man but that he was soundly converted. But if he ever did fail at first to touch a heart for God, he went back to his room and wrestled in prayer until he was shown what it was in himself that had hindered his being used by God. Yes, when we are filled with the Spirit of God, we cannot help influencing others to turn toward God. But to have power with people, we must have power with God.

The momentous question for you and me is not, however, "How does God answer prayer?" The question is, "Do I really pray?" What a marvelous power God places at our disposal. Do we for a moment think that anything displeasing to God is worth our holding on to? Dear Christian, trust Christ wholly and you will find Him wholly true.

Let us give God the chance of putting His mind into us, and we shall never doubt the power of prayer again.

Chapter 11

HINDRANCES TO PRAYER

The poet said, and we often sing,
What various hindrances we meet
In coming to the mercy seat.

Yes, indeed, they are various, but most of those hindrances are our own making.

God wants me to pray. The devil does not want me to pray and does all he can to hinder me. He knows that we can accomplish more through our prayers than through our work. He would rather have us do anything else than pray.

We have already referred to Satan's opposition to prayer:

Angels our march oppose
Who still in strength excel
Our secret, sworn, relentless foes,
Countless, invisible

But we need not fear them, nor heed them, if our eyes are ever upon the Lord. The holy angels are stronger than fallen angels, and we can leave the celestial hosts to guard us. We believe that to them, the hosts of evil, we owe those wandering thoughts that so often wreck prayer. We no sooner kneel than we remember something that should have been done, or something that we need to see to at once.

These thoughts come from without, and are surely due to the promptings of evil spirits. The only cure for wandering thoughts is to get your mind fixed upon God. Undoubtedly our worst foe is ourselves. Prayer is for a child of God—and one who is living as a child of God should pray.

The great question is: "Am I harboring any foes in my heart?" Are there traitors within? God cannot give us His best spiritual blessings unless we fulfill conditions of trust, obedience, and service. Do we not often ask earnestly for the highest spiritual gifts, without even any thought of fulfilling the necessary requirements? Do we not often ask for blessings we are not spiritually fit to receive? Dare we be honest with ourselves when we're alone in the presence of God? Dare we say sincerely, "Search me, O God, ... and see if there be any wicked way in me"? (Psalm 139:23-24). Is there anything in me which is hindering God's blessing for me and through me? We discuss the problem of prayer, but we are the problem that needs discussing or dissecting. Prayer is all right. There is no problem in prayer to the heart that is absolutely stayed on Christ.

Now we shall not quote the usual Bible texts that show how prayer may be frustrated. We merely desire that you should get a glimpse of your own heart. No sin is too small to hinder prayer, and perhaps to turn the very prayer itself into sin, if we are not willing to renounce that sin. The Moslems in West Africa have a saying, "If there is no purity, there is no prayer; if there is no prayer, there is no drinking of the water of heaven." This truth is so clearly taught in our Bible that it is amazing that any Christian should try to retain both sin and prayer. Yet very many do this. Even David cried, long ages ago, "If I regard iniquity in my heart, the Lord will not hear me" (Psalm 66:18).

And Isaiah says, "Your iniquities have separated between you and your God, and your sins have hid his face from you" (Isaiah 59:2). Surely we must all agree that it is sin in us, and not the unwillingness of God to hear, that hinders prayer. As a rule, it is some little sin, so-called, that mars and spoils the prayer life. There may be:

1. *Doubt.* Unbelief is possibly the greatest hindrance to prayer. Our Lord said that the Holy Spirit would reprove the world "of sin because they believe not on me" (John 16:9). We are not of the world, yet is there not much practical unbelief in many of us? Writing to believers, James says, "But let him ask in faith, nothing wavering. For he that wavereth ... let not that man think that he shall receive any thing of the Lord." (James 1:6-8). Some have not because they ask not (James 4:2). Others have not because they believe not.

Did you think it a little strange that we spent so much time over adoration and thanksgiving before we came to the asking? But surely, if we get a glimpse of the glorious majesty of our Lord, and the wonders of His love and grace, unbelief and doubt will vanish away as mists before the rising sun? Was this not the reason that Abraham "staggered not" (wavered not through unbelief), in that he gave God the glory due unto His name, and was therefore "fully persuaded that, what he had promised, he was able also to perform"? (Romans 4:20-21). Knowing what we do of God's stupendous love, is it not amazing that we should ever doubt?

2. Then there is *self*—the root of all sin. How selfish we are prone to be even in our good works! How we hesitate to give up anything that *self* craves for. Yet we know that a full hand cannot take Christ's gifts. Was this why the Savior, in the prayer He first taught, coupled us with everything else? "Our" is the first word. "Our Father ... give us ... forgive us ... deliver us ..." (Matthew 6:9-13).

119

Pride prevents prayer, for prayer is a very humbling thing. How hateful pride must be in the sight of God. It is God "who giveth us richly all things to enjoy" (1 Timothy 6:17). "What hast thou that thou didst not receive?" asks Paul (1 Corinthians 4:7). Surely we are not going to let *pride* and its ugly and hateful sister *jealousy* ruin our prayer life? God cannot do great things for us if they are going to turn our heads. Oh, how foolish we can be! Sometimes, when we are insistent, God does give us what we ask, at the expense of our righteousness. "He gave them their request; but sent leanness into their soul" (Psalm 106:15). O God, save us from that; save us from SELF!

Again, *self* asserts itself in criticizing others. Let this thought burn itself into your memory. The more like Jesus Christ you become, the less you will judge other people. It is an infallible test. Those who are always criticizing others have drifted away from Christ. They may still be His, but have lost His Spirit of love. Beloved, if you have a criticizing nature, use it to dissect yourself and never your neighbor. You will be able to give it full scope, and it will never be unemployed. Is this a harsh remark? Does it betray a tendency to commit the very sin it condemns? It would do so were it spoken to any one individual. But its object is to pierce armor that is seemingly invulnerable. And no one who has kept their tongue from picking and stealing the reputation of other people for one month will ever desire to go back again to backbiting. "Charity (love) suffereth long, and is kind" (1 Corinthians 13:4). Do we? Are we?

We are ourselves no better because we have managed to paint other people in worse colors than ourselves. But we enhance our own spiritual joy and living witness for Christ when we refuse to pass on disparaging information about others, or when we refrain from judging the work or lives of other people. It may be hard at first, but it soon brings untold joy, and is rewarded by the love of all around. It is most hard to keep silent in the face of modern heresies. Are we not told to "earnestly contend for the faith which was once delivered unto the saints"? (Jude 3). Sometimes we must speak out, but it should always be in the spirit of love. *Rather let error live than love die.*

Fault finding of others must be resolutely avoided even in our private prayers. Read once more the story of John Hyde praying for the cold brother. Believe me, a criticizing spirit destroys holiness of life more easily than anything else, because it is such an eminently respectable sin, and makes such easy victims of us. We need scarcely add that when a believer is filled with the Spirit of Christ, who is love, he will never tell others of the unchristian behavior he may discern in his friends. "He was most rude to me." "He is too conceited." "I can't stand that man." Remarks like those are surely unkind, unnecessary, and often untrue.

Our dear Lord suffered the contradiction of sinners against Himself (Hebrews 12:3), but He never complained or published abroad the news to others. Why should we do so? *Self* must be dethroned if Christ is to reign supreme. There must be no idols in your heart. Do you remember what God said of some leaders of religion? "These men have set up their idols in their heart,... should I be inquired of at all by them?" (Ezekiel 14:3).

When our aim is solely the glory of God, then God can answer our prayers. Christ Himself rather than His gifts should be our desire. "Delight thyself also in the LORD; and he shall give thee the desires of thine heart" (Psalm 37:4).

"Beloved, if our heart condemn us not, then we have confidence toward God. And whatsoever we ask, we receive of him, because we keep his commandments, and do those things that are pleasing in his sight" (1 John 3:21-22).

It is as true today as in the early days of Christianity that Christians ask and do not receive because they ask amiss that they may spend it on their pleasures; i.e., self (James 4:3).

3. No love in the heart is possibly the greatest hindrance to prayer. A loving spirit is a condition of believing prayer. We cannot be wrong with people and right with God. The spirit of prayer is essentially the spirit of love. Intercession is simply love at prayer.

He prayeth best who loveth best
All things both great and small;
For the great God who loveth us,
He made and loveth all.

Dare we hate or dislike those whom God loves? If we do, can we really possess the Spirit of Christ? We really must face these elementary facts in our faith if prayer is to be anything more than a mere form. Our Lord says, "Love your enemies, bless them that curse you, do good to them that hate you, and pray for them which despitefully use you, and persecute you; That ye may be the children of your Father which is in heaven: for he maketh his sun to rise on the evil and on the good, and sendeth rain on the just and on the unjust. (Matthew 5:44-45).

We venture to think that large numbers of so-called Christians have never faced this question. To hear how many Christian workers—and prominent ones, too—speak of others with whom they disagree, one must charitably suppose they have never heard that command of our Lord.

Our daily life in the world is the best indication of our power in prayer. God deals with my prayers not according to the spirit and tone that I exhibit when I am praying in public or private, but according to the spirit I show in my daily life.

Hot-tempered people can make only frigid prayers. If we do not obey our Lord's command and love one another, our prayers are nearly worthless. If we harbor an unforgiving spirit it is almost wasted time to pray. Yet a prominent minister was recently reported to have said that there are some people we can never forgive. If so, we trust that he uses an abridged form of the Lord's prayer. Christ taught us to say, "forgive us ... as we forgive." And He goes further than this. He declares, "if ye forgive not men their trespasses, neither will your Father forgive your trespasses" (Matthew 6:15). May we ever exhibit the Spirit of Christ, and not forfeit our own much needed forgiveness. How many of our readers who have not the slightest intention of forgiving their enemies, or even their offending friends, repeated the Lord's prayer today?

Many Christians have never given prayer a fair chance. It is not through conscious insincerity, but from lack of thought. The blame for it really rests upon those of us who preach and teach. We are prone to teach doctrines rather than doings. Most Christians desire to do what is right, but they regard the big things rather than the little failings in the life of love.

Our Lord goes so far as to say that even our gifts are not to be presented to God if we remember that our brother "hath ought against thee" (Matthew 5:23). If He will not accept our gifts, is it likely He will answer our prayers? It was when Job ceased contending with his enemies (whom the Bible calls his friends) that the LORD turned his captivity and gave him twice as much as he had before (Job 42:10).

How slow we are, how unwilling we are, to see that our lives hinder our prayers. And how unwilling we are to act on lines of love. Yes, we desire to win people to Christ. Our Lord shows us one way. Don't publish abroad their wrongdoings. Speak to the person alone, and "thou hast gained thy brother" (Matthew 18:15). Most of us have rather pained our brothers and sisters.

Even the home life may hinder the prayer life. See what Peter says about how we should so live in the home that our "prayers be not hindered" (1 Peter 3:1-7). We would venture to urge you to ask God to search your heart once again and to show you if there is "any root of bitterness" toward anyone (Hebrews 12:15). We all desire to do what is pleasing to God. It would be an immense gain to our spiritual life if we would resolve not to attempt to pray until we had done all in our power to make peace and harmony between ourselves and any with whom we have quarreled. Until we do this as far as lies in our power, our prayers are just wasted breath. Unkindly feelings towards another hinder God from helping us in the way He desires.

A loving life is an essential condition of believing prayer. God challenges us today to become fit persons to receive His superabundant blessings. Many of us have to decide whether we will choose a bitter, unforgiving, spirit, or the tender mercies and loving kindness of our Lord Jesus Christ. Is it not amazing that any person can halt between two opinions with such a choice in the balance? For bitterness harms the person who is bitter more than anyone else.

"And when ye stand praying, forgive, if ye have ought against any: that your Father also which is in heaven may forgive you" (Mark 11:25). So said the blessed Master. Must we not then either forgive, or cease trying to pray? What will it profit us if we spend all our time pretending to pray, when we know that we harbor unforgiveness in our heart that prevents real prayer? How the devil laughs at us because we do not see this truth.

We have God's word for it that eloquence, knowledge, faith, liberality, and even martyrdom profit a person nothing—get hold of it—nothing, unless the heart is filled with love (1 Corinthians 13:1-3).

4. Refusal to do our part may hinder God answering our prayers. Love calls forth compassion and service at the sight of sin and suffering, both here and all over the world. Love was the reason Paul's "spirit was stirred in him" as he beheld the city full of idols (Acts 17:16). We cannot be sincere when

we pray "Thy kingdom come" (Matthew 6:10) unless we are doing what we can to hasten the coming of that kingdom by our gifts, our prayers, and our service.

We cannot be truly sincere in praying for the conversion of the ungodly unless we are willing to speak a word, or write a letter, or make some attempt to bring that sinner under the influence of the Gospel. Before one of Moody's great missions, he was present at a prayer meeting where they were asking for God's blessing. Several wealthy men were there. One began to pray that God would send sufficient funds to defray the expenses. Moody at once stopped him. "We need not trouble God about that," he said quietly, "we are able to answer that prayer."

5. Praying only in secret may be a hindrance. Children of a family should not always meet their father separately. It is remarkable how often our Lord refers to united prayer—**praying in** agreement.

"When ye pray, say, *Our* Father ..." (Luke 11:2).

"If two of you shall agree on earth as touching any thing that they shall ask, it shall be done for them of my Father which is in heaven. For where two or three are gathered together in my name, there am I in the midst of them." (Matthew 18:19-20).

We feel sure that the weakness in the spiritual life of many churches can be traced to an inefficient prayer meeting, or the absence of meetings for prayer. Formal morning and evening meetings, even when reverent and without the unseemly haste that is so often associated with them, cannot take the place of less formal gatherings for prayer, in which everyone may take part. Can we not make the weekly prayer meeting a live thing and a living force?

6. Praise is as important as prayer. We must "enter into his gates with thanksgiving, and into his courts with praise: be

thankful onto him, and bless his holy name" (Psalm 100:4). At one time in his life, Praying Hyde was led to ask for four souls a day to be brought into the fold by his ministry. If on any day the number fell short of this, there would be such a weight on his heart that it was positively painful, and he could neither eat nor sleep. Then in prayer he would ask the Lord to show him what the obstacle was in himself. He invariably found that it was the lack of praise in his life. He would confess his sinfulness and pray for a spirit of praise. He said that as he praised God, seeking souls would come to him. We do not imply that we, too, should limit God to definite numbers or ways of working; but we do cry, "Rejoice! Praise God with heart and mind and soul."

It is not by accident that we are so often bidden to "rejoice in the Lord" (Philippians 4:4). God does not want miserable children, and none of His children have cause for misery. The apostle Paul, the most persecuted of men, was a man of song. Hymns of praise came from his lips in prison and out of prison. Day and night he praised His Savior. The very order of his exhortations is significant. "Rejoice evermore. Pray without ceasing. In everything give thanks: for this is the will of God in Christ Jesus concerning you" (1 Thessalonians 5:16-18).

The will of God. Get that thought into your mind. It is not an optional thing. REJOICE! PRAY! GIVE THANKS!

That is the order, according to the will of God—for you and for me. Nothing so pleases God as our praises—and nothing so blesses the Christians who pray as the praises they offer! "Delight thyself also in the LORD; and he shall give thee the desires of thine heart" (Psalm 37:4).

A missionary who had received very bad news from home, was utterly cast down. Prayer availed nothing to relieve the darkness of his soul. He went to see another missionary, no doubt seeking comfort. There on the wall was a motto:

"Try Thanksgiving." He did, and in a moment every shadow was gone, never to return.

Do we praise enough to get our prayers answered? If we truly trust Him, we shall always praise Him. For—

> *God nothing does nor suffers to be done*
> *But thou would'st do thyself*
> *Could'st thou but see*
> *The end of all events as well as He.*

A person who once overheard Martin Luther praying said, "Gracious God! What spirit and what faith is there in his expressions! He petitions God with as much reverence as if he were in the Divine presence, and yet with as firm a hope and confidence as he would address a father or a friend." Luther seemed quite unconscious that hindrances to prayer existed. They obviously did not for him.

After all that has been said, we see that everything can be summed up under one head. All hindrance to prayer arises from ignorance of the teaching of God's Word on the life of holiness He has planned for all His children, or from an unwillingness to consecrate ourselves fully to Him.

When we can truthfully say to our Father, "All that I am and have is thine," then He can say to us, "All that is mine is thine."

Chapter 12

WHO MAY PRAY?

It is only two centuries ago that six undergraduates were expelled from the University of Oxford solely because they met together in each other's rooms for extempore prayer. Whereupon George Whitefield [1714-1770] wrote to the Vice-Chancellor, "It is to be hoped that, as some have been expelled for extempore praying, we shall hear of some few others of a contrary stamp being expelled for extempore swearing." Today, thank God, no Christian in our land is hindered by society from praying. Any person may pray—but has every person a right to pray? Does God listen to everyone?

Who may pray? Is it the privilege, the right, of all men? Not everyone can claim the right to approach the King of our realm [England]. But there are certain persons and bodies of people who have the privilege of immediate access to our sovereign. The Prime Minister has that privilege. The ancient Corporation of the City of London can at anytime lay its petition at the feet of the King. The ambassador of a foreign power may do the same. He has only to present himself at the gate of the palace of the King, and no power can stand between him and the monarch. He can go at once into the royal presence and present his request. But none of these has such ease of access and such loving welcome as the King's son.

But there is the King of all kings, the God and Father of us all. Who may go to Him? Who may exercise this privilege—yes, this power—with God? We are told, and there is much truth in the remark, that in the most skeptical person or generation prayer is always underneath the surface, waiting. Has it the right to come forth at anytime? In some religions it has to wait. Of all the millions in India living in the bondage of Hinduism, none may pray except the Brahmins. A millionaire merchant of any other caste must perforce get a Brahmin—often a mere boy at school!—to say his prayers for him.

The Mohammedan cannot pray unless he has learned a few phrases in Arabic, for his Allah only hears prayers offered in what they believe to be the holy language. Praise be to God, no such restrictions of caste or language stand between us and our God. Can any person, therefore, pray?

Yes, you reply, anyone. But the Bible does not say so. Only a child of God can truly pray to God. Only a son can enter His presence. It is gloriously true that anyone can cry to Him for help; i.e., for forgiveness and mercy. But that is scarcely prayer. Prayer is much more than that. Prayer is going into "the secret place of the most High," and abiding "under the shadow of the Almighty" (Psalm 91:1). Prayer is a making known to God our wants and desires, and holding out the hand of faith to take His gifts. Prayer is the result of the Holy Spirit dwelling within us. It is communion with God. Now, there can scarcely be communion between a king and a rebel. "What communion hath light with darkness?" (2 Corinthians 6:14). In ourselves we have no right to pray. We have access to God only through the Lord Jesus Christ (Ephesians 2:18, 3:12).

Prayer is much more than the cry of a drowning man sinking in the whirlpool of sin: "Lord, save me. I am lost.

I am undone. Redeem me. Save me." Anyone can do this, and that is a petition that is never unanswered; and one, if sincere, to which the answer is never delayed. But that is not prayer in the Bible sense. Even the lions, roaring after their prey, seek their meat from God; but that is not prayer.

We know that our Lord said, "Every one that asketh receiveth" (Matthew 7:8). He did say that, but to whom? He was speaking to His disciples (Matthew 5:1-2). Yes, prayer is communion with God: the "home life of the soul," as one describes it. And I much question whether there can be any communion with Him unless the Holy Spirit dwells in the heart, and we have received the Son, and so have the right to be called "sons [children] of God" (John 1:12, Galatians 3:2).

Prayer is the privilege of a child. Children of God alone can claim from the heavenly Father the things which He hath prepared for them that love Him. Our Lord told us that in prayer we should call God "our Father." Surely only children can use that word? Paul says that it is "because ye are sons, God hath sent forth the Spirit of his Son into your hearts, crying, Abba, Father" (Galatians 4:6).

Is this what was in God's mind when, in dealing with Job's comforters, He said, "My servant Job shall pray for you: for him will I accept"? (Job 42:8). It looked as if *they* would not have been accepted in the matter of prayer. But as soon as we become children of God we must enter the school of prayer. "Behold, he prayeth," said our Lord of a man as soon as he was converted. Yet that man had said prayers all his life (Acts 9:11). Converted people not only may pray, but must pray; each person for himself, and, of course, for others. But unless and until we can truthfully call God our Father, we have no claim to be treated as children—as sons, "heirs of God, and joint heirs with Christ" (Romans 8:17)—no claim at all. Do you say this is hard? No, it is natural. Surely a child has more privileges than those who do not belong to the family.

131

But do not misunderstand me. This does not shut any person out of the kingdom of heaven. Anyone, anywhere, can cry, "God be merciful to me, a sinner." Any person who is outside the fold of Christ, outside the family of God, however bad or however good can this very moment become a child of God. Even you who are reading these words, no matter how good or how bad you may think you are, can this very moment become a child of God, if you are not one already. One look to Christ in faith is sufficient: "Look and live" (Numbers 28:8-9). God did not even say see. He says just look. Turn your face to God.

How did those Galatian Christians become children of God? By faith in Christ. "For in Christ Jesus you all children of God through faith" (Galatians 3:26). Christ will make any person a child of God by adoption and grace the moment they turn to Him in true repentance and faith. But we have no rightful claim even upon God's providence unless we are His children. We cannot say with any confidence or certainty, "I shall not want," unless we can say with confidence and certainty, "The Lord is *my* Shepherd."

A child, however, has a right to his father's care, love, protection, and provision. Now a child can only enter a family by being born into it. We become children of God by being "born again," "born of the Spirit" (John 3:3, 5). That is, by believing in the Lord Jesus Christ (John 3:16).

Having said all this as a warning, and perhaps as an explanation why some people find prayer an utter failure, we hasten to add that God [for His own sovereign reasons] sometimes hears and answers prayer even from those who have no legal right to pray—from those who are not His children, and may even deny that He exists. The Gospels tell us of not a few unbelievers who came to Christ for healing; and He never sent one away without the coveted blessing—never. They came as beggars and not as children. And even if the children must "first be filled," these others received the crumbs; yes, and more than crumbs that were freely given (Mark 7:27-30).

So today God sometimes hears the cry of unbelievers for temporal mercies. One case well known to the writer may be given as an illustration. My friend told me that he had been an atheist many years. Although an infidel, he had sung for forty years in a church choir because he was fond of music. His aged father became seriously ill two or three years ago, and lay in great pain. The doctors were helpless to relieve the sufferer. In his distress for his father, the infidel choir singer fell on his knees and cried, "O God, if there is a God, show your power by taking away my father's pain." God heard the man's piteous cry and removed the pain immediately. The atheist praised God and hurried off to his church minister to find out the way of salvation. Today he is out-and-out for Christ, giving his whole time to work for his Savior. Yes, God is greater than His promises, and is more willing to hear than we are to pray.

Perhaps the most striking of all prayers from the lips of unbelievers is that recorded of Caroline Fry, the author of *Christ Our Example*. Although possessed of beauty, wealth, position, and friends, she found that none of them satisfied her, and at length, in her utter misery, she sought God. Yet her first utterance to Him was an expression of open rebellion to and hatred of Him. Listen to it—it is not the prayer of a child of God.

O God, if Thou art a God: I do not love Thee; I do not want Thee; I do not believe there is any happiness in Thee: but I am miserable as I am. Give me what I do not seek; give me what I do not want. If Thou canst, make me happy. I am miserable as I am. I am tired of this world; if there is anything better, give it me.

What a prayer—or what *not* a prayer! Yet God heard and answered. He forgave the wanderer and made her radiantly happy and gloriously fruitful in His service.

In even savage bosoms—

There are longings, servings, yearnings
For the good they comprehend not.
And their feeble hands and helpless.
Groping blindly in the darkness,
Touch God's right hand in the darkness,
And are lifted up and strengthened.

Shall we, then, alter our question a little and ask, who has a *right* to pray?" Only children of God in whom the Holy Spirit dwells. But, even so, we must remember that we cannot come unashamed and with confidence to our Father in heaven unless we are living as a child of God should live. We cannot expect our Father to lavish His favors upon erring children. Only a faithful and sanctified child of God can pray with the Spirit, and pray with the understanding also (1 Corinthians 14:15).

But if we are children of God, nothing but sin can hinder our prayers. We, His children, have the right of access to God at any time, in any place. And He understands any form of prayer. We may have a wonderful gift of speech pouring itself out in a torrent of thanksgiving, petition, and praise like Paul; or we may have the quiet, deep, lover-like communion of a John. A brilliant scholar like John Wesley and a humble cobbler like William Carey are alike welcome at the throne of grace. Influence at the court of heaven depends not upon birth, or brilliancy, or achievement, but upon humble and utter independence upon the Son of God.

Dwight Moody attributed his marvelous success in England to the prayers of an obscure and almost unknown invalid woman. And truly the invalid saints of England could bring about a speedy revival by their prayers. Oh, that all the shut-ins would speak out.

Do we not make a mistake in supposing that some people have a gift of prayer? A brilliant Cambridge undergraduate asked me if the life of prayer was not a gift, and one which very few possessed? He suggested that just as not everyone was musical, so not everyone is expected to be prayerful. George Muller was exceptional not because he had a gift of prayer, but because he prayed. Those who cannot speak well, as God declared Aaron could, may labor in secret by intercession with those that speak the Word of God. We must have great faith if we are to have great power with God in prayer, although God is very gracious and often goes beyond our faith.

Henry Martyn was a man of prayer, yet his faith was not equal to his prayers. He once declared that he "would as soon expect to see a man rise from the dead as to see a Brahmin converted to Christ." Would James say, "Let not that man think he shall receive anything of the Lord"? (James 1:7). Henry Martyn died without seeing one Brahmin accepting Christ as his Savior. He used to retire, day by day, to a deserted pagoda for prayer. Yet he had not faith for the conversion of a Brahmin. A few months back, there knelt in that very pagoda Brahmins and Mohammedans from all parts of India, Burma, and Ceylon, now all Christians. Others had prayed with greater faith than Henry Martyn.

Who may pray? We may, but do we? Does our Lord look at us with even more pathos and tenderness than when He first uttered the words and said, "Hitherto have ye asked nothing in my name: ask, and ye shall receive, that your joy may be full" (John 16:24). If the dear Master was dependent on prayer to make His work a power, how much more are we? He sometimes prayed with "strong crying and tears" (Hebrews 5:7). Do we? Have we ever shed a prayerful tear? Well might we cry, "quicken us, and we will call upon thy name" (Psalm 80:18).

The apostle Paul's exhortation to Timothy may well be made to us all: "Stir up the gift of God, which is in thee" (2 Timothy 1:6). For the Holy Spirit is prayer's great helper. We are incapable of ourselves to translate our real needs into prayer. The Holy Spirit does this for us. We cannot ask as we ought. The Holy Spirit does this for us. It is possible for us to ask for what is harmful to us. The Holy Spirit can check this. No weak or trembling hand dare put in motion any mighty force. Can I, dare I, move the hand that moves the universe? No! Not unless the Holy Spirit has control of me.

Yes, we need divine help for prayer—and we have it. How the whole Trinity delights in prayer. The Holy Spirit dictates, the eternal Son presents the petition and intercedes, God the Father listens, and thus the answer comes down.

Believe me, prayer is our highest privilege, our gravest responsibility, and the greatest power God has put into our hands. Prayer, real prayer, is the noblest and most sublime and stupendous act that any creature of God can perform.

It is, as Samuel Taylor Coleridge declared, the very highest energy of which human nature is capable. To pray with all your heart and strength—that is the last and greatest achievement of your Christian warfare on earth.

"LORD, TEACH US TO PRAY!"

THE KNEELING CHRISTIAN STUDY GUIDE

CHAPTER 1: GOD'S GREAT NEED

1. What is the basic reason why so many Christians are defeated and discouraged?

2. Why are so few churches on fire for God?

3. What is the least attended meeting in most churches?

    a. Why do many churches not even have such a meeting?

4. Does God ever give an unnecessary or optional command? Explain your answer.

5. Has God ever made a promise that He could not, or would not, fulfill? Explain your answer.

CHAPTER 2: ALMOST INCREDIBLE PROMISES

1. Are there any promises of God that seem so incredible to you that you are having trouble believing them?

    a. If so, what are they?

    b. What do you have to do to develop the faith to believe them?

2. How many times does the Lord literally command us to ask for what we will?

a. How often each day do you ask God for something?

b. How often does God answer your prayer?

c. If not often, why not?

3. What does it mean to be a person of prayer?

4. If you prayed this morning, do you remember what you asked for?

a. If you don't remember, how will you know if your prayer is answered?

5. What help does God provide if we don't know how to pray or what we should pray for?

CHAPTER 3: "ASK OF ME AND I WILL GIVE"

1. What is all success in spiritual work dependent upon?

2. What are you looking for in your spiritual life, what is your real aim?

3. If your spiritual life is a failure, what advice do you think the Holy Spirit would give you?

4. What did John Hyde do that made him Praying Hyde?

5. What are some of the reasons that God wants us to pray?

CHAPTER 4: ASKING FOR SIGNS

1. Should you ever put God to the test concerning your prayers? Explain your answer.

2. When someone puts God to the test concerning prayer, who is really being tested?

3. Have you ever fairly tested prayer by offering up a definite prayer and expecting a definite answer?

4. Have you ever prayed and had the Spirit bear witness to you that your request was granted?

5. Does God sometimes lead us to prove Him?

a. Can you think of any examples?

CHAPTER 5: WHAT IS PRAYER?

1. Define prayer.

2. When real prayer is at its highest and best what does it reveal?

3. What two steps, or thoughts, are necessary to enter into God's presence when we pray?

4. How should you enter God's presence?

5. What should you often meditate upon to become more like Christ?

CHAPTER 6: HOW SHALL I PRAY?

1. What does it indicate if you ask and do not receive?

2. What does it mean to ask in the name of Jesus Christ?

3. What kind of a life must we live to truly pray in the name of Jesus Christ?

4. Who is God's great prayer helper? Explain your answer.

5. Will God answer prayers that are not truly prayed in Jesus' name? Explain your answer.

CHAPTER 7: MUST I AGONIZE?

1. Does God measure prayer by how long you pray? Explain your answer.
    a. If not, what does He measure it by?
2. Is prayer given to us as a burden we must bear? Explain your answer.
3. Can everyone make time for prayer? Explain your answer.
4. What is sometimes the hardest thing to do during prayer?
5. What are some of the things the devil will try to do to keep us from praying?
6. Are we called upon to agonize in prayer? Explain your answer.
    a. What examples can you find in the Bible?
    b. What examples can you find in Church history?

CHAPTER 8: DOES GOD ALWAYS ANSWER PRAYER?

1. If God does not answer one of your prayers, is it because He did not intend to answer it?
2. As a child of God should you expect God to answer every one of your prayers?
    a. Does true prayer ever go unanswered?
3. How can you know whether God's answer is no or wait.
4. What is one of the reasons that we often ask and do not receive what we ask for?
5. What must be the condition of your heart, your motives, and your desires in order for God to answer your prayers? (Consider the condition of Christ in these areas and how He said that God always heard Him.)

CHAPTER 9: ANSWERS TO PRAYER

1. Does the age of the person praying affect the answers to prayer?
a. Explain your answer.
2. What are the three things that you must have for God to answer your prayers?
3. Will criticism of anyone move them closer to Christ?
4. Will your unconverted friends be converted if no one prayers for them?

CHAPTER 10: HOW GOD ANSWERS PRAYER

1. What is one of the main ways that God speaks to us or to those for whom we're praying?
2. What is God trying to teach us by making many things dependent upon our prayers?
3. What kind of things can God not do on the earth unless we work?
4. If the most momentous question is not "How does God answer prayer," then what is it?

CHAPTER 11: HINDRANCES TO PRAYER

1. If there are any hindrances to your prayers being answered, where should you search within yourself to find them?
2. Can the devil do anything to you if …
a. There is nothing in you that belongs to him,
b. You have nothing in common,
c. He has no claim upon you?

3. Is there any sin that is too small to hinder your prayers? Explain your answer.

4. What is possibly the greatest hindrance to your prayers?

5. How will the following hinder your prayers?
   a. Doubt
   b. Self
   c. Pride
   d. Criticism
   e. Fault finding
   f. Unforgiveness
   g. Bad temper
   h. Home life
   i. Hard heart

6. What are the three things that the apostle Paul exhorts you to do in relation to God?

CHAPTER 12: WHO MAY PRAY?

1. Who does the Bible say may pray?

2. Does God accept everyone's prayer?

3. Does God hear everyone's prayer?
   a. If there are conditions to God's hearing a person's prayer, what are they?

4. What is the only prayer by a sinner that God is certain to hear and answer.

5. Does God, for His own sovereign reasons, ever answer prayers by those who have no right to pray; i.e., are not His children. Explain your answer.
   a. Can you give any examples to justify your answer?

6. As children of God, what is the only thing that will hinder our prayers?

7. Do some have a special gift of prayer, or will the Holy Spirit teach all Christians to pray—have a desire to be taught?

THE LIFE
OF PRAYER

BY

A.B. SIMPSON

BIOGRAPHY OF
A. B. SIMPSON

Albert Benjamin Simpson was born on Prince Edward Island on December 15, 1843, to James and Janet Simpson. His sister said that his birth was an answer to his mother's prayer. She lost her firstborn son when he was just a toddler. "Like little Samuel, Albert was given to the Lord from his birth. My mother told me that she gave him to the Lord to use him in life or death; to be a minister and a foreign missionary, if the Lord so willed, and he lived to grow up, and was so inclined."

When he was fourteen Simpson was torn between what he considered his duty to enter the ministry and the delights he found in the world. He knew he needed salvation, and struggled his way toward God. The God he had been brought up to know, however, was fearsome and severe. He said, "My whole religious training had left me without any conception of the sweet and simple Gospel of Jesus Christ." But he did know that "God could give in some mysterious way a wonderful change called the new birth or regeneration."

All of this caused him great inward conflict, and that combined with his poor health brought him close to a physical and emotional breakdown. At the height of his physical and emotional stress, he asked his father to pray for him, which he did, but he apparently was not able to show his son the way to peace. "No one," Simpson said, "shared with me the simple way of believing in the promises and accepting the salvation fully provided and freely offered."

One day Simpson came across a book titled, *The Gospel Mystery of Sanctification* by Walter Marshall. In it he read: "The first good work you will ever perform is to believe on the Lord Jesus Christ. Until you do this, all your works, prayers, tears, and good resolutions are vain. To believe on the Lord Jesus Christ is to believe that He saves you according to His word, that He receives and saves you here and now, for He has said: 'Him that cometh to Me I will in no wise cast out'" (John 6:37).

This was just what Simpson needed. He cast himself upon the Lord in prayer and the peace that passes all understanding swept over him and brought him rest. In one of his books he described his experience: "To my bewildered soul this was like the light from heaven that fell upon Saul of Tarsus on his way to Damascus. I immediately fell upon my knees, and looking up to the Lord, I said, Lord Jesus, Thou hast said, 'Him that cometh unto Me I will in no wise cast out.' Thou knowest how long and earnestly I have tried to come, but I did not know how. Now I come the best I can, and dare to believe that Thou dost receive me and save me, and that I am now Thy child, forgiven and saved simply because I have taken Thee at Thy word. Abba Father, Thou art mine, and I am Thine."

After finishing high school Simpson taught to earn enough money to enter Knox College in Toronto, Ontario. He graduated in 1864 and accepted the pastorate of the Knox Presbyterian Church in Hamilton, Ontario. In December 1873, he received a call to the pulpit of the Chestnut Street Presbyterian Church in Louisville, Kentucky. Five years later he went to New York City to pastor the affluent Thirteenth Street Presbyterian Church. In New York City he found a mission field at his door among the immigrant population. When he wanted to bring a hundred or so new Italian converts into the church, the Presbytery sugge... attend a different church. That inspired Simpso... Presbyterian denomination and form an indepe... where he could evangelize and minister to the mas... York City and elsewhere.

Although his work was constantly increasing, Simpson always took two or three hours each day to pray and study the Word. He said, "We cannot go through life strong and fresh on express trains, with ten minutes for lunch. We must have quiet hours, secret places of the Most High, times of waiting upon the Lord, when we renew our strength and learn to mount up on wings as eagles, and then come back, to run and not be weary, and to walk and not faint (Isaiah 40:31).... The best thing about this stillness is that it gives God a chance to work."

He encouraged believers to consider the Lord's reply to his disciples when they asked him to teach them to pray; the Lord's reply was, "Pray." Simpson said, "This is the only way we can ever learn to pray, by just beginning to do it. Prayer will teach us how to pray, and the more we pray, the more we will learn the mysteries of the heights and depths of prayer."

For his own spiritual growth in prayer, Simpson studied the writings of the mystics like Madame Jeanne Guyon and François Fénelon (full name: François de Salignac de la Mothe-Fénelon), and writings of other Christian mystics (Quietist). He liked the discipline of *listening prayer*, which is listening to the Lord speak while reading the Word. He said that when he first sought to hear the "still, small voice of God"... a pandemonium of voices reached my ears, a thousand clamoring notes from without and within, until I could hear nothing but their noise and din. Some of them were my own voice, some of them were my own questions, and some of them were my own cares, and some of them were my very prayers." Yet had not God said, "Be still, and know that I am God"? (Psalm 46:10).

By shutting out "noisy acclamations" and "unspeakable unrest," he began to hear deep within himself a *small voice* that spoke with "an inexpressible tenderness, power and comfort. As I listened, it became to me the voice of prayer, and the voice of wisdom, and the voice of duty. I did not need to think so hard, or pray so hard, or trust so hard, but that 'still, small voice' of the Holy Spirit in my heart was God's prayer in my secret soul, was God's answer to all my questions, was God's life and strength for soul and body, and became the substance of all knowledge, and all prayer, and all blessing; for it was the living God himself as my life and my all."

Activity could never substitute for prayer: "We cannot go through life strong and fresh on express trains, with ten minutes for lunch. We must have quiet hours, secret places of the Most High, times of waiting upon the Lord, when we renew our strength and learn to mount up on wings as eagles, and then come back, to run and not be weary, and to walk and not faint. ..."

In August 1881, he was miraculously healed of a chronic heart disorder while on vacation at Old Orchard Beach, Maine. After that, divine healing became an essential part of Simpson's ministry. He began meetings for healing, and associated himself with the American faith-healing movement, for which he later became a spokesman.

A. B. Simpson was one of the most important and active Christian workers of his day. He was a zealous soul-winner and was constantly evangelizing and training and encouraging Christian workers to do the same. As busy as he was, he wrote over 70 books on the Bible and the Christian life, plus hundreds of encouraging and faith-inspiring hymns and poems. He founded the Christian and Missionary Alliance, and was known around the world for preaching the "fourfold gospel," which is Christ as Savior, Sanctifier, Healer, and soon coming King.

Here is a famous anecdote about a conversation between Dr. Simpson and a reporter from the New York Journal. It clearly shows Simpson's expectation of the second coming of Christ and how he believed the Church could help to bring it about.

Reporter: "Dr. Simpson, Do you know when the Lord is coming?"

Simpson: "Yes, and I will tell you if you promise to print just what I say, references and all."

Reporter: "I promise."

Simpson: "Then put this down: 'This gospel of the kingdom shall be preached in all the world for a witness unto the nations and then shall the end come.' Matthew 24:14. Have you written the reference?"

Reporter: "Yes, what more?"

Simpson: "Nothing more."

Reporter: "Do you mean to say that you believe that when the Gospel is preached to all the nations Jesus will return?"

Simpson: "Just that."

Reporter: "I think I begin to see the daylight. I see the motivation and the motive power in this movement."

Simpson "Then you see more than some of the doctors of divinity."

In his book, *A Larger Christian Life*, Simpson wrote about his vision for the Church: "He is showing us the plan for a Christian church that is much more than an association of congenial friends to listen once a week to an intellectual discourse and musical entertainment and carry on by proxy a mechanism of Christian work; but rather a church that can be at once the mother and home of every form of help and blessing which Jesus came to give to lost and suffering men, the birthplace and the home of souls, the fountain of healing and cleansing, the sheltering home for the orphan and distressed, the school for the culture and training of God's children, the armory where they are equipped for the battle of the Lord and the army which fights those battles in His name. Such a center of population in this sad and sinful world!"

On October 28, 1919, A. B. Simpson had a stroke and went into a coma from which he never recovered. According to family members, his final words were a prayer to God for all the missionaries he had helped to send throughout the world.

For more biographical information about A. B. Simpson, see the Pure Gold Classics edition of *The Fourfold Gospel*, published by Bridge-Logos Publishers.

Photo Gallery

ALBERT BENJAMIN SIMPSON

1843–1919

Simpson at 17 – when entering Knox College

At the Crisis in Louisville, KY

Margaret Simpson during Hamilton years

During last visit to England

Margaret Henry Simpson

Simpson Homestead, Chatham, Ontario

Mr. & Mrs. Simpson

New York Gospel Tabernacle interior

Funeral procession at Nyack, New York

PREFACE

The *Life of Prayer* is a great and sacred theme! It leads us into the Holy of Holies and the secret place of the Most High. It is the very life of the Christian, and it touches the life of God himself.

We enter the sacred chamber on our knees. We still our thoughts and words, and say, "Lord, teach us to pray. Give us thy holy desires, and let our prayer be the very echo of thy will. Give us thy Spirit as our advocate within. Open our eyes to see our great high priest and advocate above, and help us so to abide in Him, and to have His Word so abiding in us, that we shall ask what we will, and it shall be done unto us."

And as in ignorance and weakness we venture to speak and think upon this vital theme, "Let the words of my mouth, and the meditation of my heart, be acceptable in thy sight, O LORD, my strength, and my redeemer" (Psalm 19:14).

And may every true word and thought of this little volume be a living experience to him who speaks and to all who hear, and so minister to the life of prayer in all our lives, that it shall bring, in some humble measure, an answer to the greatest of all prayers, and the prayer with which this opening chapter begins and to which this book is dedicated, "Our Father which art in heaven, Hallowed be thy name."

—A. B. Simpson

Chapter 1

THE PATTERN PRAYER

A nd he said unto them, when ye pray, say, Our Father which art in heaven, Hallowed be thy name. Thy kingdom come. Thy will be done, as in heaven, so in earth. Give us day by day our daily bread. And forgive us our sins; for we also forgive every one that is indebted to us. And lead us not into temptation; but deliver us from evil. (Luke 11:2-4).

This wonderful prayer was dictated by our Lord in reply to the question on the part of His disciples, "Lord, teach us to pray." His answer was to bid them pray. This is the only way we shall ever learn to pray, by just beginning to do it. And as the babbling child learns the art of speech by speaking, and the lark mounts up to the heights of the sky by beating its little wings again and again upon the air, so prayer will teach us how to pray. The more we pray, the more shall we learn the mysteries and heights and depths of prayer.

And the more we pray what the Lord bid His disciples to pray, the more we shall realize the incomparable fullness and completeness of this unequaled prayer. It is the prayer of universal Christendom, the common liturgy of the Lord's Church, the earliest and holiest recollection of every Christian child, and the latest utterance often of the departing soul.

We who have used it most have come to feel that there is no want that it does not interpret and no holy aspiration that it may not express. There is nothing else in the holy Scriptures that more fully evolves the great principles that underlie the divine philosophy of prayer.

IT TEACHES US THAT
ALL TRUE PRAYER BEGINS IN THE
RECOGNITION OF THE FATHER

It is not the cry of nature to an unknown God, but the intelligent conversation of a child with his heavenly Father. It presupposes that the one praying has become a child of God, and it assumes that the mediation of the Son has preceded the revelation of the Father. No one, therefore, can truly pray until he has accepted the Lord Jesus Christ as Savior and received through Him the child-heart in regeneration, and then been led into the realization of sonship in the family of God. The person to whom prayer is directly addressed is the Father as distinguished from the Son and the Holy Spirit. The great purpose of Christ's mediation is to bring us to God and reveal to us the Father as *our Father* in reconciliation and fellowship. It is not wrong to address the Son and Spirit in our hearts. The name Father, however, suggests the spirit of confidence, and this is essential to prayer.

The first view given of God in what is commonly called *The Lord's Prayer* is not His majesty but His paternal love. To the listening disciples this must have been a strange expression from the lips of their Lord as a pattern for them. Never had Jewish ear heard God so named, at least in His relation to the individual. He was sometimes called the *Father of the Nation,* but no sinful person had ever dared to call God his Father. Undoubtedly, the disciples had heard their Master speak in this delightful name, calling God His Father. But that they themselves should call Jehovah by such a name had never dawned upon their legal and unenlightened minds.

And yet by its use the Lord is telling us that we may and should recognize that God is our Father in the very sense in which He is His Father—because we are partakers of Jesus' sonship and His name. The name "Father" expresses the most personal and tender love, protection, care, and intimacy. It gives to prayer, at the very outset, the beautiful atmosphere of the home circle and the delightful affectionate and intimate fellowship of friend with friend

Beloved, have you learned to pray that way? Do wondering angels look down upon your closet every day to see a humble and sinful creature of the dust talking to the majestic Sovereign of the skies, as an infant lies upon its mother's breast or prattles without a fear upon her knee? Can it be said to you, "I write unto you, little children, because ye have known the Father"? (1 John 2:13).

IT TEACHES US THAT
PRAYER SHOULD RECOGNIZE THE MAJESTY AND
ALMIGHTINESS OF GOD

The words, "who art in heaven," or, rather, "in the heavens," are intended to give to the conception of God a very definite and local personality. He is not a vague influence or pantheistic presence. He is a distinct person, exalted above matter and nature and having local habitation, to which the mind is directed, and where He occupies the throne of sovereignty over all the universe. He is also recognized as above our standpoint and level, in the heavens, higher than our little world, and exalted above all other elements and forces that need His con-trolling power. It enthrones Him in the place of highest power, authority, and glory.

True prayer must ever recognize at once the nearness and greatness of God. The Old Testament, therefore, is full of sublime expressions of the majesty of God, and the more fully we realize His greatness, the more boldly will we dare to claim His intervention in prayer in all our trials and emergencies.

Beloved, have we learned, as we bow our knees in prayer, that we are talking with Him who still says to us as to Abraham, "I am El Shaddai; the Almighty God" (Genesis 17:1); to Jeremiah, "I am the LORD, the God of all flesh: is there any thing too hard for me?" (Jeremiah 32:27); to Isaiah, "Hast thou not known? hast thou not heard, that the everlasting God, the LORD, the Creator of the ends of the earth, fainteth not, neither is weary? there is no searching of his understanding" (Isaiah 40:28).

IT TEACHES US THAT
PRAYER IS NOT ONLY A FELLOWSHIP WITH GOD
BUT A FELLOWSHIP OF HUMAN HEARTS

"Our Father" lifts each of us at once out of ourselves, and, if nowhere else on earth, at least at the throne of grace, makes us members one of another. Of course, it is assumed that the first link in the fellowship is Christ, our elder brother. So there is no single heart, however isolated, but that may come with this prayer with perfect truthfulness and, hand in hand with Christ before the throne of grace, say, "Christ's prayer and mine." But, undoubtedly, it chiefly refers to the fellowship of human hearts. The highest promises made to prayer are made to those who agree—or, as the Greek more beautifully expresses it, *symphonize*—on earth. There is no place where we can love our friends so beautifully or so purely as at the throne of grace. There is no exercise in which the differences of Christians melt away as when their hearts meet together in the unity of prayer, and there is no remedy for the divisions of Christianity but to come closer to the Father, and then, being together at the throne, we shall be closer to each other.

IT TEACHES US THAT
WORSHIP IS THE HIGHEST ELEMENT
IN PRAYER

"Hallowed be thy name" is more than any petition of the Lord's Prayer. It brings us directly to God himself and makes His glory supreme, above all our thoughts and all our wants. It reminds us that the first purpose of our prayers should ever be, not the supply of our personal needs, but the worship and adoration of our God. In the ancient feasts, everything was first brought to Him, and then it was given to the worshiper for his use, and its use was hallowed by the fact that it had already been laid at Jehovah's feet. And so the spirit that can truly utter this prayer and fully enter into its meaning can receive all the other petitions of it with double blessing. Not until we have first become satisfied with God himself, and realize that His glory is above all our desires and interests, are we prepared to receive any blessing in the highest sense. And when we can truly say, "*Hallowed be thy name* no matter what comes to me," we have the substance of all blessing in our heart.

This is the innermost chamber of the Holy of Holies, and none can enter it without becoming conscious of the hallowing blessing that falls upon and fills us with the glory that we have ascribed to Him. The sacred sense of His overshadowing, the deep and penetrating solemnity, the heavenly calm, that fills the heart that can truly utter these sacred words, constitute a blessing above all other blessings that even this prayer can ask.

Beloved, have we learned to begin our prayer in this holy place, on this heavenly plane? Then, indeed, we have learned to pray.

IT TEACHES US THAT
TRUE PRAYER RECOGNIZES THE ESTABLISHMENT
OF THE KINGDOM OF GOD AS THE CHIEF
PURPOSE OF THE DIVINE WILL AND THE SUPREME
DESIRE OF EVERY TRUE CHRISTIAN

"Thy kingdom come" teaches us that we are to pray for the establishment of God's kingdom more than for our own temporal or even spiritual needs. This implies that the real remedy for all that needs prayer is the restoration of the kingdom of God. The true cause of all human trouble is that humanity is out of the divine order and the world is in rebellion against its sovereign God. Not until God's kingdom is reestablished in every heart and in all the world can the blessings that prayer desires be realized. It includes in a primary sense, of course, the establishment of the kingdom of God in the individual heart, but much more in the world at large it means the fulfillment of God's great purpose of redemption. It is, in short, the prayer for the accomplishment of redemption and its glorious consummation in the coming of our Lord and the setting up of His millennial kingdom.

What an exalted view this gives of prayer! How it raises us above our petty selfish cares and cries. It is said of a devoted minister, Dr. Backus, of Baltimore, that when told he was dying and had only half an hour to live, he asked them to raise him from his bed and place him upon his knees. There he spent the last half-hour of his life in one ceaseless prayer for the evangelization of the world. Truly that was a glorious place to end a life of prayer. But the Lord's Prayer begins with this lofty theme and teaches us that it should ever be the first concern and petition of every loyal subject of our Father's kingdom.

Must it not be true, beloved, that the failure of many of our prayers may be traced to their selfishness; i.e., the innumerable efforts we have spent upon our own interests, and the little we have ever asked for the kingdom of our Lord? There is no blessing so great as that which comes when our hearts are lifted out of *self* and become one with Christ in intercession for others and for His cause. There is no joy so pure as that of taking the burden of our Master's cause on our hearts and bearing it with Him every day in ceaseless prayer—**doing it** as though its success wholly depended upon the uplifting of our hands and the exercise of our faith. "Prayer also shall be made for him continually" (Psalm 72:15), is one of the promises respecting our blessed Lord.

Beloved, have we prayed for Jesus as much as we have for ourselves? There is no ministry that will bring more power and blessing upon the world and from which we ourselves will reap larger harvests of eternal fruit than the habit of believing, definite, and persistent prayer for the progress of Christ's kingdom, for the needs of His Church and work, for His ministers and servants, and especially for the evangelization of the world. Oh, let us awaken from our spiritual selfishness and learn the meaning of the petition, "Thy kingdom come!"

IT TEACHES US THAT TRUE PRAYER IS FOUNDED UPON THE WILL OF GOD AND HAS GOD'S WILL AS ITS LIMITATION AND ENCOURAGEMENT

"Thy will be done, as in heaven, so in earth" shows us that true prayer is not asking for things because we want them, but that the primary condition of all true prayer is the renunciation of our own will that we may desire and receive God's will instead. But having done this, and recognizing the will of our Father as the standard of our desires and petitions, we are to claim these petitions, when they are in accordance with His will, with a force and tenacity as great as the will of God itself. And so this petition of "thy will be done," instead of being a limitation of prayer, is really a confirmation of our faith, and gives us the right to claim that a petition that is conformed to His will must be fulfilled.

Therefore, there is no prayer so mighty, so sure, so full of blessing, as this little sentence at which so many of us have often trembled, "thy will be done." It is not the death-knell of all our happiness, but the pledge of all possible blessing; for if it is the will of God to bless us, we shall be blessed. Happy are they who suspend their desires until they know their Father's will, and then, asking according to His will, they can rise to the height of the Lord's own mighty promise, "If ye abide in me, and my words abide in you, ye shall ask what ye will, and it shall be done unto you" (John 15:7).

"And this is the confidence that we have in him, that, if we ask any thing according to his will, he heareth us: And if we know that he hear us, whatsoever we ask, we know that we have the petitions that we desired of him" (1 John 5:14-15). What more can we ask of ourselves and others than that God's highest will, and that for us, shall be fulfilled?

How shall we know that will? At the very least, we may always know it by His Word and promise, and we may be very sure we are not transcending its infinite bounds if we ask anything that is covered by a promise of God's holy Word. When it is, we may immediately turn that promise into an order on the very bank of Heaven and claim its fulfillment by all the power of His omnipotence and the sanctions of His faithfulness. Why, the very added clause itself, "as it is in heaven," implies that the fulfillment of this petition would change earth into a heaven, and bring heaven into every one of our lives in the measure in which we meet this lofty prayer! This petition, therefore, while it implies the spirit of absolute submission, rises to the height of illimitable faith.

Beloved, have we understood it and learned thus to pray, "Thy will be done in earth, as it is in heaven"?

IT TEACHES US THAT
PRAYER MAY INCLUDE ALL OUR NATURAL
AND TEMPORAL WANTS AND SHOULD BE
ACCOMPANIED BY THE SPIRIT OF TRUSTFUL
DEPENDENCE UPON OUR FATHER'S CARE FOR THE
SUPPLY OF ALL OUR EARTHLY NEEDS

"Give us this day our daily bread," gives to every child of God the right to claim our Father's supporting and providing love. It is wonderful how much spiritual blessing we get by praying and trusting for temporal needs. Those who try, through second causes or through ample human provision, to be independent of God's direct interposition and care, greatly curtail the fullness of their spiritual life and separate God's personal providence from the most simple and minute of life's secular interests. We are to recognize every means of support and temporal link of blessing as directly from His hand, and to commit every interest of business and life to His direction and blessing.

At the same time, it is implied that there must be in this a spirit of simplicity and daily trust. It is not the bread of future days for which we ask, but the bread of today. Nor is it always luxurious bread, the bread of affluence, the banquet and the feast, but daily bread—or rather as the best authorities translate it, "sufficient bread," bread such as He sees to be really best for us. It may not always be bread and butter. It may be just plain bread, and it may sometimes be very little bread. But God can make even a little bread sufficient, and add such a blessing and impartation of His life and strength with it that we will know, like our Master in the wilderness, that "man shall not live by bread alone, but by every word of God" (Luke 4:4). The petition implies, in short, a spirit of contentment and satisfaction with our daily lot, and a trust that leaves tomorrow's needs in His wise and faithful hand.

It states, further, that we believe that He will care for us day by day as each new tomorrow comes.

Beloved, have you learned to pray for temporal things in this way, bringing all your life to God in the spirit of daily trust and thankful contentment with your simple lot and your Father's wisdom and faithfulness?

IT TEACHES US THAT
TRUE PRAYER MUST EVER RECOGNIZE
OUR NEED OF THE MERCY OF GOD

There are two versions of this petition: "forgive us our sins" (Luke 11:4), and "forgive us our debts" (Matthew 6:12). This is not accidental. There may be an honest consciousness in the heart of the one praying that there has been no willful or known disobedience or sin, and yet there may be infinite debt, omission, and shortcoming as compared with the high standard of God's holiness and even our own ideal. The sensitive and thoroughly quickened spirit will never reach a place where it will not be sensible of so much more to which it is reaching out and God is pressing it forward, that it will not need to say, "Forgive us our debts," even where perhaps it could not conscientiously say, "Forgive us our sins."

This sense of demerit on our part throws us constantly upon the merits and righteousness of our great High Priest and makes our prayers forevermore dependent on His intercession and offered in His name. This enables the most unworthy to "come boldly unto the throne of grace" to "obtain mercy, and find grace to help in time of need" (Hebrews 4:16). We do not mean that our dear Lord encourages us to expect to be constantly sinning and repenting. The final petition of this prayer is for complete deliverance from all evil. But He graciously stoops to the lowest level, and yet grades the prayer so as to cover the experience of the highest saint—to meet the finer sense of the most sanctified spirit as well as the coarser consciousness of actual sin on the part of the humblest penitent.

This petition presupposes a very solemn spirit of forgiveness in the heart of the one praying. This is indispensable to the acceptance of the prayer for forgiveness. The Greek construction and the use of the aorist tense expresses a very practical shade of meaning; namely, that the forgiveness of the injury that has been done to us has preceded our prayer for divine forgiveness. Freely translated it should be thus expressed, "Forgive us our debts as we have already forgiven our debtors" (Matthew 6:12).

There are certain spiritual states, therefore, that are indispensable to acceptable prayer, even for the simplest mercies, and without which we cannot pray. The soul that is filled with bitterness cannot approach God in communion. It must, therefore, be true that the soul that is cherishing any other sin and sinful state is thereby hindered from access to the throne of grace. This is an Old Testament truth that all the abundant grace of the New Testament has not revoked nor weakened. "If I regard iniquity in my heart, the Lord will not hear me" (Psalm 66:18), was a lesson that even David learned in his sad and solemn experience. "I will wash mine hands in innocency: so will I compass thine altar, O LORD," is the eternal condition of acceptable communion with a holy God. The most sinful may come for mercy, but they must put away their sin and freely forgive the sins of others. Above all others there seem to be two unpardonable sins; one, the sin that willfully rejects the Holy Spirit and the Savior presented by Him—that is, the sin of willful unbelief; and the other, the sin of unforgiveness.

IT TEACHES US THAT
PRAYER IS OUR TRUE WEAPON AND SAFEGUARD
IN THE TEMPTATIONS OF LIFE, AND THAT WE MAY
RIGHTLY CLAIM THE DIVINE PROTECTION FROM
OUR SPIRITUAL ADVERSARIES

This petition, "lead us not into temptation," undoubtedly covers the whole field of our spiritual conflicts and may be interpreted, in the largest sense, of all we need to arm us against our spiritual enemies. It cannot strictly mean that we pray to be kept from all temptation, for God Himself has said, "Blessed is the man that endureth temptation (James 1:12)," and "count it all joy when ye fall into divers temptation" (James 1:2), and, "let patience have her perfect work" (James 1:4). It rather means, "Lead us not into a crisis of temptation," "and lead us so that we shall not fall under temptation or be tried above what we are able to bear." There are spiritual trials and crises that come to souls, too hard for them to bear, snares into which multitudes fall. This is God's special promise to His own, and the promise which this prayer claims; that they will not come into any such crisis, but will be kept out of situations that would be too trying, carried through the places that would be too narrow, and kept safe from peril.

This is what is meant by the word "The Lord knoweth how to deliver the godly out of temptations" (2 Peter 2:9), and also the still more gracious promise in 1 Corinthians 10:13, "There hath no temptation taken you but such as is common to man: but God is faithful, who will not suffer you to be tempted above that ye are able; but will with the temptation also make a way to escape, that ye may be able to bear it." When we think how many there are who perish in the snare, and how narrow the path often is, oh, what comfort it should give us to know that our Lord has authorized us to claim His divine protection in these awful perils to meet the wiles of the devil and the insidious foes against whom all our skill would be unavailing.

This was the Master's own solemn admonition to His disciples, in the garden in the hour and power of darkness, "Watch and pray, that ye enter not into temptation" (Matthew 26:41), and this was His own safeguard in that hour. The apostle has given it to us as the unceasing prescription of wisdom and safety in connection with our spiritual conflict, "Praying always with all prayer and supplication in the Spirit, and watching thereunto with all perseverance and supplication for all saints" (Ephesians 6:18). "Continue in prayer, and watch in the same with thanksgiving" (Colossians 4:2).

THE CROWNING PETITION OF THE LORD'S PRAYER IS A PETITION FOR ENTIRE SANCTIFICATION, INCLUDING DELIVERANCE FROM EVERY OTHER FORM OF EVIL

"Deliver us from evil." This has frequently been translated "from the evil one," but the neuter gender contradicts this and renders it most natural to translate it, as the old version does, of evil in all forms rather than the author of evil. This is more satisfactory to the Christian heart. There are many forms of evil that do not come from the evil one. We have as much cause to pray against ourselves as against the devil. And there are physical evils covered by this petition as well as special temptations.

It is a petition, therefore, against sin, sickness, and sorrow in every form in which they could be evils. It is a prayer for our complete deliverance from all the effects of Adam's fall, in spirit, soul, and body. It is a prayer that echoes the fourfold gospel and the fullness of Jesus in the highest and widest measure. It teaches us that we may expect victory over the power of sin, support against the attacks of sickness, triumph over all sorrow, and a life in which all things shall be only good and work together for good according to God's high purpose (Romans 8:28). Surely the prayer of the Holy Spirit for such a blessing is the best pledge of the answer! Let us not be afraid to claim it in all its fullness.

ALL PRAYER SHOULD END WITH PRAISE AND BELIEVING CONFIDENCE

The Lord's Prayer, according to the most correct manuscripts, really ends with "deliver us from evil," but later copies [of Matthew's Gospel] contain the closing clause, "For thine is the kingdom, and the power, and the glory for ever. Amen" (Matthew 6:13). And while it is extremely doubtful whether our Lord uttered these words, yet they have so grown into the phraseology of Christendom that we may, without danger, draw from them our closing lessons.

This doxology expresses the spirit of praise and consecration. We ascribe to God the authority and power to do what we have asked, and give the glory of it to His name. Then, in token of our confidence that He will do so, we add the Amen, which simply means, "So let it be done." It is faith ascending to the throne and humbly claiming and commanding in the name of Jesus that for which humility has petitioned. Our Lord does require this element of faith, and this acknowledgment and confirmation of His faithfulness as a condition of answered prayer. No prayer is complete therefore until faith has added its "Amen."

Such, then, are some of the principle teachings of this universal prayer, commonly called *The Lord's Prayer*. How often our lips have uttered it! Beloved, has it searched our hearts this day and shown us the imperfection, the selfishness, the smallness, the unbelief of what we call prayer? Let us henceforth repeat its meaningful words with deeper thoughtfulness and weigh them with more solemn realization

176

than we have done before. Until they come to be to us what they indeed are, the summary of all prayer, the expression of all possible need and blessing, and the language of a worship like that of the holy ranks who continually surround the throne above. Then indeed will His kingdom come and His will be done on earth as it is in heaven.

Beautiful and blessed prayer! How it recalls the most sacred associations of life. How it follows the prodigal even in his deepest downfall and his latest moments. How it expands with the deepening spiritual life of the saint. How it sends the latest aspirations and adorations of departing Christians to the throne to which they are ready to wing their way. Let it be more dear to us henceforth, more real, more deep, wider and higher, as it teaches us to pray and carries our petition to the throne of grace.

And oh, if there is any one reading these words now who has often uttered it without having any right to say, "Our Father," or any real ability to enter into its heart-searching meaning, may you this very moment, beloved reader, stop. Then with tears of memory think of the voice that once taught you its tender words years ago, but that are silent now in the molding grave, and kneel down at the feet of that mother's God, that father's God, that sister's God, that brother's God. And if you are willing to say, "Forgive us our debts, as we forgive our debtors," you may dare to add, linked in everlasting hope and fellowship with those that first voiced those words to you, "Our Father which art in heaven."

On a lonely bed in a veteran's hospital, a soldier lay dying. A Christian chaplain called to see him and tried to speak of Christ, but soldier said that he did not believe in a life after death. Once or twice the chaplain tried in vain to reach the soldier's heart, but he could not. So he simply knelt down by the bed and tenderly repeated the Lord's Prayer, slowly and solemnly. When he arose to leave, the soldier's eyes were wet with tears. He tried to brush them away and conceal his feelings, but at last broke down and said, "My mother taught me that more than fifty years ago, and it quite broke me up to hear it again."

The chaplain went on his way, not wishing to hinder the work of the Holy Spirit. The next time he called, the patient was not there. Sending for the nurse he asked about him, and was told that the soldier had died the night before. "And did he die in peace?" the chaplain asked.

"I'm sure he did," the nurse replied. "Just before he died I heard him repeating the words, 'Our Father who art in heaven.' And then I heard him say in just a whisper, 'Mother, I am coming! He is *my* Father, too!'"

Dear friend, let this old prayer become to you a holy bond with all that is dearest on earth, and a stepping stone to the very gates of Heaven!

Chapter 2

ENCOURAGEMENTS TO PRAYER

And he said unto them, Which of you shall have a friend, and shall go unto him at midnight, and say unto him, Friend, lend me three loaves; for a friend of mine in his journey is come to me, and I have nothing to set before him? And he from within shall answer and say, Trouble me not: the door is now shut, and my children are with me in bed; I cannot rise and give thee. I say unto you, Though he will not rise and give him, because he is his friend, yet because of his importunity he will rise and give him as many as he needeth. And I say unto you, Ask, and it shall be given you; seek, and ye shall find; knock, and it shall be opened unto you. For every one that asketh receiveth; and he that seeketh findeth; and to him that knocketh it shall be opened. If a son shall ask bread of any of you that is a father, will he give him a stone? or if he ask a fish, will he for a fish give him a serpent? or if he shall ask an egg, will he offer him a scorpion? If ye then, being evil, know how to give good gifts unto your children: how much more shall your heavenly Father give the Holy Spirit to them that ask him? (Luke 11:5-13).

This is our Savior's second teaching about prayer. His first was an actual example of prayer. This is an unfolding of some of the special encouragements to prayer that are afforded by the gracious care of God, our Father and friend, and also some deeper instructions respecting the nature and spirit of true prayer.

ENCOURAGEMENTS TO PRAYER

God is our Father. This had already been suggested in the opening words of the Lord's Prayer, but it is amplified in this passage by a comparison between the earthly and heavenly parent: "If ye then, being evil, know how to give good gifts unto your children: how much more shall your heavenly Father give the Holy Spirit to them that ask him?" God is not only a Father, but much more than any earthly father. How much this expresses to many of us!

There are few who cannot recall, in the memories of home, the value of a father's or a mother's love and care. Or, if they have been lacking, all the more, perhaps, has the orphaned heart felt its deep need and reached out for a father's heart and hand. Who of us has not felt in some great emergency, needing a wisdom and resource beyond our own, "Oh, if my father were only here," or, perhaps, has said to God: "If you were my earthly father now, you would sit down by my side and let me tell you of all my perplexity, and you would tell me just what to do, and then would do for me what I cannot do for myself." And yet His presence is as real as if we saw Him, and we may as freely pour our hearts out with all their fears and griefs and know that He hears and helps as no earthly father is able to do either in love or relief.

Perhaps even better than the memory of our childhood is the realization of our own fatherhood or motherhood. Who that has ever felt a parent's love can fail to understand this appeal? It is a love that neither the helplessness nor the worthlessness of its object can affect. It is a love that often has gladly sacrificed everything, even life itself, for the loved one. But it was from the bosom of God that all that love came at first, and infinitely more is still in reserve. The depth, and length, and height of this *much more love* can only be measured by the distance between the infinite and the human. Much more than you love your child does He love you; much more than you would give or sacrifice is He ready to bestow and has He already sacrificed; much more than you can trust or ask a father for, may you dare to bring to Him; much more unerring is His wisdom, unlimited His power, and inexhaustible His love. Shall we, then, with the little alphabet of our human experience, try to spell out all His love and learn the deeper meaning of the prayer, "Our Father which art in heaven"?

He is our friend. "Which of you shall have a friend?" This also finds its full significance through the actual experience of each one of us. Who has not had a friend, and more of a friend in some respects than even a father? There are intimacies not born of human blood that are the most intense and lasting bonds of earthly love. Jonathan was more to David than Jesse was, and Timothy was more to Paul than a very son. How much our friends have been to some of us! One by one let us count them over, recall each act and bond of love, and think of all that we may trust them for and all in which they stood by us.

Now, as we concentrate the whole weight of recollection and affection, let us put God in that place of confidence and think He is all that and infinitely more. Our friend! The one who is personally interested in us, who has set His heart upon us, who has made himself acquainted with us, who has come near to us in the tender and delicate intimacy of unspeakable fellowship, who has spoken to us such gracious words, who has given us such invaluable pledges and promises, who has done so much for us, who has made such priceless sacrifices, and who is ready to take any trouble or go to any expense to aid us—to Him we are coming in prayer, our friend in Heaven.

He is a friend in extremity. The case here supposed is a hard one. The one praying is in great need, has a case of suffering on hand, and is wholly without means to meet it. It may represent any emergency in our lives. Other friends are for fair weather. This is always God's time.

The friends who in our sunshine live,
When winter comes, have flown,
And he who has but tears to give
Must weep those tears alone.

But this friend has authorized us to claim His help, especially in times of need. "Call upon me," He says, "in the day of trouble: I will deliver thee, and thou shalt glorify me" (Psalm 50:15). "God is our refuge and strength, a very present help in time of trouble" (Psalm 46:1). "Thou hast known my soul in adversities" (Psalm 31:7) is the testimony of one who proved His faithful friendship under the severest pressure. "God, that comforteth those that are cast down" (2 Corinthians 7:6), "the Father of mercies, and the God of all comfort" (2 Corinthians 1:3) are His chosen names and titles.

Let us not fear, therefore, to come to Him when we have nothing to bring to Him but our grief and fear. We will be welcome. He is able for the hardest occasions, and He is seated on His throne of grace for the very purpose of giving help in time of need. Even if the case seems wholly helpless and the hour is as dark as the dark midnight of this parable, cast your burden on the Lord. Yes, all your cares, for "he careth for you" (1 Peter 5:7), and "The LORD is nigh unto them that are of a broken heart; and saveth such as be of a contrite spirit" (Psalm 34:18).

He is a friend, not only in season, but at all seasons, and at the most unseasonable times. This parable is the story of a man coming to his friend when all reasonable ground for expecting a favorable reception was out of the question. It was midnight. The door was shut, literally barred, the house closed for the night, and the time for calls long past. Nevertheless that door was opened, that petition heard, that favor granted. And whatever may be the meaning of the reluctance of the earthly friend, certainly we know that our heavenly friend assures us that none of these causes will prevent His hearing and helping in the most extreme and desperate straits and seasons. The peculiarity of God's grace is that He helps when man would refuse to help, and its highest trophies are associated with time when mercy seemed long past and hope forever dead.

Look at that wicked king, Manasseh, who for half a century was a brutal butcher of the prophets and saints of God. He had literally fed his brutality on the wreck of all that was sacred and divine. And then the hand of retribution struck him down and left him in his miserable old age a captive in a foreign prison. One would have thought that prayer from such a man was profanity and that all heaven would shut its ears at the very idea of his escaping well-deserved and merciless punishment. But in that late hour Manasseh cried to the Lord in his affliction, and the Lord heard him and had mercy on him, forgave him all his sins, and brought him again into his kingdom. And then Manasseh knew that the Lord was God. Surely no soul can ever say again that the hour is too late or the door too strongly barred for mercy.

Look at that city Nineveh, the oppressor of the nations, the proud queen of Assyria, the scourge of Israel and Judah, the boastful shrine of every abominable idolatry. At length its iniquities reached to heaven, and the prophet Jonah was sent to proclaim its speedy and certain doom. "Yet forty days, and Nineveh shall be overthrown" (Jonah 3:4). That city went upon its knees; its kings, its priests, its princes, and its peasantry were prostrated in penitential prayer. What was the result? The barred gates were opened, the doors of mercy were unlocked, the terrible decree was revoked, and Nineveh became a monument of the mercy of God. The children in its streets and the cattle in its stalls were specified as the objects of His tender compassion.

Look at King Hezekiah to whom, in the fullness of his prosperity, the message came, "Set thine house in order; for thou shalt die, and not live" (2 Kings 20:1). Surely that looked like a closing and barring of the gates of the tomb. The sentence fell on his ears like a voice of doom. But in that hour Hezekiah prayed. A poor and trembling prayer it was: "I reckoned till morning, that, as a lion, so will he break all my bones: from day even to night wilt thou make an end of me. Like a crane or a swallow, so did I chatter: I did mourn as a dove: mine eyes fail with looking upward" (Isaiah 38:13-14). Though there was little faith in that heartbroken gasp of prayer, it reached the heart of God, and the decree that had seemed imperative and inexorable, the stern word that had set a barrier to the path of life and opened the cold stone portals of what seemed an inevitable tomb, was changed, and the messenger was sent back with the gracious reprieve, "I will add unto thy days fifteen years" (2 Kings 20:6).

Such is the friend to whom we pray, who stands between us and all the mighty bars and doors of material force, of natural law, of human purpose, and even of divine judgment. He turns aside with His hands of love every bolt and bar that stands between us and the fullest blessing that He can give our trusting and obedient hearts. Shall we ever again think anything too hard, or any hour too late? He loves the hour of extremity. It is His chosen time of almighty intervention. *God will help her at the turning of the morning* is His voice to Zion.

Summoned to the dying couch of a little girl, the mighty Lord had time to tarry by the way until a poor, helpless, woman was healed by the touch of His garment. But meanwhile that little life had ebbed away, and human unbelief hastened to turn back the visit that was now too late. "Thy daughter is dead; trouble not the Master." It was then that His strong and mighty love rose to its glorious height of power and victory. "Fear not," was His calm reply; "believe only, and she shall be made whole" (Luke 8:49-50).

Yes, let us go at midnight, for He that keeps Israel neither slumbers nor sleeps. Let us go when all other doors are barred and even the heavens seem brass, for the gates of prayer are open evermore, and it is only when the sun is gone down and our pillow is but the stone of the wilderness that we behold the ladder that reaches onto heaven, with our infinite God above it and the angels of His providence ascending and descending for our help and deliverance. "Men ought always to pray, and not to faint" (Luke 18:1).

He is a friend that will not deceive us. He will not give us a stone for bread; i.e., a barren, worthless, empty answer, but a real and satisfying blessing. He will not give us a serpent when we come for a fish; i.e., a harmful gift, or one that contains a hidden snare of temptation or spiritual evil. Many of the things that we ask in our blindness have serpents coiled in their folds, but He loves us too well to give us such an answer. Sometimes, therefore, He must modify or refuse our petition if He would be our true Father in heaven. And we need not fear to trust this to Him or make the boldest requests lest they might do us harm, for He who gives the greatest blessing can give the grace to keep it from being a selfish idol or a spiritual curse. People sometimes say, "If God were to heal me or give me some temporal blessing for which I am praying, I fear it might not be best for me." Can we not trust Him for the grace as well as the gift?

185

And again, our Father will not give us a scorpion if we ask an egg; i.e., something that would leave a bitterness and a sting behind. "The blessing of the LORD, it maketh rich, and he addeth no sorrow with it" (Proverbs 10:22). How many earthly roses fade and leave a lasting thorn! How many drops from earthly cups have more dregs of poison than drops of joy! How many a love and friendship but adds to the sorrow of the parting and to the bitterness of the memory. But all that heaven gives us are everlasting joys. Let us trust Him for all we ask, and we will have eternal cause to sing of His love and faithfulness.

This friend gives full measure. "He will rise and give him as many as he needeth." In our Father's house there is bread enough and to spare. His measure is more abundantly (John 10:10). Three loaves He gave to the hungry wayfarer. These three may be suggestive of our threefold life and God's complete provision for it in every part—spirit, soul and body. Have we claimed the ample measure? Are we satisfied today and running over with superabundant life and love for the hungry wayfarers that come to us? He only asked it as a loan, but he received it as a gift, the only return required being thanks and love. So our Father and our friend is ready to supply all our need "according to his riches in glory by Christ Jesus" (Philippians 4:19). Let us come, exclaiming:

> My soul, ask what thou wilt,
> Thou canst not be too bold.
> Since His own blood for thee He spilt,
> What else can He withhold?
> Beyond thy utmost wants,
> His power and love can bless;
> To trusting souls He loves to grant
> More than they can express.

INSTRUCTIONS CONCERNING PRAYER

In its simplest form, prayer is represented as asking. "Ask, and it shall be given you" (Luke 11:9). This expresses the most elementary form of prayer—the presenting of our petitions to God in the simplest terms and manner, and we are undoubtedly taught that even the most ordinary and imperfect request that is sincerely presented at the throne of grace receives the attention and response of our heavenly Father. It is probable that no honest heart ever asks in vain, even where, through ignorance or inexperience, it may but partly understand the principles and conditions of effectual prayer. The infant's helpless cry reaches the mother's heart not more surely than the feeblest gasp of need and supplication from His children's lips.

There is a higher form of prayer, "Seek, and ye shall find" (Luke 11:9). This denotes the prayer that waits upon God until it receives an answer, and that follows up that answer in obedience to His direction until it finds all it seeks, whether of light, or health, or strength from on high.

This is the prayer that inquires of the Lord, hearkens to catch His answer, hastens to obey it, and finds, as it follows, full light, help, and blessing. For prayer is more than asking. It is a receiving, a waiting, a learning of Him, a conversation and communion in which He has much to say and we have much to learn. This is the prayer that has brought us so often His peace, His heavenly baptism of love and power, His blessed working out of the problems of our life. It is of this He says in such often-repeated promises, "Let none that wait on thee be ashamed" (Psalm 25:3). "I said not unto the seed of Jacob, Seek ye me in vain" (Isaiah 45:19). "They that seek the LORD shall not want [lack] any good thing" (Psalm 34:10). For prayer is not an asking for things so much as seeking Him and pressing into that fellowship that is beyond all other gifts, and that carries with it every needed blessing.

There is a knocking prayer, to which the promise is given, "knock, and it shall be opened unto you" (Luke 11:9). This is more than seeking. This is the prayer that surmounts the great obstacles of life, the closed doors of circumstances, the brazen gates and unyielding mountains of hindrance and opposition, and that, in the name of our ascended Lord and in the fellowship of His mediatorial rights and powers, presses through every obstacle and treads down every adversary. It is not so much the prayer that knocks at the gates of heaven and extorts an answer from an unwilling God, as the prayer that, having received the answer and promise, carries it forth against the gates of the enemy and beats them down, just as the walls of Jericho fell before the tramp and shout of Israel's believing hosts. It is the prayer that takes its place at the side of our ascended Lord and claims what He has promised to give, and even commands, in His mighty name, that which He has already commanded through His royal Priesthood and all-prevailing intercession. It is faith putting its hand on the omnipotence of God and using it in fellowship with our omnipotent head until it sees His name prevail against all that opposes His will, the crooked things made straight, the gates of brass opened, and the fetters of iron broken asunder.

It is Moses standing on the mount with God while Joshua fights in the plain below, holding up the hands of victorious faith, seeing the hosts of Joshua keep step with his uplifted hands and the battle advance or ebb as those hands went up or down, until they waved on high over a victorious field and proclaimed the memorial name, "Jehovah-Nissi, the Lord is my banner," a name which has become our watchword from generation to generation. It is written, "Because the LORD hath sworn that the LORD will have war with Amalek from generation to generation" (Exodus 17:15-16). It is when our hand is upon the throne of the Lord that He wages war with all our enemies, and they fall before His victorious will.

It is Deborah, kneeling in her tent that day when Barak led the host of Israel against the legions of Sisera, feeling in her great heart the surging tides of that glorious warfare, and knowing by the throbs of her faith and prayer when the battle waxed or waned, until she had fought it all over upon the field of vision. As she claimed the last victorious onset and commanded the last foe to flee in Jehovah's name, her exulting spirit shouted in the victory of faith, though perhaps her eyes had not seen the battlefield at all, "O my soul, thou hast trodden down strength" (Judges 5:21). Her soul had trodden down the foe, her spirit had triumphed in the conscious power of Jehovah, her faith had knocked at the gates of the enemy until the immovable wall was laid in the dust and the gates of brass were shivered into fragments and scattered as by the whirlwinds of the sky. This is "the effectual prayer" which "availeth much" (James 5:16).

We are also instructed to come in the spirit of boldness and importunity. "Because of his importunity he will rise and give him as many as he needeth." This is a very difficult passage and one that has been variously interpreted. Dr. Walker, the thoughtful author of *The Philosophy of the Plan of Salvation*, has endeavored to show in his work on the Holy Spirit that this word here means "extremity," and that the idea conveyed is not that the man is heard because of his continued prayer, but because of his extreme distress and the difficult emergency that is facing him. We cannot find, however, sufficient authority for this view. The Greek word literally means "without shamefacedness." It is the negative form of the word "shamefacedness" which occurs in 1 Timothy 2:9, and it properly means boldness and audacity. There is nothing whatever unscriptural in this truth, which, indeed, is constantly reiterated in the New Testament, that we are to come boldly to the throne of grace, and claim our redemption rights in all their fullness. "We have boldness and access," we are told, "by the faith of him" (Ephesians 3:12). "Having therefore ... boldness to enter into the holiest by the blood of Jesus,... let us draw near with a true heart in full assurance of faith" (Hebrews 10:19-22). "Let us therefore come boldly unto the throne of grace" (Hebrews 4:16).

There is no doubt that if Esther had hesitated to enter into the presence of the king at the crisis of her country's fate, she would have both lost her blessing and risked the fortunes of her nation. There is no doubt that if modest Ruth had feared to claim her lawful rights at the feet of Boaz under the law of the kinsman, she probably would never have been his bride nor the mother of the long and honored line of kings, commencing with David and ending with Jesus. And there is no doubt that our unbelieving fear and shrinking timidity have lost us many a redemption right, and that a bold and victorious confidence that claims its inheritance in the name of our risen and ascended Lord is pleasing to God. We believe this is the meaning and teaching of this beautiful parable—that we are to come boldly to our Father and friend, no matter what doors would seem to be closed or what discouragements may frown across our way. Someone has said that the secret of success in human affairs has often been audacity. There is, at least, a holy audacity in Christian life and faith that is not inconsistent with the profoundest humility and in which lies the secret of the victorious achievements of Moses, Joshua, Elijah, and Daniel in the Old Testament, and of the Syro-Phoenician woman and the glorious apostle of faith in the New Testament. As well as the Luthers and the Careys and the hundreds of others who have been pioneers of gospel truth and missionary triumph in the Christian dispensation.

Perhaps the highest ministry of prayer is prayer for others. This petition was not for the one praying, but for a friend who in his journey had come to him, and he had nothing to set before him. Literally it means a friend "who had lost his way."

How tenderly it suggests the need of those on whose behalf we have constantly to go to our heavenly friend. It is of this that the apostle James says in referring to prayer, "Confess your faults one to another, and pray one for another, that ye may be healed. The effectual fervent prayer of a righteous man availeth much" (James 5:16). And then with special reference to this very case he adds, "Brethren, if any of you do err from the truth, and one convert him; Let him know, that he which converteth the sinner from the error of his way shall ... hide a multitude of sins" (James 5:19). Thank God that we can bring to Him these cases that have lost their way—our unsaved friends, our wandering sons and daughters, our brethren who have gone back from their first love and the blessedness they knew when first they saw the Lord—and He will not refuse to hear their cry nor fail to give them the living bread.

Often our boldest prayer will be the prayer for others. For ourselves we may fear perhaps a selfish motive, but for them we know it is the prayer of love; and if it be the prayer that seeks His glory, we can claim for it His mighty and prevailing will and intercession. Oh, you who have often felt your way closed for service, this is a ministry that all can exercise, and is the mightiest ministry of life! Let us be encouraged henceforth to use it in fellowship with Him who has spent the centuries that have passed since His ascension in praying for others and representing us as our great high priest before the throne.

The last lesson that this passage teaches us about prayer is that the Holy Spirit is the source and substance of all that prayer can ask, and a gift that carries with it the pledge of all other gifts and blessings.

191

"How much more shall your heavenly Father give the Holy Spirit to them that ask him?" (Luke 11:13).

This is spoken as if there were really nothing else to ask. It is still more remarkable that in the parallel passage in Matthew the language used is, "How much more shall your Father which is in heaven give good things to them that ask him?" (Matthew 7:11). So then "the Holy Spirit" and "good things" are synonymous. He that has the Holy Spirit will have all good things. Was not that the symbolical meaning of the widow's oil in the ancient miracle? Her pot of oil, poured out into all the empty vessels, became sufficient to pay all her debts and furnish an income for all her future life. All she needed was the pot of oil; it was currency for every blessing (2 Kings 4:1-7).

So is the Holy Spirit. If you have this heavenly gift you are in touch with the throne of infinite grace and the God of infinite fullness, and there is nothing that you cannot claim. Oh, when shall we learn to seek first the kingdom of God and His righteousness, and know that all these things shall be added unto us! (Matthew 6:33).

Dean Alford (Dean of Canterbury 1857-1871; poet and translator) calls attention to a beautiful Greek construction in this closing verse in the reference to our heavenly Father. The verse, "your heavenly Father," in the original is, literally, "your Father out of heaven." In the Lord's Prayer a few verses previously it is, "Our Father which art in heaven," but here the preposition is changed and it is "your Father out of heaven." Why this blessed and stupendous change? Our Father has already begun to move toward us and to enter our hearts by the Holy Spirit whom He has sent to make a heaven below for every praying heart. So while we begin our prayer with our eyes directed upward, we end it with our being filled in our innermost being with the presence and fullness of God and the throne of His abiding grace and power.

Blessed and heavenly altar of incense, standing by the rent veil, and breathing forth its incense into the outer and inner chambers! (See Revelation 8:3-4.) oh, let us be found forever there!

> *Where heaven comes down our souls to greet;*
> *And glory crowns the Mercy Seat.*

Chapter 3

IN HIS NAME

A nd in that day ye shall ask me nothing. Verily, verily, I say unto you, Whatsoever ye shall ask the Father in my name, he will give it you. Hitherto have ye asked nothing in my name: ask, and ye shall receive, that your joy may be full. These things have I spoken unto you in proverbs: but the time cometh, when I shall no more speak unto you in proverbs, but I shall show you plainly of the Father. At that day ye shall ask in my name: and I say not unto you, that I will pray the Father for you: for the Father himself loveth you, because ye have loved me, and have believed that I came out from God. (John 16:23-27).

For Jesus' sake and *in Jesus' name* are phrases familiar to every ear and tongue in Christendom, but how little they are thoroughly understood we shall probably learn as we look at their deeper meaning. This is the profound teaching about prayer that the Lord chiefly emphasizes in His closing addresses to His disciples.

Undoubtedly it means this much at least, that we are to pray to the Father as revealed in Jesus Christ.

"Whatsoever ye shall ask the Father in my name" might be translated, "Whatsoever ye shall ask the Father as represented by me." It expresses Christ's identity with the Father. The

Father had been known to them before by many different names: "Elohim," the God of nature; "El Shaddai," the God of power; "Adonai," the God of providence; "Jehovah," the God of covenant grace; but henceforth, He is to be known as "Jehovah-Jesus," God in Christ.

This is undoubtedly implied in the language of this passage, and involved in the thought to which the Savior is giving expression. It is the same thought that He repeats in the parallel verse, "Whatsoever ye shall ask in my name, that will I do, that the Father may be glorified in the Son" (John 14:13). There it plainly expresses that the Father and Son are acting in perfect concert, and it is through the Son only that the Father is glorified and revealed or understood.

The idea may be carried so far as to do away with the distinct personality of the Father and the Son, and this, of course, would be extreme and erroneous. But bearing this in mind and recognizing fully the dual personality, it is true that the Father himself is revealed to us in the person of the Son, and that we are to ask the Father for our petitions and feel encouraged to expect His gracious answer because of what we know of Jesus, through whose presence and teachings He himself has been revealed to us. Would we come with confidence to our Savior? Let us come with the same confidence to His Father, for "He that hath seen me hath seen the Father" (John 14:9). The words that He spoke were the Father's words. The love that He manifested was the Father's love, whom He came to reveal. He is the brightness of that Father's glory, the express image of His person, and the reflection of His will and character (Hebrews 1:3). It is to God in Christ, therefore, that we are to pray—to the God and Father of our Lord Jesus Christ. To Him of whom we know nothing except through the Son, and in whom we trust as we do in Jesus himself. Thus let us learn to pray in the name of Jesus.

This expression "in the name of Jesus" denotes far more, however, than the identity of the Father and the Son. It expresses the great truth of mediation and intercession.

Not only do we come to the Father as we know Him in Jesus, but we come to Him through the mediator. There are deep necessities for this in the nature of God and the relationships of sinful people with Him. So deeply did Job realize this that he cried out for a Daysman [umpire, mediator], who "might lay his hand upon us both" (Job 9:33)—some being that could touch at once both heaven and earth and bring them into harmony and fellowship. This is just what Christ has done. His incarnation has bridged over the infinite gulf between the eternal and spiritual Deity and finite man, and His atonement has healed the awful breach that had morally and irrevocably separated the sinner from a holy God. Like the dying mother, who, with her last breath, reached out one hand to her husband and the other to her boy, and, drawing both hands together, united them upon her dying breast and covered them with her tears and benedictions. Jesus in His death has united the sinner with his offended God, praying, "Father, forgive them; for they know not what they do" (Luke 23:34), and appealing through the apostle to sinful humanity, "Be ye reconciled to God" (2 Corinthians 5:20).

But not only has Christ brought God and men into reconciliation and fellowship, but He keeps that fellowship unbroken by His ceaseless intercession. "He ever liveth to make intercession for (us)," and, therefore, "is able also to save them to the uttermost that come unto God by him" (Hebrews 7:25).

This idea of mediation is widely illustrated in the holy Scriptures. We see it in the story of Joseph and his relation to Pharaoh and the Egyptians. "Go to Joseph," was the king's response to all who came to him for relief or judgment. All the affairs of the kingdom were entrusted to his administration, and he was the mediator and channel of all communication. We see it in the beautiful story of Esther as she ventured to touch the golden scepter and stand between her people and their oppressor and danger, and by her courage and patriotism saved her nation from extinction. Still more impressively was it foreshadowed in the ministry of Moses, who at Sinai became the channel of communication between God and the terrified people. "Speak thou with us," was their cry, "but let not God speak with us lest we die" (Exodus 20:19). God consented to use Moses as the channel of His revelations to Israel and to teach the lesson of our great mediator.

But the most striking of all the ancient types of Christ our mediator was Aaron, the Hebrew high priest. It was his special office to stand between the people and God and present their worship in the most holy place and make intercession for their sins and needs. For them he passed through the open veil, stood beneath the Shekinah, presented the blood and incense at the mercy seat, and came back to them with the benediction of Jehovah. In all this he was but the type of the better ministry of the great High Priest in the true Tabernacle of heaven. There He has entered with His own blood through the rent veil of His own flesh, now to appear in the presence of God for us.

The ministry of Aaron may well express the deeper meaning of His high priesthood. Upon his heart the ancient priest continually carried, engraved in precious jewels, the names of Israel's tribes, and this was but to teach us that Christ, our great High Priest, perpetually carries upon His heart our names, engraved in imperishable characters and worn as jewels of ornament and pride, even amid the glories of the heavenly world. It does not merely mean that He prays for us occasionally or takes our petitions and presents them to His Father. That, undoubtedly, He does, but He prays for us ten thousand times when we are too ignorant or too forgetful to pray for ourselves, and every moment He holds our names before His Father in love that never forgets and ceaseless remembrance of our frailties. The ancient priest carried the names not only upon his heart but also upon his shoulders. So, upon the strong arms of His omnipotence, our ascended Lord continually bears our burdens, as strong to help as He is swift to hear.

The ancient priest bore upon his brow a beautiful and significant symbol, a coronet with jeweled letters, carrying the significant words, "Holiness to the Lord" (Exodus 28:36-38). This he was continually to bear as often as he entered the Holy Place, that he might bear the iniquities of the children of Israel in their holy things. So in the our blessed Intercessor bears upon His brow this inscription, not for Himself, for His holiness is never questioned, but as the proclamation of our holiness and perfect acceptance. He covers the imperfection of our holiest services with His perfect righteousness and keeps us constantly accepted in the presence of holy angels and the infinite and heart-searching God. What infinite meaning these figures give to the simple words, "In his name!" How wide they open the gates of prayer, and how perfect the consolation they give to the timid heart. "Seeing then that we have a great high priest, that is passed into the heavens, Jesus the Son of God, ... let us therefore come boldly unto the throne of grace, that we may obtain mercy, and find grace to help in time of need" (Hebrews 4:14-16).

"In his name," signifies that our prayers are to be grounded upon the finished work of Christ and our redemption rights through His death and atonement.

Indeed, His very intercession for us is based upon His sufferings and blood. It is on the ground of the Cross and the accomplished redemption that He claims for us all that He purchased by His blood and all the promises of the everlasting covenant.

We are all familiar with the incident of the Civil War veteran who had often pleaded for the pardon of his unworthy younger brother and saved him from the punishment of being executed for repeatedly deserting his post. But finally he had been told by his brother's commanding general that it was useless to plead any more, because if his brother repeated the offense, it would be absolutely necessary in the interests of military order that the penalty be carried out.

Unfortunately, the reckless young man soon repeated the offense, and by order of his commanding general his execution was about to take place. As the firing squad lined up, the general saw the brave old soldier standing nearby weeping, and asked him if he had anything to say for his brother. The old veteran stood up and raised the stump of his arm that had been amputated because of war wounds, and silently held it aloft while great tears rolled down his cheeks. Many wept around him as they thought of all it meant of sacrifice and devotion to his country. That was his only plea. He knew that words were useless now, but he held up the pledge of his sufferings and love for his country, and let it plead more eloquently than words for his brother's condemned life. And eloquently it did plead, for with tears running down his face the general said, "Sit down, my brave fellow, you shall have your brother's life. He is unworthy of it, but you have purchased it by your blood."

It is thus our ascended Redeemer pleads for us. He does not beg for mercy that is free and without cost, but He boldly asks for that which is His purchased right, and for which His own blood has been sacrificed. Long before the incarnation and the Cross He had entered into a covenant with His Father. God had promised by His immutable oath that if He would bear the sins of humanity and settle for all the penalties of a holy law, He would receive, as His mediatorial right, forgiveness for every penitent and believing sinner who would accept His gospel. And He would be given all the resources of grace that would be needed to achieve and bring to perfection the salvation of every sinner. Now He simply claims His redemption rights and our rights through Him by virtue of that promise.

Asking in Jesus' name, therefore, is asking that for which Jesus has suffered and died, and which He has freely and fully purchased for all His own. Surely with such a plea, we may come boldly to the throne of grace and ask as much as the precious blood of Calvary is worthy to claim. How much that is will take all eternity to tell. This is the strong ground of our prayer for salvation. Salvation has been purchased and forgiveness is the birthright of every believing penitent. This is the plea of our prayer for sanctification, "for by one offering he hath perfected forever them that are sanctified" (Hebrews 10:14). This is the foundation of our plea for physical healing, for "Himself took our infirmities, and bare our sicknesses" (Matthew 8:17), and purchased redemption for our suffering bodies. And on this ground we may claim every other needed blessing, for "He that spared not his own Son, but delivered him up for us all, how shall he not with him also freely give us all things?" (Romans 8:32).

Have we learned the meaning of His name and the power of His Cross and blood as the strong and all-prevailing plea of the believing petitioner at the throne of grace?

"IN HIS NAME," MEANS, FINALLY, IN UNION AND COMPLETE IDENTITY WITH HIM

It expresses our relation to Him as well as His relation to the Father. It means in His person, in His stead, on His account, as if the petitioner were the very Son himself. We all know something of how far a human name and introduction will go. The friend we introduce in our name is received, in some sense, as we would be received. Still more is this the case when he is commended to us on the ground of intimate relations with the one we love. The wife is received by her husband's family as if she were part of him and related to them. In his name she comes to them as he would come. Sometimes we see this relationship very strongly and strangely illustrated in the case of those who otherwise would have no claim whatever for consideration.

In the days that followed the American Civil War, many incidents were told of the tender bonds of fellowship and suffering on the battlefield or in the Southern hospital—bonds which often gave the stranger a place in a home as dear as that of the fallen soldier whom he had befriended.

One such incident is related of a wretched-looking young man who called one day at a farmhouse in the west and was refused, very naturally, by the suspicious housewife. But the stranger drew from his well-worn pocket a scrap of paper and handed it to the woman. It was the writing of her young son, and it told how this man had fought by his side and then had nursed him in the hospital until the last hour had come. In the letter her son committed his dying body and his last messages for home and mother into the hands of his friend. He asked that when his mother and father met his friend, they would receive him and love him as they had loved and cherished their son, for his sake and in his name. That was enough. The haggard face and ragged dress of the stranger were all forgotten, and the young man was clasped in that mother's arms and taken into that home circle as a son, for the sake of another.

It is thus that we become identified with Jesus, and our Father receives us in His name as He receives Him. This is what faith may claim as it comes in His name. We enter into His rights, we ask on His account, and we expect to be welcomed and loved even as He is loved. This was His own bequest to us in His intercessory prayer in the seventeenth chapter of John, "That the world may know that thou hast . . . loved them, as thou hast loved me" and "that the love wherewith thou hast loved me may be in them, and I in them" (John 17:23, 26). Is it too bold if we claim that which He himself has asked for us as our place of privilege and right?

Not only, however, may we claim His rights, we must also come in His will and spirit, and ask as He claims and only what He himself would ask. The privilege is limited by its own very nature. We cannot ask in the behalf of Christ what Christ himself would not ask if He were praying. "In his name," therefore, necessarily means in harmony with His will and at the prompting of His Spirit. We may not claim from God that which would be sinful or selfish, involve harm to another, or hindrance to the cause of Christ. All our asking must be within this eternal limit, "Thy will be done in earth, as it is in heaven." But this will is as large as the utmost of our being. Within this large and ample place there is room for every reasonable petition for spirit, soul, body, family, friends, temporal circumstances, spiritual services, and all the possibilities of human desire, hope, or blessing.

And, finally, this identity with Him implies that He will be in us as the spirit of faith, making it His prayer and supplying the spirit and conditions of effectual prevailing intercession.

Such then, beloved, is the divinely appointed channel of prayer. Oh, how it encourages the unworthy and weak to come with full assurance of faith to the mercy seat! You may be a poor sinner, but He who represents you in heaven is the righteousness of God, and bears upon His brow, above your name, the flashing jeweled coronet that inscribes your standing, "Holiness unto the Lord." You may be an obscure and insignificant disciple, but He who endorses your petition has the mightiest name in earth and heaven. You may be a timid spirit and a faint-hearted child of unbelief and fear, but He who bids you have the faith of God and who offers himself to you as the spirit of faith and prevailing prayer is the one who said on earth, "Father,... I knew that thou hearest me always" (John 11:42). "Father, I will that they

also, whom thou hast given me, be with me where I am"
(John 17:24), and in His faith you may claim with boldness
all His will, and go forth in deepest humility, but highest
confidence, saying:

> *I am not skilled to understand*
> *What God hath willed,*
> *What God hath planned,*
> *But this I know, at His right hand,*
> *Stands one who is my Savior.*

Chapter 4

THE PRAYER OF FAITH

A nd Jesus answering saith unto them, Have faith in God. For verily I say unto you, That whosoever shall say unto this mountain, Be thou removed, and be thou cast into the sea; and shall not doubt in his heart, but shall believe that those things which he saith shall come to pass; he shall have whatsoever he saith. Therefore I say unto you, What things so ever ye desire, when ye pray, believe that ye receive them, and ye shall have them. (Mark 11:22-24).

There is an unseen principle of force in the material world that is mightier far than all the physical elements that we touch and see. It is the force of attraction that, in its twofold form of cohesion and gravitation, holds the physical universe together. As the force that condenses and holds in cohesion the minutest particles of matter, it is the cause by which, in a sense, all things consist or hang together. But for this cohesive force, our bodies would dissipate into impalpable air, the raindrops and the oceans would dissolve into vapor, the mighty mountains would crumble to pieces, and the great world itself would explode in a catastrophe of wreck and dissolution. And in its wider and far-reaching application, it is the force that holds our planet in its orbit and keeps it, on its awful journey of a thousand miles a minute and more than five hundred million miles a year, from rushing into the distant fields of immensity, or diverging a hair-breadth from its unmarked path amidst the spheres, or even quivering in its course notwithstanding the terrific velocity of its career. It is the same force that holds all the planets on their aerial track, and all the systems that circle round ten thousand suns in all their spheres, without collision or catastrophe. What is this force?

It is the mighty power of gravitation—*unseen* and noiseless. There is no vibration in its mighty heart-throbs; no reverberation from its voice; no trace of its invisible but mighty arm. Yet, it is mightier than the earth that it poises in space and propels along its pathway; mightier than the mighty sun, from whose center it sweeps the circle of the solar system with its revolving circuit of planets; mightier than all the stars in all their spheres. It is the great, invisible, intangible, inaudible, impalpable secret of the material universe and all its mighty movements. How simple is this subtle force, and yet how sufficient and sublime!

But now let us ascend from the material world to the social, rational, and human sphere. There we shall find a corresponding principle that holds society together, even as the law of gravitation holds the worlds of space. What is that principle that binds the family together, that cements the friendships of life, that controls the partnerships of business, that forms the basis of commercial confidence and the greatest transactions of business, and leads men continually to stake their whole fortune and every material interest on their investments and securities? Why, it is simply confidence, trust, faith between people! Without it, the home circle would be torn with strife and wrecked with distrust and misery. Without it, political and national fabrics would collapse, and government would be impossible. Without it, business would be ruined. No single bank could stand a day without the trust of its constituents, and no security would be worth anything were people to cease to trust the promises and reliability of others. The world is adopting this very name of trust in this day for its strongest institutions. Everything now is taking the form of a commercial trust. There must be some fascination in the term, and well there may be, for it is the very cohesive principle of society, the law of gravitation for the whole social world.

Let us now carry this thought to its true plane and apply it to the great spiritual kingdom of which all natural things are but imperfect types. Should it seem strange if this law of faith were found to be the very principle of the spiritual world as it is of the natural. That it is the underlying force that holds it together, and the remedial principle that is to bring back our own lost orb to its true place in the circle of the heavens? Such indeed it is. Faith is the essential principle of the kingdom of God. It was the loss of faith that separated man from God in Eden. The fall of the race began the moment the woman listened to Satan's insinuations, "Hath God said?" (Genesis 3:1). The recovery of the race commences the moment the soul begins to trust its God. This is why faith has been made indispensable to the reception of the gospel and the salvation of the soul. This is why it is forever true, "He that believeth on the Son hath everlasting life: and he that believeth not the Son shall not see life; but the wrath of God abideth on him" (John 3:36). Faith is the gateway of salvation, and it is not strange that it should be made the gateway of prayer.

Let us consider this great subject thoughtfully and prayerfully, and may the Holy Spirit search our hearts on this solemn matter until we shall be convicted of sin because we believe not. For this is the condemnation, because they have not believed on the name of the Son of God.

Faith is necessary in order to have acceptable and effectual prayer. This our Lord very distinctly states in this passage. He commands the disciples to have faith in God, and then adds, "When ye pray, believe that ye receive them." But this is not the only place where this necessity is emphasized, for we are told in Hebrews that "without faith it is impossible to please him: for he that cometh to God must believe that he is, and that he is the rewarder of them that diligently seek him" (Hebrews 11:6). There must be a believing recognition of God's personal existence and of His goodness and graciousness, and that He does hear and answer prayer.

So, again, in speaking of prayer for healing, it is declared that "the prayer of faith shall save the sick, and the Lord shall raise him up" (James 5:15). If we would understand what James means by the prayer of faith, we have only to turn to the first chapter and hear him say, "If any of you lack wisdom, let him ask of God, that giveth to all men liberally ... but let him ask in faith, nothing wavering. For he that wavereth is like a wave of the sea driven with the wind and tossed. For let not that man think that he shall receive any thing of the Lord" (James 1:5-7). The language here is very emphatic. God will give to all, but they must take by faith what God gives, or the giving is in vain. Those who waver do not take, cannot receive. They are like that poor victim in the hospital who died in agony, with water held to his lips, but unable to swallow a single drop through the spasms that contracted his throat, arising from the most terrific of all human diseases.

There are people to whom the Lord gives the water of life, but they will not drink it. There are people whose tables God has spread with the blessings of faith, but they do not partake of its bounties. There are prayers that God has answered, but we do not enjoy the answers. There are souls whom God has long ago forgiven, but they are in darkness and despair because they did not trust His pardon. Therefore, when the troubled and despairing father came to Him about his child, crying, "I spake to thy disciples that they should cast him out; and they could not ... but if thou canst do any thing, have compassion on us, and help us," the Master simply answered, as He turned the whole question back upon the man, "If thou canst believe, all things are possible to him that believeth" (Mark 9:17-24).

It is perfectly right that God should require us to believe before He answers our prayers, because faith is the law of the New Testament and the gospel dispensation. The apostle Paul speaks of two laws in the third chapter of Romans, the law of works and the law of faith. The former has been superseded, and the principle on which the whole gospel is based is the law of faith. "To him that worketh not, but believeth on him that justifieth the ungodly, his faith is counted for righteousness" (Romans 4:5).

We have already suggested why this law has been adopted. No doubt in the light of eternity we shall find many reasons for it that we could not now fully apprehend, but it is enough to know that as it was through unbelief that men fell, so it is through faith that they must be restored. In a word, we must come back to the point from which we started in a wrong direction. When Bunyan's pilgrim found that he had lost his roll on the Hill of Difficulty, he simply went back to the place where he had lost it and started on again. And so we must begin at the point of departure from God, by learning to trust Him. God is bound to act upon this principle if it be the law of this dispensation, and He cannot justly acknowledge our plea if we do not present it according to the prescribed rule.

If this is true, it works most solemnly in both directions. On one side it is gloriously certain, "According to your faith be it unto you" (Matthew 9:29). Yet, on the other side it may be just as true, "According to your unbelief it shall be unto you." It may be that God for consistency or balance is required to keep His word to those who doubt Him as well as to those who believe Him, and that the enemy of souls might even accuse Him of falsehood and inconsistency if He answered the prayer of unbelief. He has announced this as the principle of His throne of grace, the very law on which petitions will receive attention and consideration. Surely, therefore, we cannot afford to disregard His sacred statement or venture into His presence expecting our unbelieving complaint and insulting doubts and insincerities to bring any blessing from His hand.

But faith is not only the law of the Christian dispensation, it is also a mighty force in the spiritual world. We are touching now upon a subject that the wisest spirits can but dimly comprehend, but upon which, perhaps, there is light enough to be well assured that the very act of believing for anything that God has promised is an actual creative force and produces effects and operations of the most important character. Indeed it seems that faith is the very principle upon which God Himself acts, and the secret of His power in creating matter and in commanding the events of providence. "He spake, and it was done; he commanded, and it stood fast" (Psalm 33:9). When the disciples wondered at the withering of the fig tree, Jesus simply said it was an act of divine faith. It was the faith of God that produced it, and then He commanded them to "have faith in God." [The literal interpretation of this passage should be, for so it is in the Greek, "Have the faith of God."]

The faith of God must mean the faith that God himself exercises. In the fourth chapter of Romans we are told a little about this faith of God, when it is said that Abraham acted like Him "who quickeneth the dead, and calleth those things which be not as though they were" (Romans 4:17). He commands that which is not and expects it and believes in the efficacy of His own command without a shadow of hesitation. Thus He sees it instantly or ultimately accomplished. And even for the things that lie in the future in His purpose, He counts them as if they were present or past. The lapse of time is nothing in His mind and involves no uncertainty as to the results. He so believes in the things that are not, but which He has foretold and promised, that He calls them by the names of actual realities. He called Abraham "the father of many nations," before he even had a child, and made him call himself by the same significant name (Genesis 17:5). He calls Jesus Christ "His only begotten Son" (John 3:16), "the Lamb slain from the foundation of the world" (Revelation 13:8), and the Cross was as real to the Father ages ago as it is now. He speaks of you and me as if we were already sitting in the heavenly palaces in the ages to come, and shining like the sun in the kingdom of our Father.

It was this faith in Jesus Christ that commanded and compelled the quickening of Lazarus in his tomb. It was a resistless force, a divine power that actually moved upon second causes and compelled their obedience. If that faith of God is in us, it will be a corresponding force, and there shall be in us that effectual working prayer which availeth much (James 5:16). So at the very moment we are offering our prayer and believing for it, faith is moving something or upon some heart, and making someone conscious of the presence of the power of God.

Surely this is reason enough, then, that we should pray in faith. It is a spiritual force that God requires of us to cooperate with, to enter into, to use with Him and for His glory. The mighty forces of nature must have man's cooperation or they are lost and wasted. The electricity goes to waste if we do not constrain it to our will and use it according to its own laws. And so God's omnipotence must be taken hold of by our faith and actually used, in deep humility but holy confidence, for the carrying through of His own great purposes.

Could we see what is behind the curtains of the invisible world, we would be able to trace living streams of spiritual influence passing from the heavens at the very instant that our prayer of faith is ascending from some lonely closet, and see it lighting upon the exact persons whose names we are holding up before the throne. Two streams of heavenly power would be distinctly visible—one an ascending line of prayer from the kneeling petitioner, and the other a descending current of power upon some far distant heart. Such phenomena have actually been traced in innumerable instances.

While Elijah was praying on Mount Carmel, the clouds were actually marshaling on the distant horizon. While Jacob was praying at Peniel, the heart of Esau, as he lay in his tent that night, was going back to early memories, and melting into the tender welcome which he gave at that noontide to his once hated brother. While some of God's intercessors have been holding up special fields in far distant lands, it has been found that at the moment they prayed showers of blessing descended on that special field that they were praying for. While some weeping wife or mother has been praying for her husband or boy, that husband or boy was being converted hundreds of miles away. Faith is a force mightier than any force upon the earth. It can heal lepers, move mountains of rock and stone, raise the dead, part the seas, close the heavens. In requiring us, therefore, to pray in faith, God simply requires us to join hands with him in the exercise of His own almighty power, and be partakers of His mighty working.

The faith that God requires of us in prayer is essential to our own spiritual welfare. Even if it added no direct exterior result in the actual answer, it would be abundantly repaid in the blessing that believing prayer brings to our own spirit. How it quiets our fears, tranquilizes our agitation, and stills our troubled spirit! How it enables us to submit to God and say "thy will be done" as we never can until we believe that His will for us is only love and blessing. Indeed, so wonderful are the subjective benefits of prayer that many go so far as to say that this is all the value of prayer. This would be a very foolish conclusion to adopt, for it would be a strange blessing if we were only comforted by an imaginary dream that had no objective reality. Take away the actual reality of God and the facts of prayer, and you take away the foundation of our subjective comfort. For if God is not real and the answer not actual, why, then, our comfort is a lie and our peace an unreal dream. But if we know God is real, and that His promise will be actually fulfilled, then indeed we can rest our troubled heads upon His breast and our hearts upon His promises, and be still and know that He is God (Psalm 46:10).

How self-possessed and restful are the hearts that have learned to trust God for all they ask! How sweetly these two thoughts are combined in the gracious words of the apostle in Philippians: "Be careful for nothing; but in every thing by prayer and supplication with thanksgiving let your requests be made known unto God. And the peace of God, which passeth all understanding, shall keep your hearts and minds through Christ Jesus" (Philippians 4:6-7). There we have the injunction to pray about everything. The requirement is to pray without care, doubt, or anxiety, but with thanksgiving that we will receive what we pray for, and then comes the promise that the peace of God shall keep our hearts and minds through Jesus Christ.

But God requires our trust in order to keep us from hindering His answer to our prayer by our own restless activity or flight. When we ask God to do anything for us, we must give Him time to do it, and carefully avoid rushing off in unbelieving haste to do something that would probably quite hinder His plan. Many a time, if God were to come with the answer to our prayer, He would find that we were not there, but had simply run away in fear and doubt, first firing our gun like a sentinel, and then getting off as fast as our limbs could carry us. Suppose Israel had not believed God when they cried to Him at the Red Sea, but had rushed back upon their foes or forward into the deep or away into the mountains, where God could never have answered their prayer by dividing the sea. To prevent this He had to say to them first, "Stand still, and see the salvation of the LORD," and then bid them go forward in His way and claim it (Exodus 14:13).

If Joshua's hosts had not believed God and marched around Jericho at His command, they never would have found the answer that was awaiting their seventh circuit on the seventh day. In the thirtieth chapter of Isaiah, we find the prophet pleading with his people to be quiet and not hinder the deliverance that they had asked God to give them from Sennacherib and his army. But instead of this, they insisted upon doing something to help themselves; they sent an emissary into Egypt for an alliance with Pharaoh. The prophet warned them without avail that the Egyptians would help in vain, and that their strength was to sit still. "In quietness and in confidence shall be your strength; and ye would not. But ye said, No; for we will flee upon horses." And God answered, Get all the horses you want; you will need them soon, for "they that pursue you be swift" (Isaiah 30:15-16). Then the prophet adds, "Therefore will the LORD wait, that he may be gracious unto you," for "blessed are all they that wait for him" (Isaiah 30:18).

In due time they found out their Egyptian alliance was a broken reed and a reed that pierced the hand that leaned upon it. The Egyptians were helpless, and Sennacherib, furious that they should have gone to Egypt, returned with a fierce and cruel scorn, and bade his caged prisoners prepare for their doom. Then they were shut up to faith and cried to the Lord alone, and lo! in a moment, without any of their contriving, God sent an angel at night, who simply swept along the line of Syrian tents, shook his fiery wings above those slumbering hosts, and their vital breath ceased and the morning saw an army of corpses, and the caged and invested city found itself gloriously free! (Isaiah 37: 36).

So God requires us to trust Him and be still until He brings His answer to us and works it out in our lives. Without faith we are sure to do something to hinder Him or get out of the place where we can receive the answer in its fullness.

It is spiritually reasonable to believe—i.e., have faith—for an answer that we do not yet see. How can I believe for that which I do not know or see to be actually so? Simply because if you did see and know from other evidence, it would not be faith at all, but believing from the evidence of your senses. You only have faith when you do not see. "Faith is the evidence of things not seen" (Hebrews 11:1). God's way for us is to believe first, on the simple evidence of His promise, and to continue to believe without other evidence until we have proved our faith without sight. Then He will permit us to see and know by the demonstration of the fact itself.

This is nothing more than what we are doing every day in the affairs of human life. Millions of dollars are invested in our commercial exchanges every week on the simple faith of a telegram or an item of news in the daily papers. Values are bought and sold on paper where the actual realities have not been seen by either party. Securities are constantly negotiated by those who buy them on simple trust. Every time we send a telegram and act upon it, we are venturing on simple faith in the operator that dispatches it, on the wire that carries it, and the messenger boy that delivers it. We do not see it go, nor do we see it received, but we rest, and probably take most important action on the certainty that it has gone and that the matter has been settled. It is surely very humiliating that we cannot put the same confidence in God's Word as we do in the fidelity of a messenger boy.

Then again, we are constantly in the habit of recognizing things as done, when, in fact, they are only decided and long weeks and even months must intervene before we see the actual accomplishment. A friend of mine had an application for a pension before Congress. It meant everything to her and her helpless husband and family. On one side was a life of toil and suffering; on the other, comfort and happiness for those she loved better than her life. There was considerable delay and uncertainty, but at last the message was flashed across the wires from Washington one day, and she quickly hastened to tell me the glad news, with tears of joy. She said, "I have got my husband's pension, praise the Lord!"

But if one of our critics had been there, I suppose he would have said, "Madam, you are telling a story; you have not a single dollar of your pension, and won't have a single dollar of it for months to come." And the critic, in one sense, would have been right, for she herself told me in the same breath, "It will be several months before we have it actually, for it has to go through a great deal of red tape, but that does not make any difference." And so the dear woman went ahead in simple faith, and long before she had the money, all the arrangements for her future life were made as calmly and surely as if she had the first installment deposited in the bank. To her, the decree of the supreme authority was enough. The question of time meant nothing, and she could truthfully say, even in the face of the critic, "I have my pension." Honestly and actually she did have all that was necessary to make it certain and to give her the benefit of it.

And so the moment our petition reaches the throne of God, we are justified in believing that we have just what we ask and in saying, like her, "I have got my answer, praise the Lord!" This was what God intended to teach Daniel when He sent the angel from heaven, after he had been praying twenty-one days, to say to him, "From the first day that thou didst set thine heart to understand, and to chasten thyself before thy God, thy words were heard, and I am come for thy words. But the prince of the kingdom of Persia withstood me one and twenty days" (Daniel 10:12-13). In the very beginning his prayer reached the throne above, and he was justified all those three weeks in counting the answer given, but the delivery of the blessing and even the message was hindered by the opposition of the enemy. But all the opposition of earth or hell cannot hinder God's purposes, and to His mind and the mind of faith, they are as certain from the beginning as after they have taken form like the solid mountains and become the facts and memories of actual life.

Indeed, all God's promises to His children are gauged on this pattern. To the penitent sinner Christ's word was instant and final, "Thy faith hath saved thee" (Luke 7:50). To the disciples His message of cleansing was, "Now ye are clean through the word which I have spoken unto you" (John 15:3). To the sick and suffering the decree always went forth, "Be thou clean," "Receive thy sight," "Be it unto thee even as thou wilt," "Thy son liveth," **"According to your faith be it unto you"** (Luke 5:13; Luke 18:42; Matthew 15:28; John 4:50; Matthew 9:29). To Abraham the promise that carried with it all the promises of the future was in the perfect tense, "a father of many nations have I made thee" (Genesis 17:5). And the explanation given was that God, as the basic principle of His government, "calleth those things which be not as though they were" (Romans 4:17). This very thing that so many shrink from is the essence of all true faith, and the lack of it teaches the fine line of demarcation between effectual faith and that which is only hope.

Shall we then, beloved, recognize the reasonableness of faith and rise to something higher than the mere reasoning of probability and the mere hope and encouragements to which people can rise without the need of God at all? Shall we count God's Word more true than all our evidences and feelings, than all the endorsements of people, than all the actual evidences of its fulfillment, for even the latter may not be abiding, but "the word of God ... abideth for ever" (1 Peter 1:23), and "one jot or one tittle shall in no wise pass from the law, till all be fulfilled" (Matthew 5:18).

Let us learn to be very deliberate in our prayers. Many persons pour out a reckless mass of ill-considered supplication very much as a child blows soap bubbles into the air, scarcely expecting ever to see them again. It is doubtful if such persons go through the mental effort of believing or attempting to believe that they will receive even one in ten of these petitions. Certainly, if they should receive even that few, it would take a very busy life to hold all the answers and turn them to practical account. The habit of asking indiscriminately wears out the very power of believing. It is a pity ever to ask anything from God that we have to abandon or confess to be of no significance. It is a very serious thing to take the name of our God in vain, and everything asked in His name without meaning or effect is of this character. Every time we find our prayers ineffectual we are weakened for our next attempt, and after a time, like iron heated and cooled successively, the temper of our faith is worn out and its very fiber disintegrated like rusty metal. If we would ever learn the prayer of faith, we must learn to pray with thoughtful deliberation and carefully weigh our words before the Lord as He has weighed His promises, for "the words of the LORD are pure words: as silver tried in a furnace" (Psalm 12:6). The secret of faith is always to endeavor to ascertain, before we ask, whether we are asking according to His will, and then to take the simple stand of John the beloved: "If we ask any thing according to his will, he heareth us: and if we know that he hear us, whatsoever we ask, we know that we have the petitions that we desired of him" (1 John 5:14-15).

Let us cultivate the habit of definitely believing when we have truly prayed. Let us commit the matter to God and recognize it from that time forward as one of the things He has promised and passed, and a thing for which we cannot pray again in the sense of an unsettled question. Faith is a matter of definite will, to a certain extent at least. We must choose to believe and fix our will as the sailor sets his helm; then God will swell our sails and hold our helm for us in the attitude in which we set it. We cannot create the faith, but we can choose to believe, and God will sustain us in our choice and uphold us in our trust.

We must claim the faith of God, the Spirit of Jesus, the enabling of His trust, to sustain ours. We choose to believe, but He must enable us to claim even His own promises. This follows, of course, consistently with the whole doctrine of Christ's indwelling life. We must trust Him for our faith as well as for our love and holiness, but in each case we must yield ourselves and choose to stand in the position assumed, and then throw ourselves upon Him to sustain us. This He will do, baptizing us with such a spirit of prayer and confidence that we will be enabled to claim and humbly command the blessing that He has already decreed.

Then we must stand fast, and not be shaken by either delay or apparent denial, drawing comfort and encouragement even from His seeming refusals. Until at last, our Lord shall look upon us as He did the Syro-Phoenician woman, with admiring love, and say: "Great is thy faith: be it unto thee even as thou wilt" (Matthew 15:28).

Beloved, let us realize that God is educating us for higher destinies, and placing upon us, day by day, heavier loads of discipline, that we may thereby be trained for the mightier activities of faith, which, in the eternal world, we are to share with our enthroned Lord. Let us not stagger under these loads, but like Abraham of old, be "strong in faith, giving glory to God; and being fully persuaded that, what he had promised, he was able also to perform" (Romans 4:20-21), and we shall find that "our light affliction, which is but for a moment," has worked out for us "a far more exceeding and eternal weight of glory" (2 Corinthians 4:17).

Chapter 5

HINDRANCES TO PRAYER

"That your prayers be not hindered." (1 Peter 3:7).

THE GREATEST HINDRANCE TO THE LIFE OF PRAYER IS SIN

"The Lord's hand is not shortened, that it cannot save; neither his ear heavy, that it cannot hear: but your iniquities have separated between you and your God, and your sins have hid his face from you, that he will not hear" (Isaiah 59:1-2). God would rather let Israel be defeated at Ai and go into captivity to Babylon, notwithstanding the prayers of Joshua in the one case, or any other great Old Testament saint in the other, if the answering of these prayers would have given approval to the sin of His people. Yes, even that beautiful and consecrated temple must be consumed to ashes, and the very name of Jehovah dishonored by His enemies, rather than sin be sanctioned in the slightest degree by a holy God.

"If I regard iniquity in my heart, the Lord will not hear me" (Psalm 66:18). Even considering sin in our hearts will hinder our prayers. The apostle John most clearly adds his testimony to this heart-searching truth when he tells us that, "If our heart condemn us, God is greater than our heart, and knoweth all things. Beloved, if our heart condemn us not, then have we confidence toward God. And whatsoever we ask, we receive of him, because we keep his commandments, and do those things that are pleasing in his sight" (1 John 3:20-22).

The old farmer, who tried to get peace with God at the altar by the prayers of the saints, was quite right when he told them one night that the Lord would never answer their prayers "so long as that ox is in the wrong stall." He hurried away to return his neighbor's property, and came back the next night with shining face and light heart to testify to the blessing that came the moment he put the hindrance away.

God can hear the prayers of the saints who sin, or else none of us could have access to the throne of grace, but this is a different matter from expecting Him to answer our prayers while we are deliberately committing sin without an honest purpose to abstain from it. This is insolent presumption in the face of heaven. The sin may be confessed and put away, and the Lord will freely bless. But when we pray with an evil conscience and wrong intent and expect God to countenance our disobedience and presumption, He will speak to us the same message He gave to the leaders of Israel in the fourteenth chapter of Ezekiel:

> Son of man, these men have set up their idols in their heart, and put the stumbling block of their iniquity before their face: should I be enquired of at all by them? Therefore speak unto them, and say unto them, Thus saith the Lord GOD; Every man of the house of Israel that setteth up his idols in his heart, and putteth the stumbling block of his iniquity before his face, and cometh to the prophet; I the LORD will answer him that cometh according to the multitude of his idols; ... For every one of the house of Israel, or of the stranger that sojourneth in

Israel, which separateth himself from me, and setteth up his idols in his heart, and putteth the stumbling block of his iniquity before his face, and cometh to a prophet to enquire of him concerning me; I the LORD will answer him by myself: And I will set my face against that man, and will make him a sign and a proverb, and I will cut him off from the midst of my people; and ye shall know that I am the LORD. (Ezekiel 14:3-8)

This will frequently be found to be the cause of long unanswered prayers and the failure of God's people to enter into the fullness of the blessing they are seeking. God is searching their hearts and bringing to their remembrance long-forgotten sins with which He wants them to deal thoroughly. When we are at some secret crisis of life, therefore, seeking entire sanctification, the baptism of the Holy Spirit, the healing of some critical and alarming disease, the life of some precious friend, or deliverance in some great emergency, God searches the heart as with eyes of flame, and brings to our conscience things long buried in oblivion, and enables us to search and try our ways and lay open all our heart before Him. Then we may receive His blessing unhindered and unbounded and know the blessedness of the person "whose transgression is forgiven, whose sin is covered,... and in whose spirit there is no guile" (Psalm 32:1-2).

Beloved, let us search and try our ways, and turn again unto the Lord. Let us be willing to say, "Search me, O God, and know my heart: try me, and know my thoughts, and see if there be any wicked way in me, and lead me in the way everlasting" (Psalm 139: 23-24). Let us bring every Achan to the light and to the sentence of death, and we will find that even sin cannot hinder our prayers nor our perfect blessing if it is truly put away. When it is, the valley of Achor will become the very door of hope, and the place of forgiven sin and self-crucifixion will be marked as the starting point of a new and higher life of usefulness (Joshua 7:1-25).

ANOTHER HINDRANCE TO PRAYER IS SELFISHNESS AND EARTHLY DESIRE

"Ye ask, and receive not," says the Apostle James, "because ye ask amiss, that ye may consume it upon your lusts" (James 4:3). God cannot give us all the things that our carnal nature clamors for any more than we would give our child the gleaming razor for which its little hands reach out in such eager desire. They would often be more hurtful to us than the keen edge of the steel to the thoughtless child. Many a good thing may be desired from an earthly and selfish motive and in a carnal spirit. Many people seek forgiveness to escape the remorse of a guilty conscience and that they may be at ease to go on again in a life of godless selfishness. Most people, who have no true sense of honor, are quite willing to be accepted as candidates for heaven if God will let them enjoy the pleasures of the world on their way. Prayer for healing may be simply the expression of the desire to get free from pain and be able to enjoy the pleasures of life. Even Simon Magus wanted the power of the Holy Spirit from a thoroughly base and unholy motive. Things that God in other circumstances would be quite willing to give us, He has often had to refuse us sense they would really separate us from Him. At a later period of our lives we find Him able and willing to give us the same things without reserve, because, in the meanwhile, we have been able to lay them all on His altar, to be used to His glory and in union with Him.

Therefore, the Lord's Prayer, as we have already seen, begins with the prostration of our whole being at the feet of God and the threefold consecrating prayer, "Hallowed be thy name, thy kingdom come, thy will be done" (Matthew

6:10). We cannot be trusted to ask anything for ourselves until our spirit is truly consecrated to God.

This is the meaning of that profound promise in the thirty-seventh Psalm, "Delight thyself also in the LORD: and he shall give thee the desires of thine heart" (Psalm 37:4). The heart that has found its joy in God cannot desire anything that God cannot grant. He gives it first its desires and then their fulfillment.

Beloved, have not many of your unanswered prayers been thoroughly selfish ones? Have not your very longings for your own spiritual good been prompted either by a slavish fear or a narrow self-love? Have not your prayers for the salvation of your children and friends been as selfish as your desire to see them well settled in life, and perhaps you have never once offered a petition for anyone else's child or made an effort to bring them to Christ? It is all right that we should seek these blessings for ourselves and for our own, but if it be a true spirit of prayer and union with God, there will be something higher than mere selfish or human love or desire.

AN INSURMOUNTABLE BARRIER TO ANSWERED PRAYER IS THE SPIRIT OF STRIFE AND BITTERNESS

"When ye stand praying," our Savior said to His disciples, "forgive, if ye have ought against any" (Mark 11:25). "Let none of you imagine evil in your hearts against his neighbor" (Zechariah 8:17), is the message of the prophet Zechariah to the people of the restoration, as he teaches them the secret of God's blessing in their critical trials. Job had to pray for his enemies and banish from his heart every particle of bitter feeling toward the men who had tormented him through months of sickness with their ignorance, misconstruction, and offensive interference, before God turned his captivity and restored him to more than his former blessings. One reason why the disciples could not claim the casting out of the demon from the suffering child was that they had disputed by the way which should be the greatest. The spirit of cherished animosity, lurking prejudice, sullen vindictiveness, or cold disdain will as effectively obstruct our communication and intimacy with heaven as a speck upon the crystalline lens of the eye will obstruct our vision, or the crossing of the wires of the electric machinery of a building will leave us in darkness.

There are a great many crossed wires in Christ's Church, and the consequence is dark hearts and mournful cries, "Hath God forgotten to be gracious?" (Psalm 77:9). "How long, O Lord, will you not hear my prayer?" Just this long, beloved, "If thou bring thy gift to the altar, and there rememberest that thy brother hath ought against thee; leave there thy gift before the altar, and go thy way; first be reconciled to thy brother, and then come and offer thy gift" (Matthew 5:24-25).

The spirit of prayer is essentially a spirit of love. Frequently when we are at some crisis of prayer and very much is hanging upon God's answer, perhaps life itself, or something more precious than life, we shall find ourselves confronted with just such a test as this. Someone will be thrown across our path where all the strength of the natural heart, with its dislikes, prejudices, and self-wills, will be laid hold of by the enemy to hinder our victory. Oh, let us remember at such an hour that we cannot hurt another by our irritation or retaliation, but we can deeply wound ourselves and hinder the blessing of our God! In the presence of infinite love, no breath of hate can live one moment. The simple lines of the old English poet are sweetly true:

> He prayeth best who loveth best,
> All things both great or small,
> For the great God who loveth us,
> He made and loveth all.

It is especially with respect to this matter of love that the apostle John speaks of our heart condemning us in prayer, and above all other things it is perhaps that which we are most likely to over-look and God is least likely to pass by. "The greatest thing in the world," as Professor Drummond so happily styles it, "is love, and it is the one business of life to learn it."

Beloved, is this hindering your prayers? Can you think this moment of some brother or sister from whom you are wrongly estranged. Some person whom you treat with studied harshness, neglect, perhaps disdain, or possibly with injury and injustice. Some word that you have spoken against another, and which you should not have spoken even if true. Some word to which you have listened against another, and never should have heard except in that persons presence. Some cherished suspicion, criticism, or judgment where you have no business even to think evil? May God help you to see the way to discover some cause of unanswered prayer!

THE HABIT OF DOUBT IS A HINDRANCE TO PRAYER

"He that wavereth is like a wave of the sea driven with the wind and tossed. For let not that man think that he shall receive anything of the Lord" (James 1:6-7). This is strong language, but there is no doubt that the sin of unbelief, according to the divine standpoint, is the most hurtful of all spiritual conditions. It destroys contact of the soul with God as effectively as the cutting of a telegraph wire would prevent the transmission of a message. We have already seen that the word *receive* in this passage of James means *take*, and that it denotes, not so much God's anger with the unbelief, for He does "give liberally and upbraideth not" (James 1:5), but it refers to the inability of the person to take what God gives. Doubt shuts up our whole spiritual sensibilities and capacities

227

and renders us incapable of absorbing and appropriating the blessing that is offered us at the time.

God holds us responsible for our doubt but does not require us to produce, by our own will, the faith that brings us into contact with His love and blessing, for this is His impartation. But He does require us to prevent it from running out, as from leaking vessels, through all the openings of our miserable doubts. There is one thing that we can all do—we can refuse to doubt. We can refuse to entertain the questioning and fear, the morbid apprehension and subtle Satanic insinuation. If we do this, God will do the rest and enable us to stand fast in faith, and press forward to the fullness of His blessing.

This is where the enemy concentrates his strongest attacks, waiting when the hour of trial comes and our prayer seems to be refused and delayed. He hurls all his shafts of fire and evil suggestion into our trembling hearts to try to drive us from our confidence and get us to betray our own cause by consenting to his wicked questionings. Therefore Christ has said, "Whosoever shall say unto this mountain, Be thou removed, and be thou cast into the sea; and shall not doubt in his heart, ... he shall have whatsoever he saith" (Mark 11:23). "Abraham... staggered not at the promise of God through unbelief; but was strong in faith, giving glory to God" (Romans 4:20). So we are to hold fast the faith we have professed without wavering, for, "He is faithful that promised" (Hebrews 10:23). "Now the just shall live by faith: but if any man draw back, my soul shall have no pleasure in him. (Hebrews 10:38). God waits to give His blessing to the Christians who stand their ground, and who, when the blessing comes, are there to claim it.

But perhaps you say, "I have already doubted, and forfeited my blessing. Is it then too late to receive the answer?" No, not if you will repent of your doubt as you would of any other sin. Then immediately bring forth fruits meet for repentance by refusing from henceforth and forevermore to be betrayed into the same sin. Often we will find that such a fall becomes the occasion of thoroughly convincing us of the sin of doubting and curing us of it forever.

Beloved, have you been trifling with God in this matter of prayer and defrauding yourself of the blessings for which you have already suffered so much? May the Lord set your face this day like a flint, and fix your feet on the rock and stay your soul upon God!

OUR PRAYERS WILL BE HINDERED IF WE STAND ON FORBIDDEN GROUND, OR IN ANYTHING HOLD BACK FROM THE MASTER'S WILL

It is not necessary that there should be willful sin or actual vice and transgression of moral law. It may simply be disobedience to the Spirit's voice in some definite leading to service or testimony. We have known many instances of persons who did not receive the full answers to their prayers for the baptism of the Holy Spirit until they had definitely obeyed the voice of God in some particular thing where they had been shrinking or hesitating. We have known many sad cases of persons who have failed to receive the answer to their prayer for healing because they were standing in some forbidden place, holding back their testimony for God, from timidity or the fear of man, or failing to take some step of faith to which the Holy Spirit was calling. It was not until after months or even years of striving with God and bitter sorrow that they learned the lesson, and in prompt and thorough obedience received perfect deliverance and wondrous blessing.

The Bible has some very solemn instances of people of God standing on forbidden ground and finding their power and defense departing from them. The mighty Samson lost all his hold upon God the moment he left his place of separation. Abraham had no power while in a compromising attitude in Egypt. Jacob had no vision of God during the years of his wandering. And even the good Josiah lost his heavenly protection and sacrificed his precious life because he stepped beyond the divine will and went unbidden against Pharaoh Necho, king of Egypt, who warned him of his fate if he persisted in his rash presumption. There is not one of us who stands on consecrated ground but would probably lose even life itself if we persisted in disobeying the distinct call of God to special service or pressing forward where He had said no.

It is a very solemn thing for those who are walking in the Spirit to trifle with His voice or be disobedient to His least command. Such disobedience may interrupt all communication and hinder all prayer.

FORBIDDEN MEANS MAY AS EFFECTUALLY INTERRUPT OUR FATHER'S BLESSING

It is possible to ask God's help in a proper manner and spirit, and then immediately go to work to help Him to fulfill our prayer in an unlawful manner. No doubt Jacob sincerely asked God for the coveted blessing, but he proceeded afterwards to take the most unworthy means to accomplish his purpose, and involved himself in years of waiting and sorrow. No doubt Moses sincerely asked God to deliver Israel by His hand when forty years of age, but he proceeded in the most rash and improper manner to accomplish his patriotic desire by slaying an Egyptian, and involving himself in crime and peril from the hand of the king. Undoubtedly Abraham thought that his compromise about Hagar was going to assist God in fulfilling His promise of a son, but he only silenced the heavenly voice for many years and brought upon himself domestic strife and trouble, hindering the object he had at heart. No doubt Saul of Tarsus sincerely prayed for salvation for many years, but he sought it by his own righteousness and missed his aim by not submitting himself to the righteousness of God. Similarly, his whole race today are praying in vain for mercy that they reject by rejecting God's only appointed way.

Many souls pray for sanctification but fail to enter into the blessing because they do not intelligently understand and believingly accept God's appointed means by Jesus Christ and the indwelling of the Spirit. Many prayers for the salvation of others are hindered because those who pray take the wrong course to bring about the answer and resort to means that are wholly fitted to defeat the worthy object. We know many a wife who is pleading for her husband's soul and hoping to win him by avoiding anything that may offend him, yielding to all his worldly tastes in the vain hope of attracting him to Christ. Far more effective would be an attitude of fidelity to God and fearless testimony to Him, such as God could bless.

Many a church asks the Lord for His blessing, and then goes to work to defeat it by methods of worldly conformity that God never can tolerate. Many a congregation wonders why it is so poor and struggling and its prayer for financial resources never answered, and yet it may be found that its financial methods are wholly unscriptural and often unworthy of ordinary self-respect, and such as a decent worldly institution would not stoop to depend upon. When we ask God for any blessing, we must allow Him to direct the steps that are to bring the answer. God will give His power to every heart that will let Him hold the reins. God's answer must be brought by His own messengers, and the steps that we take in bringing about the answer must be based on His absolute direction.

Take, for example, the course of David the second time the Philistines invaded his realm after his coronation. Suppose David had done just what he had done before and marched directly against them and then asked God to bless him. He would have been defeated, for this time the command was entirely different from the previous occasion. "Thou shalt not go up; but fetch a compass behind them," that is, take a circuitous course, march away from them first, then around by a flank movement, "and come upon them over against the mulberry trees. And let it be, when thou hearest the sound of a going in the tops of the mulberry trees, that then thou shalt bestir thyself: for then shall the Lord go out before thee, to smite the host of the Philistines" (2 Samuel 5:24-25). Here we see that the answer was dependent on explicit obedience to the Lord's directions.

Is this not the reason, beloved, of many of our unanswered prayers? Have we waited for our Master's orders and sought the answer in the direction that He bade? Oh, how solemn are the words of the prophet Zechariah respecting one of God's most precious promises, "This shall come to pass if ye diligently obey the voice of the LORD your God" (Zechariah 6:15). And that is but the echo of God's word concerning Abraham, "I know him, that he will command his children and his household after him, and they shall keep the way of the LORD, to do justice and judgment; that the LORD may bring upon Abraham that which he hath spoken of him" (Genesis 18:19).

PERHAPS THE GREATEST HINDRANCE TO
EFFECTUAL PRAYER, AND NO DOUBT TO THE LIFE
OF PRAYER, IS IGNORANCE CONCERNING THE
HOLY SPIRIT AND THE INTERIOR LIFE

With so many, prayer is the hasty utterance of the mere natural heart. It is little more than the cry of a suffering brute or the wail of an almost unconscious babe. True, God hears the faithless cry of human misery, but this is not prayer. The voice that always reaches the Father's ear is the voice of a trusting child and the Holy Spirit breathing in the heart of that child. True prayer should be His prompting, and it is because most persons know Him so little, and walk with Him at such a distance, that they are comparative strangers to the language of heavenly communion.

The life of prayer is an interior life, a spiritual life, and many people do not know this, and do not want it. It holds too constant a check upon the heart, it requires too utterly that we should walk softly with our God. Most people like to be their own masters, and the habit of walking step by step with God and submitting every thought and desire to an inward monitor is intolerable to their arrogant self-will, or at least unfamiliar to their experience.

But this is truly the very element of the life of prayer. It is an interior life. Its home is "the secret place of the most High," and its dwelling, "the shadow of the Almighty" (Psalm 91:1). It is the intercourse of an inseparable divine companionship. It is Enoch walking with God. It is Elisha clinging to his master and saying, "As the Lord liveth, and as thy soul liveth, I will not leave thee" (2 Kings 2:2). It is the very breathing of the inner man, and is as necessary and constant as the pulsation of a human heart and the respiration of a human bosom.

Beloved, is not this the difficulty, after all, about your prayers? Are they not the spasmodic cries of great emergencies rather than the habitual communication of a heavenly life? If you were accustomed to walk always by His side, you would not get so far that you need to call so loudly and so long in the hour of extremity. It is the habit of constant prayer that prepares us for the great conflicts of prayer, and those, who in this neglect the moment, will find themselves unprepared for the emergencies. God is calling you to a closer walk with Him, to open your heart for His continual abiding, and to receive into your breast the Spirit of grace and supplications. He will inspire all your petitions and bear them on the strong wings of His love and power to the Lord on high, through whom you shall receive the answer of that Father who ever answers the prayer which He inspires.

We sometimes see it advertised by our great financial houses that they have a private wire with all the great centers of trade. If you possess in your heart the Holy Spirit, you have a private wire to the throne of God, and at any moment you can open and maintain direct communication with heaven and bring all its legions, if need be, to your immediate aid. O beloved, surely it is worth your while to yield yourself to a consecrated life and to allow your loving Lord to make your heart His temple and His throne, where prayer will ever be the familiar and unbroken communication of a happy child with the Father who is ever at hand.

Oh, how happy those are who are within continual reach of the supply of every need and the balm for every wound. Sorrow may overshadow, Satan may assail, difficulty may encompass on every side, but, through prayer, relief is always new. Thus the victorious spirit returns fresh from every conflict with a strength that Phoenix-like rises from its own ashes and grows with each renewing in freshness and gladness.

A South American traveler tells of a curious conflict that he once witnessed between a little quadruped and a terrific and poisonous snake of great size. The little creature seemed no match for its antagonist that threatened to destroy it and its helpless brood by a blow, but it fearlessly faced its mighty enemy and rushing in its face struck him with a succession of fierce and telling blows, but received at the onset a deep and apparently fatal wound from his poisonous fangs, which flashed for a moment with an angry fire, and then fastened themselves deep into the flesh of the daring little assailant. For a moment it seemed as if all was over, but the wise little creature immediately retired into the forest and hastening to the plantain tree eagerly devoured a portion of its leaves, and immediately came back, apparently fresh and restored, to renew the fray with fresh vigor and determination. Again and again this strange spectacle was repeated. The serpent ferociously attacked, greatly exhausted, and again and again wounded its antagonist to death. But the little creature successively repaired to its simple prescription and returned to renewed victory. In about an hour or two, the battle was over, the mammoth reptile lay still and dead, and the little victor was unharmed in the midst of its nest and brood, who had been thus saved from destruction.

How often we are wounded by the dragon's sting, wounded it would seem to death; and if we had to go through some long ceremony to reach the source of life, we would surely faint and die. But, blessed be His name, there is ever for us a plant of healing as near at hand as that which the forest holds in its shade, to which we may continually repair and come back refreshed, invigorated, transfigured, like Him. When He prayed on the mount, He shone with the brightness of celestial light. After He prayed in the garden, He arose triumphant over the fear of death, having been strengthened from on high to accomplish the mighty battle of our redemption.

Oh, the victories of prayer! They are the mountain tops of the Bible. They take us back to the plains of Mamre, to the fords of Peniel, to the prison of Joseph, to the triumphs of Moses, to the victories of Joshua, to the deliverances of David, to the miracles of Elijah and Elisha, to the whole story of the Master's life, to the secret of Pentecost, to the keynote of Paul's unparalleled ministry, to the lives of saints and the deaths of martyrs, to all that is most sacred and sweet in the history of the Church and the experience of the children of God. And when, for us, the last conflict shall have passed, and the footstool of prayer shall have given place to the harp of praise, the scenes of time that shall be gilded with eternal radiance shall be those often linked with deepest sorrow and darkest night, over which we have written the inscription, "JEHOVAH-SHAMMA: the Lord was there!" Only that which God touched shall be remembered or worth remembering forever. These are imperishable memorials. Oh, that henceforth they may cover every pathway and every step of life's journey, and that we may recognize whatever comes as but another call to prayer and another opportunity for God to manifest His glory and erect the everlasting memorial of His victorious love!

We close this little message with the thought with which we began its first chapter; namely, that the way the Lord taught His disciples to pray was by starting them at once to pray.

Begin this moment to pray for the very first thing that comes to your heart as a need, and go right on turning everything into prayer until you have to stop in the very fullness of your heart and turn it all into praise. And "now unto him that is able to do exceeding abundantly above all that we ask or think, according to the power that worketh in us, unto him be glory in the church by Christ Jesus throughout all ages, world without end. Amen" (Ephesians 3:20-21).

THE LIFE OF PRAYER
STUDY GUIDE

CHAPTER 1: THE PATTERN OF PRAYER

1. What prayer is a pattern for all prayers?
2. How should all true prayer begin?
3. What should all true prayer recognize about God?
4. In what way is prayer a "fellowship of human hearts"?
5. What is the highest element in prayer? Explain your answer.
6. What should all true prayer recognize about the kingdom of God?

    a. How should such recognition change your view of prayer?

7. What is true prayer founded upon?

    a. How does this foundation affect the limitations of prayer?

    b. Does that foundation encourage or discourage you?

8. What should we learn to trust God for every day?

    a. What may be included in the things for which we trust Him?

9. What does true prayer teach us that we constantly need from God? (See Hebrews 4:16.)

   a. How does having "iniquity in your heart" affect your prayers?

10. Prayer is a weapon and safeguard against what? Explain your answer.

11. What is the spiritual state that will keep you continually safe from temptations and other forms of evil? Explain your answer.

12. How should you end all your prayers?

13. Does everyone have the right to pray the "Our Father"? Explain your answer.

CHAPTER 2: ENCOURAGEMENTS TO PRAYER

1. Does the Lord's comparison between your heavenly Father and earthly fathers encourage you to pray? Explain your answer.

2. When you pray to your heavenly Father for others, do you claim His abundant provisions for them? Explain your answer.

3. When you pray, do you pray with boldness and persistence?

   a. If you do, what Scriptures justify your praying that way?

4. There are what might be called three forms of prayer:

   a. What is the simplest form?

   b. What is the next higher form?

   c. What is the highest form?

5. Explain in detail why the last form is the highest form of prayer.

6. What is the highest ministry of prayer?

7. Why can you often pray bolder for others than for yourself?

8. Have you received the "gift of the Holy Spirit"?

a. If you have, what effect should it have upon your praying?

b. If you have not, what is your response to the Lord's statement that "your heavenly Father [will] give the Holy Spirit to them that ask Him"?

CHAPTER 3: IN HIS NAME

1. Explain what it means to pray "in Jesus' name"?

2. Why is it necessary that Christ be your mediator with God?

3. What are some of the functions of Christ as our High Priest?

4. "In His name" signifies that your prayers are to be grounded upon what?

5. Why is it necessary for you to "enter the Holiest *by the blood of Jesus*"?

a. Can you enter any other way?

b. Can you enter without the blood?

c. If you do not recognize and acknowledge the blood of Jesus and pray anyway, are you actually praying? Explain your answer.

6. What is the ultimate meaning in regard to our relationship to Jesus—our identification with Him—when we pray "in His name"?

7. Explain what it means for Jesus to be God's "divinely appointed channel of prayer."

CHAPTER 4: THE PRAYER OF FAITH

1. Define "the prayer of faith."
2. What is the greatest force in the natural world? Explain your answer.
3. What is the greatest force in the spiritual world? Explain your answer.
4. If the Bible says, "the prayer of faith shall save the sick, and the Lord shall raise him up," why are so few healed when Christians pray for them.
5. Why is faith the essential principle of the kingdom of God?
6. Explain the difference between the two laws:
    a. The law of works
    b. The law of faith
7. What does "the faith of God" mean?
8. If you ask God for something, why is it essential that you give Him time to do it?
9 If you know that your prayer has reached the throne of God, what are you justified in believing?
10. What is the secret of faith that will enable you to pray effectually?

CHAPTER 5: HINDRANCES TO PRAYER

1. What is the greatest hindrance to a life of prayer?
2. Do you have a right to expect God to answer your prayers if you are deliberately committing sin?
3. Explain why selfishness and earthly desires are a hindrance to prayer.
4. Why is doubt such a strong hindrance to prayer?
5. What is perhaps the greatest hindrance to effectual prayer and a life of prayer? Explain your answer.

6. When His disciples asked the Lord to teach them to pray, what was the first thing He told them to do?

a. How can you apply His answer to yourself?

THE TRUE VINE

MEDITATIONS FOR A MONTH ON JOHN 15:1-16

The mystery which hath been hid from ages and from generations, but now is made manifest to his saints: To whom God would make known what is the riches of the glory of this mystery among the Gentiles; which is Christ in you, the hope of glory (Colossians 1:26-27).

BY

ANDREW MURRAY

ONLY A BRANCH

"I am the vine, ye are the branches" (John 15:5).

Tis only a little Branch,
"A thing so fragile and weak,
But that little Branch hath a message true
To give, could it only speak.

"I'm only a little Branch,
I live by a life not mine,
For the sap that flows through my tendrils small
Is the life-blood of the vine.

"No power indeed have I
The fruit of myself to bear,
But since I'm part of the living vine,
Its fruitfulness I share.

"Dost thou ask how I abide?
How this life I can maintain?-
I am bound to the vine by life's strong band,
And I only need remain.

"Where first my life was given,
In the spot where I am set,
Upborne and upheld as the days go by,
By the stem which bears me yet.

"I fear not the days to come,
I dwell not upon the past,
As moment by moment I draw a life,
Which for evermore shall last.

"I bask in the sun's bright beams,
Which with sweetness fills my fruit,
Yet I own not the clusters hanging there,
For they all come from the root."

A life which is not my own,
But another's life in me:
This, this is the message the Branch would speak,
A message to thee and me.

Oh, struggle not to "abide,"
Nor labor to "bring forth fruit,"
But let Jesus unite thee to himself,
As the vine Branch to the root.

So simple, so deep, so strong
That union with Him shall be:
His life shall forever replace thine own,
And His love shall flow through thee.

For His Spirit's fruit is love,
And love shall thy life become,
And for evermore on His heart of love
Thy spirit shall have her home.

—Freda Hanbury

BIOGRAPHY OF
ANDREW MURRAY

Andrew Murray was born in South Africa to Dutch Reformed Church missionaries Andrew and Maria Murray. When he was ten, he and his older brother John were sent to live with an uncle in Scotland, where they received their formal education. Before returning home, they both decided to enter the ministry and took theological studies at the University of Utrecht in Holland. On May 9, 1848, after Andrew and John finished their university studies, the Hague committee of the Dutch Reformed Church ordained them both. It was Andrew's 20th birthday, and he was the youngest candidate for the ministry ever ordained by the church.

When they returned to South Africa, John, because he was the oldest, was put in charge of the church in the well-established and respected town of Burgersdorp, while Andrew was sent to the church at Bloemfontein, a remote frontier territory of nearly 50,000 miles and 12,000 people.

In 1854 Andrew was asked by church officials to go to England to help with certain church businesses and to recruit pastors. When he returned in March 1855, he stopped at Cape Town before returning to Bloemfontein. There he met a Miss Emma Rutherford. After corresponding for several months, they were married on July 2, 1856.

Murray started producing books almost from the beginning of his ministry. The deeper Christian life was his favorite subject in his writing and preaching, with prayer being a close second. The subjects of most of his books did not come from his theological studies but from his personal life and experiences. Before he wrote or preached about anything, however, he made certain it was solidly based upon the Scriptures. Over his lifetime he wrote more than 250 books. Regardless of the subject matter, each of his books emphasized a closer relationship with God, the Lord Jesus Christ, and the Holy Spirit.

In *The Secret of Adoration*, he wrote, "Take time. Give God time to reveal himself to you. Give yourself time to be silent and quiet before Him, waiting to receive, through the Spirit, the assurance of His presence with you, His power working in you. Take time to read His Word; and read it as if in His presence, so that from it you may know what He asks of you and what He promises you. Let the Word create around you and within you a holy atmosphere, a holy heavenly light, in which your soul will be refreshed and strengthened for the work of daily life."

Because of pain in his arms Murray was not able to do his own writing, so Emma wrote down all his sermons and took dictation from him. After Emma died in 1904, their daughter Annie took her place as his secretary. In later writing about her father, Annie described his method of work in his latter years.

He sits up very straight in his study chair, and dictates in a loud, clear voice, as though he were actually addressing his audience. His hours of work are usually from 9 or 10 until 11 in the forenoon, during which time two or three chapters of a book are completed. He is very particular about punctuation, and always says, "New paragraph," pointing with long, slender, finger to the exact spot on the paper where the new line must commence, and "full stop," "comma," "colon," "semi-colon," as the sense may require. Should his secretary perpetrate some mistake or other in spelling, he would make some playful remark like: "You will have to go back to the kindergarten, you know."

At 11 o'clock he would say: "Now give me ten minutes' rest; or no, let us write some letters for a change." Then half a dozen letters would be quickly dictated, in reply to requests for prayer for healing, for the conversion of unconverted relations, for the deliverance of friends addicted to drink, or, it might be, business letters. He always dictated in a tone of great earnestness, and was specially anxious to get a great deal into a page. "Write closer, closer," he often repeated. When near the end of the foolscap page, he said: "Now the last four lines for a prayer"; and then he would fold his hands, close his eyes, and actually pray the prayer which ended the written meditation.

In the Foreword of one of his several books on prayer, Murray wrote the below about the reason for the book, most of which applies as well for this book. It came about as a result of a conference of Dutch ministers in South Africa in 1912. A professor at their theological seminary had written a letter to the ministers of the Dutch Reformed Church about the low state of the spiritual life in the Church. He asked the ministers whether it was not time for them to come together and in God's presence to find out what might be the cause of the evil. He further wrote, "If only we study the conditions in all sincerity, we shall have to acknowledge that our unbelief and sin are the cause of the lack of spiritual power; that this condition is one of sin and guilt before God, and nothing less than a direct grieving of God's Holy Spirit."

About this, Murray wrote:

> His invitation met with a hearty response. Our four theological professors, with more than two hundred ministers, missionaries, and theological

students, came together with the above words as the keynote of our meeting. From the very first, in the addresses there was the tone of confession as the only way to repentance and restoration. At a subsequent meeting the opportunity was given for testimony as to what might be the sins which made the life of the Church so feeble. Some began to mention failings that they had seen in other ministers, either in conduct, or in doctrine, or in service. It was soon felt that this was not the right way; each must acknowledge that in which he himself was guilty.

The Lord graciously so ordered it that we were gradually led to the sin of prayerlessness as one of the deepest roots of the evil. No one could plead himself free from this. Nothing so reveals the defective spiritual life in minister and congregation as the lack of believing and unceasing prayer. Prayer is in very deed the pulse of the spiritual life. It is the great means of bringing to minister and people the blessing and power of heaven. Persevering and believing prayer means a strong and an abundant life.

When once the spirit of confession began to prevail, the question arose as to whether it would be indeed possible to expect to gain the victory over all that had in the past hindered our prayer life. In smaller conferences held previously, it had been found that many were most anxious to make a new beginning and yet had not the courage to expect that they would be able to maintain that prayer life which they saw to be in accordance with the Word of God. They had often made the attempt but had failed. They did not dare to make any promise to the Lord to live and pray as He would have them; they felt it impossible.

Such confessions gradually led to the great truth, that the only power for a new prayer life is to be found in an entirely new relation to our blessed Savior. It is as we see in Him the Lord who saves us from sin—the sin of prayerlessness, too—and our faith yields itself to a life of closer interaction with Him, that a life in His love and fellowship will make prayer to Him the natural expression of our soul's life. Before we parted, many were able to testify that they were returning with new light and new hope to find in Jesus Christ strength for a new prayer life.

Andrew Murray died on January 18, 1917, just four months before his eighty-ninth birthday.

For more biographical information about Andrew Murray, see the Pure Gold Classic books *Absolute Surrender* and *Humility*, published by Bridge-Logos Publishers.

Photo Gallery

ANDREW MURRAY

1828–1917

Murray as a young student.   *Murray at age 43.*

*The Murray family in 1873. Andrew is in the back row
with his arm affectionately around Emma.*

Professor Murray age 70.

Andrew Murray (center) and his family about 1880.

Andrew Murray and Emma Murray

*Andrew Murray shortly before his death
on January 18, 1917.*

257

PREFACE

I have felt drawn to try to write what young Christians might easily understand, and what will help them to obtain that position in which their Christian life will be a success. In the parable of the vine there is not one of the principal temptations and failures of the Christian life that is not met. The nearness, the all-sufficiency, the faithfulness of the Lord Jesus, the naturalness, the fruitfulness of a life of faith, are so revealed, that it is as if one could with confidence say, "Let the parable enter into my heart, and all will be right."

May the blessed Lord give the blessing. May He teach us to study the mystery of the vine in the spirit of worship, waiting for God's own teaching.

—Andrew Murray

THE TRUE VINE

MEDITATIONS FOR A MONTH ON JOHN 15:1-16

1

THE VINE

"I am the true vine" (John 15:1).

All earthly things are the shadows of heavenly realities—the expression, in created visible forms, of the invisible glory of God. The life and the truth are in heaven; on earth we have figures and shadows of the heavenly truths. When Jesus says, "I am the true vine," He tells us that all the vines of earth are pictures and emblems of himself. He is the divine reality, of which they are the created expression. They all point to Him, and preach Him, and reveal Him. If you would know Jesus, study the vine.

How many eyes have gazed on and admired a great vine with its beautiful fruit. Come and gaze on the heavenly vine until your eyes turn from all else to admire Him. How many, in a sunny climate, sit and rest under the shadow of a vine. Come and be still under the shadow of the true vine, and rest under it from the heat of the day. What countless numbers rejoice in the fruit of the vine! Come, take, and eat of the heavenly fruit of the true vine, and let your soul say, "I sat down under his shadow with great delight, and his fruit was sweet to my taste" (Song of Solomon 2:3).

"I am the true Vine." This is a heavenly mystery. The earthly vine can teach you much about this vine of heaven. Many interesting and beautiful points of comparison suggest themselves, and help us to get an understanding of what Christ meant. But such thoughts do not teach us to know what the heavenly vine really is, in its cooling shade and its life-giving fruit. The experience of this is part of the hidden mystery, which none but Jesus himself, by the Holy Spirit, can unfold and impart.

"I am the true vine." The vine is the living Lord, who himself speaks, and gives, and works all that He has for us. If you would know the meaning and power of that word, do not think to find it by thought or study. These may help to show you what you must get from Him to awaken desire and hope and prayer, but they cannot show you the vine. Jesus alone can reveal himself. He gives the Holy Spirit to open the eyes to gaze upon himself, to open the heart to receive himself. He must himself speak the word to you and me.

"I am the true vine." And what are you to do if you want the mystery, in all its heavenly beauty and blessing, opened up to you? With what you already know of the parable, bow down and be still, worship and wait, until the divine Word enters your heart, and you feel His holy presence with you and in you. The overshadowing of His holy love will give you the perfect calm and rest of knowing that the vine will do all.

"I am the true vine." He who speaks is God, in His infinite power able to enter into us. He is man, one with us. He is the crucified One, who won a perfect righteousness and a divine life for us through His death. He is the glorified One, who from the throne gives His Spirit to make His presence real and true. He speaks—oh, listen, not to His words only, but to *Him*, as He whispers secretly day by day, "I am the true vine! All that the vine can ever be to its branch, I will be to you."

Holy Lord Jesus, the heavenly vine of God's own planting, I beseech you, reveal yourself to my soul. Let the Holy Spirit, not only in thought, but in experience, give me to know all that you, the Son of God, are to me as the true vine.

2

THE HUSBANDMAN

"And my Father is the husbandman" (John 15:1).

A vine must have a husbandman to plant and watch over it, to receive and rejoice in its fruit. Jesus says, "My Father is the husbandman." He was the vine of God's planting. Everything He was and did, He owed to the Father; in everything He was and did He only sought the Father's will and glory. He became man to show us what a creature should be to its creator. He took our place, and the spirit of His life before the Father was ever what He seeks to make ours: "Of him, and through him, and to him are all things" (Romans 11:36). He became the true vine, that we might be true branches. Both in regard to Christ and ourselves, the words teach us the two lessons of absolute dependence and perfect confidence.

"My Father is the husbandman." Christ ever lived in the spirit of what He once said: "The Son can do nothing of himself" (John 5:19). A vine is totally dependent on a husbandman for the place where it is to grow, for its fencing in, and for its watering and pruning. In the same way, Christ was entirely dependent on His Father every day for the wisdom and the strength to do the Father's will. As He said in the previous chapter, "the words that I speak unto you I speak not of myself: but the Father that dwelleth in me, He doeth the works" (John 14:10). This absolute dependence had as its blessed counterpart the most blessed confidence that He had nothing to fear—the Father could not disappoint Him. With such a husbandman as His Father, He could enter death and the grave. He could trust God to raise Him up. All that Christ is and has, He has, not in himself, but from the Father. *My Father is the husbandman.* That is as blessedly true for us as for Christ.

Christ is about to teach His disciples about their being branches. Before He ever uses the word, or speaks at all of abiding in Him or bearing fruit, He turns their eyes heavenward to the Father watching over them, and working everything in them. At the very root of all Christian life lies the thought that God is to do everything, that our work is to give and leave ourselves in His hands, in the confession of utter helplessness and dependence, in the assured confidence that He gives all we need. The great lack of the Christian life is that, even where we trust Christ, we leave God out of the count. Christ came to bring us to God.

Jesus lived the life of a man exactly as we have to live it. Christ the vine points to God the husbandman. As He trusted God, let us trust God, that everything we should be and have, as those who belonged to the vine, will be given us from above. Isaiah said: "A vineyard of red wine. I the LORD do keep it; I will water it every moment: lest any hurt it, I will keep it night and day" (Isaiah 27:2-3). Before we begin to think of fruit or branches, let us have our heart filled with the faith. As glorious as the vine is, so is the husbandman. As high and holy as is our calling, so mighty and loving is the God who will work it all. As surely as the husbandman made the vine what it was to be, will He make each branch what it is to be. Our Father is our husbandman, the certainty of our growth and fruit.

Blessed Father, we are your husbandry. Oh, that you may have honor of the work of your hands! O my Father, I desire to open my heart to the joy of this wondrous truth: My Father is the husbandman! Teach me to know and trust you, and to see that the same deep interest with which you cared for and delighted in the vine, extends to every branch and to me.

3

THE BRANCH

"Every branch in me that beareth not fruit he taketh away" (John 15:2)

Here we have one of the chief words in the parable of the branch. A vine needs *branches*. Without branches it can do nothing, can bear no fruit. As important as it is to know about the vine and the husbandman, it is equally important to know what the branch is. Before we listen to what Christ has to say about it, let us first of all take in what a branch is, and what it teaches us of our life in Christ. A branch is simply a bit of wood, brought forth by the vine for the one purpose of serving it in bearing its fruit. It is of the very same nature as the vine, and has one life and one spirit with it. Just think a moment of the lessons this suggests. There is the lesson of entire consecration.

The branch has but one object for which it exists, one purpose to which it is entirely given up. That is, to bear the fruit the vine wishes to bring forth. And so the believer has but one reason for being a branch—but one reason for existence on earth—that the heavenly vine may bring forth His fruit. Happy the soul that knows this, that has consented to it, and that says, "I have been redeemed and I live for one thing. As exclusively as the natural branch exists only to bring forth fruit, so do I. As exclusively as the heavenly vine exists to bring forth fruit, so do I. I have been planted by God into Christ, and I have wholly given myself to bear the fruit the vine desires to bring forth."

There is the lesson of perfect conformity. The branch is exactly like the vine in every aspect—the same nature, the same life, the same place, the same work. In all this they are inseparably one. And so believers need to know that they are partakers of the divine nature, and have the very nature and spirit of Christ in them, and that their one calling is to yield themselves to a perfect conformity to Christ. The branch is a perfect likeness of the vine; the only difference is, the one is great and strong, and the source of strength, the other little and feeble, ever needing and receiving strength. Even so the believer is, and is to be, the perfect likeness of Christ.

There is the lesson of absolute dependence. The vine has its stores of life and sap and strength, not for itself, but for the branches. The branches are and have nothing but what the vine provides and imparts. Believers are called to, and it is their highest blessedness to enter upon, a life of entire and unceasing dependence upon Christ. Day and night, every moment, Christ is to work in them all they need.

And then the lesson of undoubting confidence. The branch has no cure. The vine provides all. The branch has but to yield itself and receive. It is the sight of this truth that leads to the blessed rest of faith, the true secret of growth and strength: "I can do all things through Christ which strengtheneth me" (Philippians 4:13). What a life would come to us if we only consented to be branches! Dear child of God, learn the lesson. You have but one thing to do: Only be a branch—nothing more, nothing less! Just be a branch. Christ will be the vine that gives all. And the husbandman, the mighty God, who made the vine what it is, will as surely make the branch what it ought to be.

Lord Jesus, reveal to me the heavenly mystery of the branch, in its living union with the vine, in its claim on all its fullness. And let your all-sufficiency, holding and filling your branches, lead me to the rest of faith that knows that you work all things.

4

THE FRUIT

"Every branch in me that there is not fruit, he taketh away" (John 15:2)

"Fruit." This is the next great word we have: the vine, the husbandman, the branch, the fruit. What has our Lord to say to us of fruit? Simply this—that fruit is the one thing the branch is for, and that if it bear not fruit, the husbandman takes it away. The vine is the glory of the husbandman; the branch is the glory of the vine; the fruit is the glory of the branch. If the branch bring not forth fruit, there is no glory or worth in it; it is an offense and a hindrance; the husbandman takes it away. The one reason for the existence of a branch, the one mark of being a true branch of the heavenly vine, the one condition of being allowed by the divine husbandman to share the life the vine is bearing fruit.

And what is fruit? Something that the branch bears, not for itself, but for its owner; something that is to be gathered and taken away. The branch does indeed receive it from the vine sap for its own life, by which it grows thicker and stronger. But this supply for its own maintenance is entirely subordinate to its fulfillment of the purpose of its existence—bearing fruit. It is because Christians do not understand or accept this truth, that they so fail in their efforts and prayers to live the branch life. They often desire it very earnestly; they read and meditate and pray, and yet they fail and wonder why. The reason is very simple: they do not know that fruit-bearing is the one thing they have been saved for. Just as entirely as Christ became the true vine with the one object, you have been made a branch with the one object of bearing fruit for the salvation of sinners. The vine and the branch are equally under the unchangeable law of fruit-bearing as the one reason for their existence. Christ and the believer, the heavenly one and the branch, have equally their place in the world exclusively for one purpose—to carry God's saving love to sinners. Hence the solemn word: *Every branch that beareth not fruit, He taketh it away.*

Let us specially beware of one great mistake. Many Christians think their own salvation is the first thing. The second is their temporal life and prosperity, with the care of their family. Then what time and interest is left may be devoted to fruit-bearing, to the saving of sinners. No wonder that in most cases very little time or interest can be found. No, Christian, the one object for which you have been made a member of Christ's body is that you carry out the saving work of the head. The one object God had in making you a branch is that Christ may through you bring life to sinners. Your personal salvation, your business and care for your family, are entirely subordinate to this. Your first aim in life, your first aim every day, should be to know how Christ desires to carry out His purpose in and through you.

Let us begin to think as God thinks. Let us accept Christ's teaching and respond to it. The one object of my being a branch, the one mark of my being a true branch, the one condition of my abiding and growing strong, is that I bear the fruit of the heavenly vine for dying sinners to eat and live. And the one thing of which I can have the most perfect assurance is that, with Christ as my vine, and the Father as my husbandman, I can indeed be a fruitful branch.

Our Father, you come seeking fruit. Teach us, we pray, to realize how truly this is the one object of our existence, and of our union to Christ. Make it the one desire of our hearts to be branches, so filled with the Spirit of the vine, as to bring forth fruit abundantly.

5

MORE FRUIT

"And every branch that beareth fruit, he cleanseth, that it may bear more fruit" (John 15:2)

The thought of fruit is prominent in the eye of Him who sees things as they are. Fruit is so truly the one thing God has set His heart upon, that our Lord, after having said that the branch that bears no fruit is taken away, at once adds that where there is fruit, the one desire of the husbandman is more fruit. As the gift of His grace, as the token of spiritual vigor, as the showing forth of the glory of God and of Christ, as the only way for satisfying the need of the world, God longs and equips you for more fruit.

"More fruit." This is a very searching word. As churches and individuals we are in danger of nothing so much as self-contentment. The secret spirit of Laodicea—we are rich and increased in goods, and have need of nothing—may prevail where it is not suspected. The divine warning— "thou art wretched, and miserable, and poor" (Revelation 3:17) —finds little response just where it is most needed. Let us not rest content with the thought that we are taking an equal share with others in the work that is being done, or that people are satisfied with our efforts in Christ's service, or even point to us as examples. Let our only desire be to know whether we are bearing all the fruit Christ is willing to give through us as living branches, in close and living union with himself. Whether we are satisfying the loving heart of the great husbandman, our Father in Heaven, in His desire for more fruit.

"More fruit." The word comes with divine authority to search and test our life. The true disciple will heartily surrender to its holy light, and will earnestly ask that God show what there may be lacking in the measure or the character of the fruit he bears. Do let us believe that the Word is meant to lead us on to a fuller experience of the Father's purpose of love, of Christ's fullness, and of the wonderful privilege of bearing much fruit in the salvation of sinners.

"More fruit." The word is a most encouraging one. Let us listen to it. It is just to the branch that is bearing fruit that the message comes: more fruit. God does not demand this as Pharaoh the taskmaster, or as Moses the lawgiver, without providing the means. He comes as a Father, who gives what He asks, and works what He commands. He comes to us as the living branches of the living vine, and offers to work the more fruit in us, if we but yield ourselves into His hands. Shall we not admit the claim, accept the offer, and look to Him to work it in us?

"That it may bear more fruit." Do let us believe that as the owner of a vine does everything to make the fruit production as rich and large as possible, the divine husbandman will do all that is needed to make us bear more fruit. All He asks is that we set our heart's desire on it, entrust ourselves to His working and care, and joyfully look to Him to do His perfect work in us. God has set His heart on more fruit. Christ waits to work it in us. Let us joyfully look up to our divine husbandman and our heavenly vine, to ensure our bearing more fruit.

Our Father who is in Heaven, you are the heavenly husbandman, and Christ is the heavenly vine. I am a heavenly branch, partaker of His heavenly life, to bear His heavenly fruit. Father, let the power of His life so fill me, that I may ever bear more fruit, to the glory of your name.

6

THE CLEANSING

"Every branch that beareth fruit, He cleanseth it, that it may bear more fruit" (John 15:2)

There are two remarkable things about the vine. There is not a plant of which the fruit has so much spirit [juice, sap] in it, of which spirit can be so abundantly distilled as the vine. And there is not a plant that so soon runs into wild wood that hinders its fruit, and therefore needs the most merciless pruning. I look out of my window here on large vineyards: the chief care of the vinedresser is the pruning. You may have a trellis vine rooting so deep in good soil that it needs neither digging, nor fertilizing, nor watering. But pruning cannot be dispensed with, if it is to bear good fruit. Some trees need occasional pruning, others bear perfect fruit without any, but the vine must have it. And so our Lord tells us, here at the very outset of the parable, that the one work the Father does to the branch that bears fruit is, "He cleanseth it, that it may bear more fruit."

Consider a moment what this pruning or cleansing is. It is not the removal of weeds or thorns, or anything from without that may hinder the growth. No, it is the cutting off of the long shoots of the previous year, the removal of something that comes from within, that has been produced by the life of the vine itself. It is the removal of something that is a proof of the vigor of its life. The more vigorous the growth has been, the greater the need for the pruning. It is the honest, healthy wood of the vine that has to be cut away. And why? Because it would consume too much of the sap to fill all the long shoots of last year's growth—the sap must be saved up and used for fruit alone. The branches, sometimes eight and ten feet long, are cut down close to the stem, and nothing is left but just one or two inches of wood, enough to bear the grapes. It is when everything that is not needful for fruit-bearing has been relentlessly cut down, and just as little of the branches as possible has been left, that full, rich, fruit may be expected.

What a solemn, precious lesson! It is not to sin only that the cleansing of the Husbandman here refers. It is to our own religious activity, as it is developed in the very act of bearing fruit. It is this that must be cut down and cleansed away. In working for God, we have to use our natural gifts of wisdom, or eloquence, or influence, or zeal. And yet they are ever in danger of being unduly developed, and then trusted in. And so, after each season of work, God has to bring us to the end of ourselves, to the consciousness of the helplessness and the danger of all that is of ourselves, to feel that we are nothing. All that is to be left of us is just enough to receive the power of the life-giving sap of the Holy Spirit. What is of ourselves must be reduced to its very lowest measure. All that is inconsistent with the most entire devotion to Christ's service must be removed. The more perfect the cleansing and cutting away of all that is of self, the less of surface over which the Holy Spirit is to be spread, so much the more intense can be the concentration of our whole being, to be entirely at the disposal of the Spirit.

This is the true circumcision of the heart, the circumcision of Christ. This is the true crucifixion with Christ: "Always bearing about in the body the dying of the Lord Jesus, that the life also of Jesus might be made manifest in our body" (2 Corinthians 4:10). Blessed cleansing, God's own cleansing! How we may rejoice in the assurance that we shall bring forth more fruit.

Oh our holy husbandman, cleanse and cut away all that there is in us that would make a fair show, or could become a source of self-confidence and glorying. Lord, keep us very low, that no flesh may glory in your presence. We do trust you to do your work.

7

THE PRUNING KNIFE

"Already ye are clean because of the word I have spoken unto you" (John 15:3)

What is the pruning knife of this heavenly husbandman? It is often said to be affliction. By no means in the first place. How would it then fare with many who have long seasons free from adversity, or with some on whom God appears to shower down kindness all their life long? No, it is the Word of God that "is quick, and powerful, and sharper than any two-edged sword, piercing even to the dividing asunder of soul and spirit, and of the joints and marrow, and is a discerner of the thoughts and intents of the heart" (Hebrews 4:12). It is only when affliction leads to this discipline of the Word that it becomes a blessing. The lack of this heart-cleansing through the Word is the reason why affliction is so often unsanctified. Not even Paul's thorn in the flesh could become a blessing until Christ's Word, "My strength is made perfect in weakness" (2 Corinthians 12:9), had made him see the danger of self-exaltation, and made him willing to rejoice in infirmities.

The Word of God's pruning knife. Jesus says: "Ye are already clean, because of the word I have spoken unto you." How searchingly that word had been spoken by Him, out of whose mouth there went a sharp two-edged sword, as he had taught them! In various ways, He told them, "except you deny yourself, lose your life, forsake all, hate father and mother, you cannot be my disciple, you are not worthy of me"—or as He humbled their pride, or reproved their lack of love, or foretold their all forsaking Him. From the opening of His ministry in the Sermon on the Mount, to His words of warning on the last night, His Word had tried and cleansed them. He had discovered and condemned all there was of self. They were now emptied and cleansed, ready for the incoming of the Holy Spirit.

It is as the soul gives up its own thoughts, and humanity's thoughts of what is religion, and yields itself heartily, humbly, patiently, to the teaching of the Word by the Spirit, that the Father will do His blessed work of pruning and cleansing away all of our fleshly nature and self that mixes with our work and hinders His Spirit. Let those who would know all the husbandman can do for them, all the vine can bring forth through them, seek earnestly to yield themselves heartily to the blessed cleansing through the Word. Let them, in their study of the Word, receive it as a hammer that breaks and opens up, as a fire that melts and refines, as a sword that lays bare and slays all that is of the flesh. The word of conviction will prepare for the word of comfort and of hope, and the Father will cleanse them through the Word. All you who are branches of the true choose once, each time you read or hear the Word, wait first of all on Him to use it for His cleansing of the branch. Set your heart upon His desire for more fruit.

Trust Him as husbandman to work it. Yield yourselves in simple childlike surrender to the cleansing work of His Word and Spirit, and you may count upon it that His purpose will be fulfilled in you.

Father, I pray, cleanse me through your Word. Let it search out and bring to light all that is of self and the flesh in my religion. Let it cut away every root of self-confidence, that the vine may find me wholly free to receive His life and Spirit. O my holy husbandman, I trust you to care for the branch as much as for the vine. You only are my hope.

8

ABIDE

"Abide in me, and I in you" (John 15:4)

When a new graft is placed in a vine and it abides there, there is a twofold process that takes place. The first is in the wood. The graft shoots its little roots and fibers down into the stem, and the stem grows up into the graft, and what has been called the structural union is effected. The graft abides and becomes one with the vine, and even if the vine were to die, the graft will still be one wood with it. Then there is the second process, in which the sap of the vine enters the new structure, and uses it as a passage through which sap can flow up to show itself in young shoots and leaves and fruit. Here is the vital union. Into the graft that abides in the stock, the stock enters with its sap to abide in it. When our Lord says: "Abide in me, and I in you," He points to something analogous to this. "Abide in me" refers more to that which we have to do. We have to trust and obey, to detach ourselves from all else, to reach out after Him and cling to Him, to

275

sink ourselves into Him. As we do this, through the grace He gives, a character is formed, and a heart prepared for the fuller experience, which is, "I in you." God strengthens us with might by the Spirit in the inner man, and Christ dwells in the heart by faith (Ephesians 3:16:17).

Many believers pray and long very earnestly for the filling of the Spirit and the indwelling of Christ, and wonder that they do not make more progress. The reason is often this, the "I in you" cannot come because the "abide in me" is not maintained. "There is one body, and one Spirit" (Ephesians 4:4). Before the Spirit can fill, there must be a body prepared. The graft must have grown into the stem, and be abiding in it before the sap can flow through to bring forth fruit. It is as in lowly obedience we follow Christ, even in external things, denying ourselves, forsaking the world, and even in the body seeking to be conformable to Him, as we thus seek to abide in Him, that we shall be able to receive and enjoy the "I in you." The work urged on us, "Abide in me," will prepare us for the "I in you" work undertaken by Him.

"In." The two parts of the injunction have their unity in that central deep meaning word "in." There is no deeper word in Scripture. God is in all. God dwells in Christ. Christ lives in God. We are in Christ. Christ is in us. Our life taken up into His and His life received into ours are a divine reality that words cannot express—we are in Him and He in us. The words, "Abide in me and I in you," tell us to believe this divine mystery, and to count upon our God the husbandman, and Christ the vine, to make it divinely true. No thinking or teaching or praying can grasp it, it is a divine mystery of love. As little as we can effect the union can we understand it. Let us look upon this infinite, divine, omnipotent vine loving us, holding us, working in us. Let us in the faith of His working abide and rest in Him, ever turning heart and hope to Him alone. And let us count upon Him to fulfill in us the mystery of "Ye in me, and I in you."

Blessed Lord, you bid me to abide in you. How can I, Lord, except you show yourself to me, waiting to receive and welcome and keep me? I pray you show me how you as vine undertake to do everything. To be occupied with you is to abide in you. Here I am, Lord, a branch, cleansed and abiding, resting in you, and awaiting the inflow of your life and grace.

9

EXCEPT YE ABIDE

"As the branch cannot bear fruit of itself, except it abide in the vine; no more can ye, except ye abide in me"
(John 15:4).

We know the meaning of the word *except*. It expresses some indispensable condition, some inevitable law. "The branch cannot bear fruit of itself, *except* it abide in the vine. No more can ye, *except* ye abide in me." There is but one way for the branch to bear fruit, there is no other possibility, it must abide in unbroken communion with the vine. Not of itself, but only of the vine, does the fruit come. Christ had already said, "Abide in me." In nature the branch teaches us the lesson so clearly. It is such a wonderful privilege to be called and allowed to abide in the heavenly vine. One might have thought it needless to add these words of warning, but Christ knows so well what a renunciation of self is implied in the words, "Abide in me." How strong and universal the tendency would be to seek to bear fruit by our own efforts. How difficult it would be to get us to believe that actual, continuous abiding in Him is an absolute necessity! He insists upon the truth—the branch cannot bear fruit of itself. Except it abide, it cannot bear fruit. "No more can ye, except ye abide in me."

277

But must this be taken literally? Must I, as exclusively, manifestly, unceasingly, and absolutely as the branch abides in the vine, be equally given up to find my whole life in Christ alone? I must indeed. The *except ye abide* is as universal as the *except it abide*. The *no more can ye* admits of no exception or modification. If I am to be a true branch, if I am to bear fruit, if I am to be what Christ as the vine wants me to be, my whole existence must be as exclusively devoted to abiding in Him as the natural branch is devoted to abiding in its vine.

Let me learn the lesson. Abiding is to be an act of the will and the whole heart. Just as there are degrees in seeking and serving God, "not with a perfect heart" (2 Chronicles 25:2), or "with the whole heart (Psalm 119:2)," so there may be degrees in abiding. In regeneration the divine life enters us, but does not all at once master and fill our whole being. This comes as matter of command and obedience. There is unspeakable danger of our not giving ourselves with our whole heart to abide. There is unspeakable danger of our giving ourselves to work for God, and to bear fruit, with but little of the true abiding, the wholehearted losing of ourselves in Christ and His life. There is unspeakable danger of much work with but little fruit, for lack of this one thing needful.

We must allow the words, "not of itself," "except it abide," to do their work of searching and exposing, of pruning and cleansing, all that there is of self-will and self-confidence in our life. Our blessed Lord desires to call us away from ourselves and our own strength, to himself and His strength. Let us accept the warning, and turn with great fear and self-distrust to Him to do His work. "Your life is hid with Christ in God" (Colossians 3:3). That life is a heavenly mystery, hid from the wise even among Christians, and revealed unto babes. The childlike spirit learns that life is given from heaven every day and every moment to the soul that accepts the teaching, "not of itself," "except it abide," and seeks its all in the vine. Abiding in the vine then comes to be nothing more nor less than the restful surrender of the soul to let Christ have all and work all, as completely as in nature the branch knows and seeks nothing but the vine.

Abide in me. I have heard, my Lord, that with every command, you also give the power to obey. With your "rise and walk," the lame man leaped, I accept your word, "Abide in me," as a word of power that gives power, and even now I say, yes, Lord, I will, I do abide in you.

10

THE VINE

"I am the vine, ye are the branches" (John 15:5)

In the previous verse Christ had just said, "Abide in me." He had then announced the great unalterable law of all branch-life on earth or in heaven: "not of itself," "except it abide." In the opening words of the parable He had already said, "I am the vine." He now repeats the words. He would have us understand—note well the lesson, simple as it appears, it is the key of the abiding life—that the only way to obey the command, "Abide in me," is to have eye and heart fixed upon Him. "Abide in me ... I am the true vine." Yes, study this holy mystery until you see Christ as the true vine, bearing, strengthening, supplying, inspiring all His branches, being and doing in each branch all it needs, and the abiding will come of itself. Yes, gaze upon Him as the true vine, until you feel what a heavenly mystery it is, and are compelled to ask the Father to reveal it to you by His Holy Spirit. If

God reveals the glory of the true vine to you, if you see what Jesus is and waits to do every moment, you cannot but abide. The vision of Christ is an irresistible attraction, it draws and holds us like a magnet. Listen always to the living Christ still speaking to you, and waiting to show you the meaning and power of His Word, "I am the vine."

How much weary labor there has been in striving to understand what abiding is, how much fruitless effort in trying to attain it! Why was this? Because the attention was turned to the abiding as a work we have to do, instead of the living Christ in whom we were to be kept abiding, and who himself was to hold and keep us. We thought of abiding as a continual strain and effort. We forget that it means rest from effort to one who has found the place of his abode. Do notice how Christ said, in effect, "Abide in me; I am the vine that brings forth, and holds, and strengthens, and makes fruitful the branches. Abide in me, rest in me, and let me do my work. I am the true vine, all I am, and speak, and do is divine truth, giving the actual reality of what is said. I am the vine, only consent and yield thy all to me, I will do all in thee."

It sometimes comes that souls who have never been specially occupied with the thought of abiding, are abiding all the time, because they are occupied with Christ. Not that the word abide is not needful. Christ used it so often because it is the essential key to the Christian life. But He would have us understand it in its true sense, as if He himself said, "Come out of every other place, and every other trust and occupation, come out of self with its reasonings and efforts, come and rest in what I shall do. Live out of thyself; abide in me. Know that thou art in me; thou needest no more; remain there in me."

"I am the vine." Christ did not keep this mystery hidden from His disciples. He revealed it first in words here, then in power when the Holy Spirit came down. He will reveal it to us too, first in the thoughts and confessions and desires these words awaken, then in power by the Spirit. Do let us wait on Him to show us all the heavenly meaning of the mystery. Let each day, in our quiet time, in the inner chamber with Him and His Word, our chief thought and aim be to get the heart fixed on Him, in the assurance: all that a vine ever can do for its branches, my Lord Jesus will do, is doing, for me. Give Him time, give Him your ear, that He may whisper and explain the divine secret: "I am the vine."

Above all, remember, Christ is the vine of God's planting, and you are a branch of God's grafting. Ever stand before God, *in Christ*; ever wait for all grace from God, *in Christ*; ever yield yourself to bear the more fruit the husbandman asks, *in Christ*. And pray much for the revelation of the mystery that all the love and power of God that rested on Christ is working in you, too. "I am God's vine," Jesus says to you, "all I am I have from Him, all I am is for you, and God will work it in you."

I am the vine. Blessed Lord, speak that word into my soul. Then will I know that all your fullness is for me. And that I can count upon you to stream it into me, and that my abiding is so easy and so sure when I forget and lose myself in the adoring faith that the vine holds the branch and supplies its every need.

11

YE THE BRANCHES

"I am the vine, ye are the branches" (John 15:5)

Christ had already said much of the branch, and now He comes to the personal application, and says, in effect, "Ye are the branches of whom I have been speaking. As I am the vine, engaged to be and do all the branches need, so I now ask you, in the new dispensation of the Holy Spirit whom I have been promising you, to accept the place I give you, and to be my branches on earth."

The relationship He seeks to establish is an intensely personal one. It all hinges on the two little words *I* and *You*. And it is as intensely personal for us as it was for the first disciples. Let us present ourselves before our Lord until He speaks to each of us in power and our whole soul feels the truth of His words: "I am the vine; you are the branch." Dear disciple of Jesus, however young or feeble, hear His voice: "You are the branch." You must be nothing less. Let no false humility, no carnal fear of sacrifice, no unbelieving doubts as to what you feel able for, keep you back from saying, "I will be a branch, with all that may mean—a branch, very feeble, but yet as like the vine as can be, for I am of the same nature, and receive of the same Spirit. A branch, utterly helpless, and yet just as manifestly set apart before God and people, as wholly given up to the work of bearing fruit, as the vine itself. A branch, nothing in myself, and yet resting and rejoicing in the faith that knows that He will provide for all. Yes, by His grace, I will be nothing less than a branch, and all He means it to be, that through me He may bring forth His fruit."

"You are the branch." You need be nothing more. You need not for one single moment of the day take upon you the responsibility of the vine. You need not leave the place of entire dependence and unbounded confidence. You need,

282

least of all, to be anxious as to how you are to understand the mystery, or fulfill its conditions, or work out its blessed aim. The vine will give all and work all. The Father, the husbandman, watches over your union with and growth in the vine. You need be nothing more than a branch. Only a branch! Let that be your watchword. It will lead in the path of continual surrender to Christ's working, of true obedience to His every command, of joyful expectancy of all His grace. Is there anyone who now asks, "How can I learn to say this correctly, 'Only be a branch!' and to live it out?" Dear soul, the character of a branch, its strength, and the fruit it bears, depend entirely upon the vine. And your life as branch depends entirely upon your understanding of what our Lord Jesus is. Therefore never separate the two words, "I the vine—you the branch." Your life and strength and fruit depend upon what your Lord Jesus is! Therefore worship and trust Him. Let Him be your one desire and the one occupation of your heart. And when you feel that you do not and cannot know Him fully, then just remember it is part of His responsibility as vine to make himself known to you. He does this not in thoughts and conceptions, but in a hidden growth within the life that is humbly and restfully and entirely given up to wait on Him. The vine reveals itself within the branch. Thence comes the growth and fruit. Christ dwells and works within His branch—only be a branch, waiting on Him to do all. He will be to you the true vine. The Father himself, the divine husbandman, is able to make you a branch worthy of the heavenly vine. You will not be disappointed.

Ye are the branches. This word, too Lord! O speak it in power onto my soul. Let not the branch of the earthly vine put me to shame, but as it only lives to bear the fruit of the vine, may my life on earth have no wish or aim, but to let you bring forth fruit through me.

12

MUCH FRUIT

He that abideth in me, and I in him, the same bringeth forth much fruit (John 15:5).

Our Lord had spoken of fruit, more fruit. He now adds the thought of *much fruit*. There is in the vine such fullness, the care of the divine husbandman is so sure of success, that the *much fruit* is not a demand, but the simple promise of what must come to the branch that lives in the double abiding— is he in Christ, and Christ in him. "The same bringeth forth much fruit." It is certain.

Have you ever noticed the difference in the Christian life between work and fruit? A machine can do work, but only life can bear fruit. A law can compel work, but only love can spontaneously bring forth fruit. Work implies effort and labor, but the essential idea of fruit is that it is the silent, natural, and restful produce of our inner life. The gardener may labor to give his apple tree the digging and fertilizing, the watering and the pruning it needs, but he can do nothing to produce the apple. "The fruit of the Spirit is love, peace, joy" (Galatians 5:22).

The healthy life bears much fruit. The connection between work and fruit is perhaps best seen in the expression, "fruitful in every good work" (Colossians 1:10). It is only when good works come as the fruit of the indwelling Spirit that they are acceptable to God. Under the compulsion of law and conscience, or the influence of inclination and zeal, Christians may be most diligent in good works, and yet find that they have but little spiritual result. There can be no reason but this—their works are from their own efforts, instead of being the fruit of the Spirit, the restful and natural outcome of the Spirit's operation within us.

284

Let all workers come and listen to our holy vine as He reveals the law of sure and abundant fruitfulness: "He that abideth in me, and I in him, the same bringeth forth much fruit." The gardener cares for one thing—the strength and healthy life of his tree. When the tree is strong and healthy, the fruit will follow naturally. If you would bear fruit, see that your inner life is perfectly right, and that your relation to Christ Jesus is clear and close. Begin each day with Him, so that you will know in truth that you are abiding in Him and He in you. Christ says that nothing less will do. It is not your willing and running, it is not by your might or strength, but "by my Spirit, saith the Lord" (Zechariah 4:6). Meet each new engagement, undertake every new work, with an ear and heart open to the Lord's voice: "He that abideth in me, beareth much fruit." See to the abiding, and He will see to the fruit, for He will give it in you and through you.

Christian, it is Christ who must do all! The vine provides the sap, the life, and the strength. The branch waits, rests, receives, and bears the fruit. Oh, the blessedness of being only branches through whom the Spirit flows and brings God's life to sinners!

I pray you, take time and ask the Holy Spirit to give you understanding of the unspeakably solemn place you occupy in the mind of God. He has planted you into His Son with the calling and the power to bear much fruit. Accept that place. Look much to God, and to Christ, and expect joyfully to be what God has planned to make you, a fruitful branch.

Much fruit! So be it, blessed Lord Jesus. It can be, for you are the vine. It shall be, for I am abiding in you. It must be, for your Father is the husbandman that cleanses the branch. Yes, much fruit, out of the abundance of your grace.

13

YOU CAN DO NOTHING

"Apart from me ye can do nothing" (John 15:5)

In everything the life of the branch is to be the exact counterpart of that of the vine. Of himself Jesus said, "The Son can do nothing of himself." As the outcome of that entire dependence, He could add, "... what things soever he [the Father] doeth, these also doeth the Son likewise" (John 5:19). As the Son He did not receive His life from the Father once for all, but moment by moment. His life was a continual waiting on the Father for all He was to do. And so Christ says of His disciples, "Ye can do nothing apart from me." He means it literally. To everyone who wants to live the true disciple life, to bring forth fruit and glorify God, the message comes— you can do nothing. What had been said, "He that abideth in me, and I in him, the same beareth much fruit," is here enforced by the simplest and strongest of arguments. The Lord says, in effect, "Abiding in me is indispensable, for of yourselves you can do nothing to maintain or act out the heavenly life."

A deep conviction of the truth of this word lies at the very root of a strong spiritual life. As little as I created myself, as little as I could raise a person from the dead, can I give myself the divine life. As little as I can give it myself, can I maintain or increase it. Every motion is the work of God through Christ and His Spirit. It is as you believe this, that you will take up that position of entire and continual dependence, which is the very essence of the life of faith. With your spiritual eye see Christ every moment supplying grace for every breathing and every deepening of your spiritual life. With your whole heart say *Amen* to the word that says, *You can do nothing.* And just because you do, you can also say: "I can do all things through Christ which strengtheneth me" (Philippians 4:13). The sense of helplessness, and the abiding to which it compels, leads to true fruitfulness and diligence in good works.

"Apart from me ye can do nothing." What a plea and what a call every moment to abide in Christ! We have only to go back to the vine to see how true it is. Look again at that little branch—utterly helpless and fruitless except as it receives sap from the vine—and learn that the full conviction of not being able to do anything apart from Christ is just what you need to teach you to abide in your heavenly vine. It is this that is the great meaning of the pruning Christ spoke of—all that is self must be brought low, that our confidence may be in Christ alone. "Abide in me"—much fruit! "Apart from me"—nothing! Should there be any doubt as to what we shall choose?

The one lesson of the parable is: As surely and naturally as the branch abides in the vine, you can abide in Christ. For this, He is the true vine—for this, God is the husbandman— for this, you are a branch. Shall we not cry to God to deliver us forever from the "apart from me," and to make the "abide in me" an unceasing reality? Let your heart go out to what Christ is and can do, to His divine power and His tender love to each of His branches, and you will say evermore confidently, "Lord! I am abiding; I will bear much fruit. My weakness is my strength. So be it. Apart from you, nothing. In you, much fruit."

Apart from you I am nothing. Lord, I gladly accept the arrangement: I nothing—you everything. My nothingness is my highest blessing, because you are the vine that gives and works everything. So be it, Lord! I, nothing, ever waiting on your fullness. Lord, reveal to me the glory of this blessed life.

287

14

WITHERED BRANCHES

"If a man abide not in me, he is cast forth as a branch, and is withered; and they gather them, and cast them into the fire, and they are burned" (John 15:6)

The lessons these words teach are very simple and very solemn. A person can come to such a connection with Christ, that he counts himself to be in Him, and yet he can be cast forth. There is such a thing as not abiding in Christ, which leads to withering up and burning. There is such a thing as a withered branch, one in whom the initial union with Christ appears to have taken place, and in whom yet it is seen that his faith was but for a time. What a solemn call to look around and see if there are not withered branches in our churches, to look within and see whether we are indeed abiding and bearing fruit. And what may be the cause of this not abiding. With some it is that they never understood how the Christian calling leads to holy obedience and to loving service. They were content with the thought that they had believed and were safe from hell. There was neither motive nor power to abide in Christ—they knew not the need of it. With others it was that the cares of the world, or its prosperity, choked the Word (Mark 4:19). They had never forsaken all to follow Christ. With still others it was that their religion and their faith was in the wisdom of men, and not in the power of God. They trusted in the means of grace, or in their own sincerity, or in the soundness of their faith in justifying grace. They had never sought an entire abiding in Christ as their only safety.

No wonder that when the hot winds of temptation or persecution blew, they withered away. They were not truly rooted in Christ. Let us open our eyes and see if there are not withered branches all around us in the churches. Young men whose confessions were once bright, but who are growing cold. Old men who have retained their profession, but out of whom the measure of life that was once there has died out. Let ministers and believers take Christ's words to heart, and see and ask the Lord whether there is nothing to be done for branches that are beginning to wither. And let the word *abide* ring through the Church until every believer has caught it. There is no safety but in a true abiding in Christ.

Let each of us turn within. Is our life fresh, green, and vigorous, bringing forth its fruit in its season? (See Psalm 1:3, 92: 13-14; Jeremiah 17:7-8.) Let us accept every warning with a willing mind, and let Christ's "if a man abide not" give new urgency to His "abide in me." To the upright soul the secret of abiding will become ever simpler—just the consciousness of the place in which He has put me, just the childlike resting in my union with Him, and just the trustful assurance that He will keep me. Oh, do let us believe there is a life that knows of no withering, that is ever green, and that brings forth fruit abundantly!

Withered! O my Father, watch over me, and keep me, and let nothing ever for a moment hinder the freshness that comes from a full abiding in the vine. Let the very thought of a withered branch fill me with holy fear and watchfulness.

15

WHATSOEVER YE WILL

If ye abide in me, and my words abide in you, ask
whatsoever ye will, and it shall be done unto you
(John 15:7)

The whole place of the branch in the vine is one of
unceasing prayer. Without interruption it is ever calling,
"O my vine, send the sap I need to bear your fruit." And its
prayers are always answered. It asks what it needs, what it
will, and it is done.

The healthy life of the believer in Christ is equally one of
unceasing prayer. Consciously or unconsciously, the believer
lives in continual dependence. The Word of the Lord, "You
can do nothing," has taught that asking and receiving must
not be broken any more than the continuance of the branch
in the vine is broken. The promise of our text gives us infinite
fullness. "Ask whatsoever ye will, and it shall be done unto
you."

The promise is given in direct connection with fruit-
bearing. Limit it to yourself and your own needs, and you rob
it of its, and you rob yourself of the power of appropriating
it. Christ was sending His disciples out, and they were ready
to give their life for the world. So He gave to them the way
to the treasures of Heaven. Their prayers would bring the
Spirit and the power they needed for their work.

The promise is given in direct connection with the coming
of the Spirit. The Spirit is not mentioned in the parable, just
as the sap of the vine is not mentioned. But both are meant
all through. In the chapter preceding the parable, our Lord
had spoken of the Holy Spirit in connection with their inner
life—He would be with them and dwell in them (14:16-17).
In the next chapter He speaks of the Holy Spirit in connection
with their work—He would come to them, convict the world,

and glorify Him (16:7-14). To avail ourselves of the unlimited prayer promises, we must be Christians who are filled with the Spirit, and wholly given up to the work and glory of Jesus. The Spirit will lead us into the truth of its meaning and the certainty of its fulfillment. Let us realize that we can only fulfill our calling to bear much fruit, by praying much. In Christ are hid all the treasures that sinners around us need. In Him all of God's children are blessed with all spiritual blessings. He is full of grace and truth (John 1:14). But it needs prayer, much prayer, strong believing prayer, to bring these blessings down. And let us equally remember that we cannot appropriate the promise without a life given up for others. Many try to take the promise, and then look round for what they can ask. This is not the way, it's the very opposite. Get your heart burdened with the need of souls and the command to save them, and the power will come to claim the promise.

Let us claim it as one of the revelations of our wonderful life in the vine. He tells us that if we ask in His name, in virtue of our union with Him, whatever it is, it will be done for us. Souls are perishing because there is too little prayer. God's children are feeble because there is too little prayer. We bear so little fruit because there is so little prayer. Faith in this promise would make us strong to pray. Let us not rest until it has entered into our heart, and drawn us in the power of Christ to continue to labor and strive in prayer until the blessing comes in power. To be a branch means not only bearing fruit on earth, but power in prayer to bring down blessing from Heaven. Abiding fully means praying much.

"Ask what ye will." O my Lord, why is it that our hearts are so little able to accept these words in their divine simplicity? Oh, help me to see that we need nothing less than this promise to overcome the powers of the world and Satan! Teach us to pray in the faith of this your promise.

16

IF YE ABIDE

*"If ye abide in me, and my words, abide in you, ask
whatsoever ye will, and it shall be done unto you"*
(John 15:7)

The reason the vine and its branches are such a true
parable of the Christian life is that all nature has one source
and breathes one spirit. The plant world was created to be to
us an object lesson teaching us our entire dependence upon
God, and our security in that dependence. He that clothes the
lilies will much more clothe us. He that gives the trees and
the vines their beauty and their fruits, making each what He
meant it to be, will much more certainly make us what He
would have us to be. The only difference is what God works
in the trees is by a power of which they are not conscious.
He wants to work in us with our consent. This is the nobility
of humanity, that we have a will that can cooperate with
God in understanding, approving, and accepting what He
offers to do.

"If ye abide." Here is the difference between the branch
of the natural and the branch of the spiritual vine. The former
abides by force of nature. The latter abides, not by force of
will, but by a divine power given to the consent of the will.
Such is the wonderful provision God has made—what the
power of nature does in the one case, the power of grace will
do in the other. The branch can abide in the vine.

"If ye abide in me ... ask whatsoever ye will." If we are
to live a true prayer life, with the love, power, and experience
of prayer marking it, there must be no question about the
abiding. And if we abide, there need be no question about the
liberty of asking what we will, and the certainty of its being
done. There is the one condition: "If ye abide in me." There

must be no hesitation about the possibility or the certainty of it. We must gaze on that little branch and its wonderful power of bearing such beautiful fruit until we truly learn to abide.

And what is its secret? Be wholly occupied with Jesus. Sink the roots of your being in faith and love and obedience deep down into Him. Come away out of every other place to abide here. Give up everything for the inconceivable privilege of being a branch on earth of the glorified Son of God in Heaven. Let Christ be first. Let Christ be all. Do not be occupied with the abiding—be occupied with Christ! He will hold you, He will keep you abiding in Him. He will abide in you.

"If ye abide in me, and my words abide in you." This He gives as the equivalent of the other expression: "I in you. If my words abide in you" Abide not only in meditation, memory, love, and faith, but all these words entering into your will, your being, and constituting your life. If they transform your character into their own likeness, and you become and are what they speak and mean, ask what you will and it will be done for you. Your words to God in prayer will be the fruit of Christ and His words living in you.

"Ask whatsoever ye will, and it shall be done unto you." Believe in the truth of this promise. Set yourself to be an intercessor for others—a fruit-bearing intercessor, ever calling down more blessing. Such faith and prayer will help you wonderfully to abide wholly and unceasingly.

"If ye abide." Yes, Lord, the power to pray and the power to prevail must depend on this abiding in you. As you are the vine, you are the divine intercessor, who breathes your spirit in us. Oh, for grace to abide simply and wholly in you, and ask great things!

17

THE FATHER GLORIFIED

"Herein is my Father glorified, that ye bear much fruit"
(John 15:8)

How can we glorify God? Not by adding to His glory or bringing Him any new glory that He has not. But simply by allowing His glory to shine out through us, by yielding ourselves to Him, that His glory may manifest itself in us and through us to the world. In a vineyard or a vine bearing much fruit, the owner is glorified, as it tells of his skill and care. In the disciple who bears much fruit, the Father is glorified. Before men and angels, proof is given of the glory of God's grace and power. God's glory shines out through the disciple. This is what Peter means when he writes, "if any man minister, let him do it as of the ability which God giveth: that God in all things may be glorified through Jesus Christ" (1 Peter 4:11). As a Christian works and serves in a power that comes from God alone, God gets all the glory. When we confess that the ability came from God alone, the one who does the work, and they who see it, equally glorify God. It was God who did it. People judge by the fruit of a garden of what the gardener is. People judge of God by the fruit that the branches of the vine of His planting bears. Little fruit brings little glory to God. It brings no honor to either the vine or the husbandman. "Herein is my Father glorified, that ye bear much fruit."

We have sometimes mourned our lack of fruit as a loss to ourselves and to others, with complaints of our feebleness as the cause. Let us rather think of the sin and shame of little fruit as robbing God of the glory He should get from us. Let us learn the secret of bringing glory to God, serving with the ability that God gives. The full acceptance of Christ's words,

"You can do nothing"; the simple faith in God, who works all in all; the abiding in Christ through whom the divine husbandman does His work and gets much fruit—this is the life that will bring glory to God.

"Much fruit." God asks for it, see that you give it. God can be content with nothing less, so you be content with nothing less. Let these words of Christ—*fruit, more fruit, much fruit*—abide in you until you think as He does. Be prepared to take from Him, the heavenly vine, what He has for you. *Much fruit: herein is my Father glorified.* Let the very height of the demand be your encouragement. It is so entirely beyond your power that it throws you entirely upon Christ, your true vine. He can, He will, make it true in you. God asks for much fruit because He needs much fruit. He does not ask fruit from the branches of His vine for show, to prove what He can do. No, He needs it for the salvation of sinners—it is in that He is to be glorified. Throw yourself in much prayer on your vine and your husbandman. Cry to your God and Father to give you fruit to bring to others. Take the burden of the hungry and the perishing on you—as Jesus did when He was moved with compassion—and your power in prayer, and your abiding, and your bearing much fruit to the glory of the Father will have a reality and a certainty you never knew before.

"The Father glorified." Blessed prospect—God glorifying himself in me, showing forth the glory of His goodness and power in what He works in me, and through me. What a motive to bear much fruit, just as much as He works in me! Father, glorify yourself in me.

18

TRUE DISCIPLES

*Herein is my Father glorified, that ye bear much fruit: so
shall ye be my disciples* (John 15:8)

Are those who do not bear *much fruit* not disciples?
They may be, but in a backward and immature stage. Of
those who bear much fruit, Christ says, in effect, "These are
my disciples, such as I would have them be—these are true
disciples." Just as we say of someone in whom the idea of
manliness is realized: That is a man! So our Lord tells who
are disciples after His heart, worthy of the name: *Those
who bear much fruit.* We find this double sense of the word
disciple in the Gospel. Sometimes it is applied to all who
accepted Christ's teaching. At other times it includes only
the inner circle of those who followed Christ wholly, and
gave themselves to His training for service. The difference
has existed throughout all ages. There have always been a
smaller number of God's people who have sought to serve
Him with their whole heart, while the majority have been
content with a very small measure of the knowledge of His
grace and will.

And what is the difference between this smaller inner
circle and the many who do not seek admission to it? We
find it in the words *much fruit.* With many Christians the
thought of personal safety, which at their first awakening
was a legitimate one, remains to the end the one aim of their
religion. The idea of service and fruit is always a secondary
and very subordinate one. The honest longing for much fruit
does not trouble them. Souls that have heard the call to live
wholly for their Lord, to give their life for Him as He gave
His for them, can never be satisfied with this. Their cry is

to bear as much fruit as they possibly can, as much as their Lord ever can desire or give in them.

"Bear much fruit: so shall ye be My disciples" Let me beg you to consider these words most seriously. Do not be content with the thought of gradually doing a little more or better work. In this way it may never come. Take the words, *much fruit*, as the revelation of your heavenly vine of what you must be, of what you can be. Accept fully the impossibility, the utter folly of attempting it in your strength. Let the words call you to look anew upon the vine, an undertaking to live out its heavenly fullness in you. Let them awaken in you once again the faith and the confession, "I am a branch of the true vine. I can bear much fruit to His glory, and the glory of my Father."

We need not judge others. But we see in God's Word everywhere two classes of disciples. Let there be no hesitation as to where we take our place. Let us ask Him to reveal to us how He asks and claims a life wholly given up to Him, to be as full of His Spirit as He can make us. Let our desire be nothing less than perfect cleansing, unbroken abiding, closest communion, abundant fruitfulness—true branches of the true vine.

The world is perishing, the Church is failing, Christ's cause is suffering, Christ is grieving on account of the lack of wholehearted Christians, bearing much fruit. Though you scarce see what it implies or how it is to come, say to Him that you are His branch to bear much fruit, and that you are ready to be His disciple in His own meaning of the word.

"My disciples." Blessed Lord, much fruit is the proof that you the true vine has in me a true branch, a disciple wholly at your disposal. Give me, I pray you, the childlike consciousness that my fruit is pleasing to you, what you consider much fruit.

19

THE WONDERFUL LOVE

"Even as the Father hath loved me, I also have loved you"
(John 15:9)

Here Christ leaves the language of parable, and speaks plainly of the Father. Much as the parable could teach, it could not teach the lesson of love. All that the natural vine does for the branch, it does under the compulsion of a law of nature. There is no personal living love to the branch. We are in danger of looking to Christ as a Savior and a supplier of every need, appointed by God, accepted and trusted by us, without any sense of the intensity of personal affection in which Christ embraces us, and in which alone our life can find its true happiness. Christ seeks to point us to this. And how does He do so? He leads us once again to himself, to show us how identical His own life is with ours. Even as the Father loved Him, He loves us. His life as a vine dependent on the Father was a life in the Father's love. That love was His strength and His joy. In the power of that divine love resting on Him He lived and died. If we are to live like Him, as branches to be truly like our vine, we must share in this, too. Our life must have its breath and being in a heavenly love as much as His. What the Father's love was to Him, His love will be to us. If that love made Him the true vine, His love can make us true branches. "Even as the Father hath loved me, I also have loved you."

"Even as the Father hath loved Me." And how did the Father love Him? The infinite desire and delight of God to communicate to the Son all He had himself, to take the Son into the most complete equality with himself, to live in the Son and have the Son live in Him—this was the love of God to Christ. It is a mystery of glory of which we can form no

298

conception, we can only bow and worship as we try to think of it. And with such a love, with this very same love, Christ longs in an infinite desire and delight to communicate to us all He is and has, to make us partakers of His own nature and blessedness, to live in us and have us live in Him. And now, if Christ loves us with such an intense, such an infinite divine love, what is it that hinders it triumphing over every obstacle and getting full possession of us? The answer is simple. Even as the love of the Father to Christ, so His love to us is a divine mystery, too high for us to comprehend or attain to by any effort of our own. It is only the Holy Spirit who can shed abroad and reveal—in its all-conquering power without interruption —this wonderful love of God in Christ. It is the vine itself that must give the branch its growth and fruit by sending up its sap. It is Christ who must by His Holy Spirit dwell in the heart. Then we shall know and have in us the love that passes all understanding.

"As the Father loved me, so have I loved you." Shall we not draw near to the personal living Christ, and trust Him, and yield all to Him, that He may love this love into us? Just as He knew and rejoiced every hour—the Father loves me— we too may live in the unceasing consciousness that as the Father loved Him, so Christ loves us.

"As the Father loved me, so have I loved you." Dear Lord, I am only beginning to understand how exactly the life of the vine is to be that of the branch, too. You are the vine, because the Father loved you, and poured His love through you. And so you love me, and my life as branch is to be like yours, a receiving and a giving out of heavenly love.

20

ABIDE IN MY LOVE

"Even as the Father hath loved me, I also have loved you: abide ye in my love" (John 15:9).

"Abide ye in My love." We speak of a man's home as his abode. Our abode, the home of our soul, is to be the love of Christ. We are to live our life there, to be at home there all the day. This is what Christ means our life to be, and what He really can make it. Our continuous abiding in the vine is to be an abiding in His love. You have probably heard or read of what is called *the higher* or *the deeper life*, of *the richer* or *the fuller life*, of *the life abundant*. And you possibly know that some have told of a wonderful change by which their life of continual failure and stumbling had been changed into a very blessed experience of being kept and strengthened and made exceeding glad. If you asked them how it was this great blessing came to them, many would tell you it was simply this—that they were led to believe that this abiding in Christ's love was meant to be a reality, and that they were made willing to give up everything for it, and then enabled to trust Christ to make it true to them.

The love of the Father to the Son is not a sentiment—it is a divine life, an infinite energy, an irresistible power. It carried Christ through life and death and the grave. The Father loved Him and dwelt in Him, and did all for Him. So the love of Christ to us, too, is an infinite living power that will work in us all He delights to give us. The feebleness of our Christian life is that we do not take time to believe that this divine love does really delight in us, and will possess and work all in us. We do not take time to look at the vine bearing the branch so entirely, working all in it so completely. We strive to do for ourselves what Christ alone can, what Christ—oh, so lovingly—longs to do for us.

This is the secret of the change we spoke of, and the beginning of a new life—the soul seeing this infinite love willing to do all, and giving itself up to it. "Abide ye in my love." To believe that it is possible so to live moment by moment, to believe that everything that makes it difficult or impossible will be overcome by Christ himself, to believe that love really means an infinite longing to give itself wholly to us and never leave us, and in this faith to cast ourselves on Christ to work it in us—this is the secret of the true Christian life. How can we come to this faith? Turn away from the visible if you would see and possess the invisible. Take more time with Jesus, gazing on Him as the heavenly vine, living in the love of the Father, wanting you to live in His love.

Turn away from yourself and your efforts if you would have your heart filled with Him and the certainty of His love. Abiding means going out from everything else to occupy one place and stay there. Come away from all else, and set your heart on Jesus and His love. That love will awaken your faith and strengthen it. Occupy yourself with that love, worship it, wait for it. You may be sure it will reach out to you, and by its power take you up into itself as your abode and your home.

"Abide in my love." Lord Jesus, I see it, it was you abiding in your Father's love that made you the true vine, with your divine fullness of love and blessing for us. Oh, that I may even so, as a branch, abide in your love, for its fullness to fill me and overflow on all around.

21

OBEY AND ABIDE

"If ye keep my commandments, ye shall abide in my love"
(John 15:10).

In our former meditation, reference was made to the entrance into a life of rest and strength that has often come through a true insight into the personal love of Christ, and the assurance that that love indeed meant that He would keep the soul. In connection with that transition, and the faith that sees and accepts it, the word *surrender* or *consecration* is frequently used. The soul sees that it cannot claim the keeping of this wonderful love unless it yields itself to a life of entire obedience. It sees, too, that the faith that can trust Christ for keeping it from sinning must prove its sincerity by venturing at once to trust Him for strength to obey. In that faith it dares to give up and cut off everything that has hitherto hindered it, and to promise and expect to live a life that is well pleasing to God.

This is the thought we have here now in our Savior's teaching. After having in the words, "Abide in my love," spoken of a life in His love as a necessity, because it is at once a possibility and an obligation, He states what its one condition is: "If ye keep my commandments, ye shall abide in my love." This is surely not meant to close the door to the abode of His love that He had just opened up. Not in the most distant way does it suggest the thought that some are too ready to entertain—that since we cannot keep His commandments, we cannot abide in His love. No, the precept is a promise. "Abide in my love" could not be a precept if it were not a promise. So the instruction as to the way through this open door points to an attainable ideal. The love that invites to her blessed abode reaches out the hand, and enables us to keep the commandments. Let us not fear, in the strength of our ascended Lord, to take the vow of obedience, and give ourselves to the keeping of His commandments. Through His will, loved and done, lies the path to His love.

Only let us understand well what it means. It refers to our performance of all that we know to be God's will. There may be things doubtful, of which we are not sure. A sin of ignorance has still the nature of sin in it. There may be involuntary sins, which rise up in the flesh, which we cannot control or overcome. With regard to these God will deal in due time in the way of searching and humbling, and if we are simple and faithful, give us larger deliverance than we dare expect. But all this may be found in a truly obedient soul. Obedience has reference to the positive keeping of the commandments of our Lord, and the performance of His will in everything in which we know it. This is a possible degree of grace, and it is the acceptance in Christ's strength of such obedience as the purpose of our heart, of which our Savior speaks here. Faith in Christ as our vine, in His enabling and sanctifying power, fits us for this obedience of faith, and secures a life of abiding in His love.

"If ye keep My commandments, ye shall abide in My love" It is the heavenly vine unfolding the mystery of the life He gives. It is to those abiding in Him to whom He opens up the secret of the full abiding in His love. It is the wholehearted surrender in everything to do His will that gives access to a life in the abiding enjoyment of His love.

Obey and abide. Gracious Lord, teach me the lesson that it is only through knowing your will that one can know your heart, and it is only through doing your will that one can abide in your love. Lord, teach me that as worthless as is the doing in my own strength, so essential and absolutely indispensable is the doing of faith in your strength, if I would abide in your love.

303

22

YE, EVEN AS I

*"If ye keep my commandments, ye shall abide in my love,
even as I have kept my Father's commandments,
and abide in His love"* (John 15:10).

We have had occasion more than once to speak of the perfect similarity of the vine and the branch in nature, and therefore in purpose. Here Christ speaks no longer in a parable, but tells us plainly of how His own life is the exact model of ours. He had said that it is by obedience alone that we can abide in His love. He now tells that this was the way in which He abode in the Father's love.

As the vine, so the branch. His life, strength, and joy had been in the love of the Father, but it was only by obedience that He abode in it. We may find our life, strength, and joy in His love all the day, but it is only by an obedience like His that we can abide in it. Perfect conformity to the vine is one of the most precious of the lessons of the branch. It was by obedience that Christ as the vine honored the Father as the husbandman. In the same way, it is by obedience that the believer as the branch honors Christ as the vine.

Obey and abide. That was the law of Christ's life as much as it is to be that of ours. He was made like us in all things, that we might be like Him in all things. He opened up a path in which we may walk even as He walked. He took our human nature to teach us how to wear it, and show us how obedience, since it is the first duty of the creature, is the only way to abide in the favor of God and enter into His glory. Now He comes to instruct and encourage us, and asks us to keep His commandments, even as He kept His Father's commandments and abides in His love.

The divine fitness of this connection between obeying and abiding, between God's commandments and His love, is easily seen. God's will is the very center of His divine perfection. As revealed in His commandments, it opens up the way for the creature to grow into the likeness of the Creator. In accepting and doing His will, I rise into fellowship with Him. Therefore, when the Son came into the world He said, "I come to do thy will, O God" (Hebrews 10:9). This was the place and this would restore the blessings of God's abiding love to the creature. This was what was lost in the Fall. This was what Christ came to restore. This is what, as the heavenly vine, He asks of us and imparts to us, that even as He by keeping His Father's commandments abode in His love, we should keep His commandments and abide in His love.

"Ye, ... even as I" The branch cannot bear fruit except as it has exactly the same life as the vine. Our life is to be the exact counterpart of Christ's life. It will be to the same measure that we believe in Him as the vine imparting himself and His life to His branches. "Ye, ... even as I," the vine says: one law, one nature, one fruit. Do let us take from our Lord the lesson of obedience as the secret of abiding. Let us confess that simple, implicit, universal obedience has too little taken the place it should have. Christ died for us as enemies, when we were disobedient. He took us up into His love. Now that we are in Him, His word to us is, "Obey and abide; ye, even as I." Let us give ourselves to a willing and loving obedience. He will keep us abiding in His love.

"Ye, even as I." O my blessed vine, who make the branch in everything partake of your life and likeness, in this, too, I am to be like you. As your life is in the Father's love through obedience, so mine is in your love. Savior, help me, that obedience may indeed be the link between you and me.

305

23

JOY

"These things have I spoken unto you, that my joy may be in you, and that your joy may be fulfilled" (John 15:11).

If any one asks the question, "How can I be a happy Christian?" our Lord's answer is very simple. He says, "these things" about the vine and the branches, "have I spoken to you, that my joy may be in you, and that your joy may be fulfilled." He says, in effect, "You cannot have my joy without my life. Abide in me, and let me abide in you, and my joy will be in you." All healthy life is a thing of joy and beauty. Live fully the branch life, and you will have His joy in full measure.

To many Christians, the thought of a life wholly abiding in Christ is one of strain and painful effort. They cannot see that the strain and effort only come as long as we do not yield ourselves unreservedly to the life of Christ in us. The meaning of the very first words of the parable have not yet opened up to them. "I am the true vine. I undertake everything and provide for everything. I ask nothing of the branch but that it yields wholly to me, and allows me to do everything. I work to make and keep the branch all that it ought to be." Should it not be an infinite and unceasing joy to have the vine thus work everything, and to know that it is the blessed Son of God in His love who is each moment bearing us and maintaining our life?

"That my joy may be in you." We are to have Christ's own joy in us. What is Christ's own joy? There is no joy like love. There is no joy but love. Christ had just spoken of the Father's love and His own abiding in it, and of His having loved us with that same love. His joy is nothing but the joy of love, of being loved and of loving. It was the joy of receiving His Father's love and abiding in it, and then the joy of passing on that love and pouring it out on sinners. It is this joy He wants us to share. The joy of being loved by the Father and by Him. The joy of, in our turn, loving and living for those around us. This is just the joy of being truly branches. Abiding in His love and then giving up ourselves in love to bear fruit for others. Let us accept His life as He gives it in us as the vine, His joy will be ours—the joy of abiding in His love, the joy of loving like Him, of loving with His love.

"And that your joy may be fulfilled." That it may be complete, that you may be filled with it. How sad that we should so need to be reminded that as God alone is the fountain of all joy, "God my exceeding joy" (Psalm 43:4), the only way to be perfectly happy is to have as much of God, as much of His will and fellowship, as possible. Religion is meant to be in everyday life a thing of unspeakable joy. Why do so many complain that it is not? Because they do not believe that there is no joy like the joy of abiding in Christ and in His love, and being branches through whom He can pour out His love on a dying world. Oh, that Christ's voice might reach the heart of all young Christians and persuade them to believe that His joy is the only true joy, that His joy can become ours and truly fill us, and that the sure and simple way of living in it is to abide as branches in Him our heavenly vine. Let the truth enter deep into us—as long as our joy is not full, it is a sign that we do not yet know our heavenly vine correctly. Every desire for a fuller joy must move us forward to abide more simply and more fully in His love.

My joy—your joy. In this, too, it is as the vine so the branch. All the vine in the branch. Your joy is our joy. Your joy in us, and our joy fulfilled. Blessed Lord, fill me with your joy—the joy of being loved and blessed with a divine love, the joy of loving and blessing others.

24

LOVE ONE ANOTHER

"This is my commandment, that ye love one another"
(John 15:12).

God is love. His whole nature and perfection is love,
living not for himself, but to dispense life and blessing. In His
love He brought forth the Son, that He might give everything
to Him. In His love He brought forth creatures that He might
make them partakers of His holiness (Hebrews 12:10).

Christ is the Son of God's love, the bearer, the revealer,
the communicator of that love. His life and death were all
love. Love is His life, and the life He gives. He only lives to
love, to live out His life of love in us, to give himself in all
who will receive Him. The very first thought of the true vine
is love—and living only to impart His life to the branches.

The Holy Spirit is the Spirit of love. He cannot impart
Christ's life without imparting His love. Salvation is nothing
but love conquering and entering into us. We have just as
much of salvation as we have of love. Full salvation is perfect
love.

No wonder that Christ said, "A new commandment I
give unto you, That ye love one another; as I have loved you,
that ye also love one another." (John 13:34). The branch is
not only one with the vine, but with all its other branches.
They drink one spirit, they form one body, they bear one
fruit. Nothing can be more unnatural than that Christians
should not love one another, even as Christ loved them. The
life they received from their heavenly vine is nothing but love.
This is the one thing He asks above all others. "By this shall
all men know that ye are my disciples, if ye have love one to
another" (John 13:35). As the special sort of vine is known

by the fruit it bears, the nature of the heavenly vine is to be judged by the love His disciples have for one another.

See that you obey this commandment. Let your *obey and abide* be seen in this. Love your brethren as the way to abide in the love of your Lord. Let your vow of obedience begin here. Love one another. Let your relationships with the Christians in your own family be holy, tender, Christ-like love. Let your thoughts of the Christians around you be, before everything else, in the spirit of Christ's love. Let your life and conduct be the sacrifice of love. Give yourself up to think of their sins or their needs, to intercede for them, to help and to serve them. Be in your church or circle the embodiment of Christ's love. The life Christ lives in you is love. Let the life in which you live it out be all love. You say, "But you write as if all this was so natural and simple and easy. Is it at all possible thus to live and thus to love?" My answer is: Christ commands it, you must obey. Christ means it. So you must obey or you cannot abide in His love.

"But I have tried," you say, "and failed. I see no possibility of living like Christ." That is because you have failed to take in the first words of the parable. In essence, "I am the true vine. I give all you need as a branch, I give all that I have." I pray you, let the sense of past failure and present feebleness drive you to the vine. He is all love. He loves to give. He gives love. He will teach you to love, even as He loved.

Love one another. Dear Lord Jesus, you are all love. The life you gave us is love. Your new commandment, and your badge of discipleship is, "Love one another." I accept the charge. With the love with which you love me and I love you, I will love my brethren.

25

EVEN AS I HAVE LOVED YOU

"This is my commandment, that ye love one another, even as I have loved you" (John 15:12).

This is the second time our Lord uses the expression "even as I." The first time it was of His relation to the Father, keeping His commandments, and abiding in His love. Even so we are to keep Christ's commandments and abide in His love. The second time He speaks of His relation to us as the rule of our love to our brothers and sisters: "Love one another, as I have loved you." In each case His disposition and conduct is to be the law for ours. It is again the truth we have more than once insisted on, which is perfect likeness between the vine and the branch.

"Even as I." But is it not a vain thing to imagine that we can keep His commandments and love all Christians, even as He kept His Father's, and as He loved us? And must not the attempt end in failure and discouragement? Undoubtedly, if we seek to carry out the injunction in our strength, or without a full apprehension of the truth of the vine and its branches. But if we understand that the "even as I" is just the one great lesson of the parable, the one continual language of the vine to the branch, we will see that it is not the question of what we feel able to accomplish, but of what Christ is able to work in us.

These high and holy commands—"Obey, even as I, Love, even as I"—are just meant to bring us to the consciousness of our inability, and through that to waken us to the need, beauty, and sufficiency of what is provided for us in the vine. We shall begin to hear the vine speaking every moment to the branch: "Even as I. Even as I. My life is your life, and you have a share in all my fullness. The Spirit is in you, and the fruit that comes from you is just the same as the fruit that comes from me. Do not be afraid, but let your faith grasp each "even as I" as the divine assurance that because I live in you, you may and can live like me."

But if this really is the meaning of the parable, if this really is the life a branch may live, why do so few realize it? Because they do not know the heavenly mystery of the vine. They know much of the parable and its beautiful lessons. But the hidden spiritual mystery of the vine in His divine omnipotence and nearness, bearing and supplying them all the day. This they do not know, because they have not waited on God's Spirit to reveal it to them.

"Love one another, even as I have loved you." How are we to begin if we are really to learn the mystery? We begin with the confession that we need to be brought to an entirely new mode of life, because we have never yet known Christ as the vine in the completeness of His quickening and transforming power. We have surrendered to be cleansed from all that is of self, and to be detached from all that is in the world, so that we may live only and wholly as Christ lived for the glory of the Father. Then with the faith that this "even as I" is indeed what Christ is ready to make true, the vine will maintain the life in the branch that is wholly dependent upon Him. "Even as I." Ever again it is, my blessed Lord, as the vine so the branch—one life, one spirit, one obedience, one joy, one love.

Lord Jesus, in the faith that you are my vine, and that I am your branch, I accept your command as a promise, and take your "even as I" as the simple revelation of what you work in me. Yes, Lord, as you have loved, I will love.

311

26

CHRIST'S FRIENDSHIP: ITS ORIGIN

"Greater love hath no man than this, that a man lay down his life for his friends" (John 15:13).

In the three verses of John 15:13-15, our Lord speaks of His relation to His disciples under a new aspect—that of friendship. He points us to the love from which friendship on His side has its origin (v.13), to the obedience on our part by which it is maintained (v.14), and then to the holy intimacy to which it leads (v.15).

Our relation to Christ is one of love. In speaking of this previously, He showed us what His love was in its heavenly glory—the same love with which the Father had loved Him. Here we have it in its earthly manifestation—He laid down His life for us. "Greater love hath no man than this, that a man lay down his life for his friends." Christ does indeed long to have us know that the secret root and strength of all He is and does for us as the vine is love. As we learn to believe this, we will feel that here is something that we not only need to think and know about, but a living power, a divine life that we need to receive within us. Christ and His love are inseparable; they are identical. God is love, and Christ is love. God and Christ and the divine love can only be known by having them, by their life and power working within us. "This is eternal life, that they know thee" (John 17:3). There is no knowing God but by having the life. The life working in us alone gives the knowledge. It is the same with the love. If we would know it, we must drink of its living stream, we must have it shed forth by the Holy Spirit in us.

"Greater love hath no man than this, that a man lay down his life for his friends." The life is the most precious thing a man has. The life is all he is. The life is himself. Sacrificing your life is the highest measure of love. When a man gives his life, he holds nothing back, he gives all he has and is. It is this our Lord Jesus wants to make clear to us concerning His mystery of the vine—with all He has He has placed himself at our disposal. He wants us to count Him our very own. He wants to be wholly our possession, that we may be wholly His possession. He gave His life for us in death not merely as a passing act that when accomplished was done with, but as making himself ours for eternity. Life for life; He gave His life for us to possess that we might give our life for Him to possess. This is what is taught by the parable of the vine and the branch, in their wonderful identification, in their perfect union.

It is when we know something of this, not by reason or imagination, but deep down in the heart and life, that we shall begin to see what should be our life as branches of the heavenly vine. He gave himself to death. He lost himself that we might find life in Him. This is the true vine, who only lives to live in us. This is the beginning and the root of that holy friendship to which Christ invites us.

Great is the mystery of godliness! Let us confess our ignorance and unbelief. Let us cease from our own understanding and our own efforts to master it. Let us wait for the Holy Spirit who dwells within us to reveal it. Let us trust His infinite love, which gave its life for us, to take possession and rejoice in making us wholly its own.

His life for His friends. How wonderful the lessons of the vine, giving its very life to its branches. And Jesus gave His life for His friends. And that love gives itself to them and in them. My heavenly vine, teach me how wholly you long to live in me.

27

CHRIST'S FRIENDSHIP: ITS ORIGIN

"Ye are my friends, if ye do whatsoever I command you"
(John 15:14).

Our Lord has said what He gave as proof of His friendship: He gave His life for us. He now tells us what our part is to be—to do the things that He commands. He gave His life to secure a place for His love in our hearts to rule us. The response His love calls us to, and empowers us for, is that we do what He commands us. As we know the love for which he died, we shall joyfully obey its commands. As we obey the commands, we shall know the love more fully. Christ had already said, "If ye keep my commandments, ye shall abide in my love." He considers it necessary to repeat the truth again. The one proof of our faith in His love, the one way to abide in it, the one mark of being true branches is, to do the things that He commands us. He began with absolute surrender of His life for us. He can ask nothing less from us. This alone is a life in His friendship. This truth, of the imperative necessity of obedience, doing all that Christ commands us, has not the place in our Christian teaching and living that Christ meant it to have. We have given a far higher place to privilege than to duty. We have not considered implicit obedience as a condition of true discipleship.

The secret thought that it is impossible to do the things He commands us, and that therefore it cannot be expected of us—and a subtle and unconscious feeling that sinning is a necessity—have frequently robbed both precepts and promises of their power. Our whole relationship to Christ has become clouded and lowered. The waiting on His teaching, the power to hear and obey His voice, and through obedience to enjoy His love and friendship, have been weakened by the terrible mistake. Do let us try to return to the true position, take Christ's words as most literally true, and make nothing less the law of our life then, "Ye are my friends, if ye do whatsoever I command you." Surely our Lord asks nothing less than that we heartily and truthfully say, "Yes, Lord, what you command, that will I do."

These commands are to be done as a proof of friendship. The power to do them rests entirely in our personal relationship to Jesus. For a friend I would do what I would not for another. The friendship of Jesus is so heavenly and wonderful, it comes to us as the power of a divine love entering in and taking possession. The unbroken fellowship with Him is so essential to it, that it implies and imparts a joy and a love that make the obedience a delight. The liberty to claim the friendship of Jesus, the power to enjoy it, the grace to prove it in all its blessedness—all come as we do the things He commands us.

Is not the one thing needful for us that we ask our Lord to reveal himself to us in the dying-love by which He proved himself our friend, and then listen as He says to us, "you are my friends." As we see what our friend has done for us, and what unspeakable blessedness it is to have Him call us friends, the doing His commands will become the natural fruit of our life in His love. We will not fear to say, "Yes, Lord, we are your friends, and we do whatsoever you command us."

"If ye do." Yes, it is in doing that we are blessed, that we abide in His love, that we enjoy His friendship. "If ye do whatsoever I command you."

Oh, my Lord, let your holy friendship lead me into the love of all your commands, and let the doing of your commands lead me ever deeper into your friendship.

315

28

CHRIST'S FRIENDSHIP: ITS INTIMACY

"Henceforth I call you not servants; for the servant knoweth not what his lord doeth: but I have called you friends; for all things that I heard of my Father I have made known unto you" (John 15:15).

The highest proof of true friendship, and one great source of its blessedness, is the intimacy that holds nothing back, and admits the friend to share our inmost secrets. It is a blessed thing to be Christ's servant. His redeemed ones delight to call themselves His slaves. Christ had often spoken of the disciples as His servants. In His great love our Lord now says, in effect, "No longer do I call you servants." With the coming of the Holy Spirit a new era was to be inaugurated. "The servant knoweth not what his Lord doeth" The servant has to obey without being consulted or admitted into the secret of all his master's plans. "But I have called you friends, for all things that I heard from my Father, I have made known unto you." Christ's friends share with Him in all the secrets the Father has entrusted to Him.

Let us think what this means. When Christ spoke of keeping His Father's commandments, He did not mean merely what was written in Holy Scripture, but those special commandments that were communicated to Him day by day, and from hour to hour. It was of these He said, "For the Father loveth the Son, and sheweth him all things that himself doeth: and he will shew him greater works than these" (John 5:20). All that Christ did was God's working: "... the Father that dwelleth in me, he doeth the works" (John 14:10). God showed it to Christ so that He could carry out the Father's will and purpose with full understanding and approval, and not as man often does, blindly and unintelligently. As one who stood in God's counsel, He knew God's plan. This now is the blessedness of being Christ's friends. We do not, as servants, do His will with little spiritual insight into its meaning and aim, but as an inner circle are admitted into some knowledge of God's more secret thoughts. From the day of Pentecost on, Christ was to lead His disciples by the Holy Spirit into the spiritual apprehension of the mysteries of the kingdom, of which He had hitherto spoken only by parables.

Friendship delights in fellowship. Friends hold council. Friends dare trust to each other what they would not for anything have others know. What is it that gives a Christian access to this holy intimacy with Jesus? That gives him the spiritual capacity for receiving the communications Christ has to make of what the Father has shown Him? "Ye are my friends, if ye do whatsoever I command you." It is loving obedience that purifies the soul. That refers not only to the commandments of the Word, but to that blessed application of the Word to our daily life, which none but our Lord himself can give. But as these are waited for in dependence and humility and faithfully obeyed, the soul becomes prepared for ever closer fellowship, and the daily life may become a continual experience:

"I have called you friends; for all things that I have heard of my Father I have made known unto you."

I have called you friends. What an unspeakable honor! What a heavenly privilege! O Savior, speak the word with power into my soul: "I have called you my friend, whom I love, whom I trust, to whom I make known all that passes between my Father and me."

29

ELECTION

"Ye did not choose me, but I chose you, and appointed you that ye should go and bear fruit" (John 15:16).

The branch does not choose the vine, or decide on which vine it will grow. The vine brings forth the branch, when it will and where it will. Even so Christ says, "Ye did not choose me, but I chose you." But some will say is not the difference between the branch in the natural and in the spiritual world the fact that man has a will and the power to choose, and that it is in virtue of his having decided to accept Christ, his having chosen Him as Lord, that he is now a branch? This is undoubtedly true. Yet it is only half a truth. The lesson of the vine, and the teaching of our Lord, points to the other half, the deeper and divine side of our being in Christ. If He had not chosen us, we would never choose Him. Our choosing Him was the result of His choosing us, and taking hold of us. In the very nature of things, it is His prerogative as vine to choose and create His own branch. We owe all we are to *the election of grace.* If we want to know Christ as the true vine, the sole origin and strength of the branch life, and ourselves as branches in our absolute, most blessed, and most secure dependence upon Him, let us drink deep of this blessed truth: "Ye did not choose me, but I chose you."

Why does Christ say this? That they may know what the object is for which He chose them, and find, in their faith in His election, the certainty of fulfilling their destiny. Throughout Scripture this is the great object of the teaching of election. "He also did predestinate us to be conformed to the image of His Son" (to be branches in the image and likeness of the vine) (Romans 8:29). "Chosen ... that we should be holy" (Ephesians 1:4). "Chosen to salvation through sanctification of the Spirit" (2 Thessalonians 2:13). "Elect according to ... sanctification of the Spirit, unto obedience" (1 Peter 1:2). Some have abused the doctrine of election, and others, for fear of its abuse, have rejected it because they have overlooked this teaching. They have occupied themselves with its hidden origin in eternity, with the inscrutable mysteries of the counsels of God, instead of accepting the revelation of its purpose in time and the blessings it brings into our Christian life.

Just think what these blessings are. In our verse, Christ reveals His twofold purpose in choosing us to be His branches: that we may bear fruit on earth, and have power in prayer in Heaven. What confidence the thought that He has chosen us for this gives. Because he has chosen us, He will not fail to prepare us for carrying out His purpose. What assurance that we can bear fruit that will abide, and can pray so as to obtain. What a continual call to the deepest humility and praise, to the most entire dependence and expectancy. He would not choose us for what we are not prepared for, or what He could not prepare us for. He has chosen us; therefore, it is certain that He will do everything in us.

Let us listen in silence of soul to our holy vine saying to each of us, "You did not choose me." And let us reply, "Yes, Lord, but you chose me. Amen, Lord." Ask Him to show what this means. In Him, the true vine, your life as a branch has its divine origin, its eternal security, and the power to fulfill His purpose. From Him to whose will of love you owe all, you may expect all. In Him, His purpose, His power, His faithfulness, and His love let me abide.

"I chose you." Lord, teach me what it means that you have set your heart on me, and chosen me to bear fruit that will abide, and to pray prayers that will prevail. In this, your eternal purpose, my soul would rest itself and say, "What He chose me for I will be. I can be. I shall be."

30

ABIDING FRUIT

"I chose you, and appointed you, that ye should go and bear fruit, and that your fruit should abide" (John 15:16).

There are some fruits that will not keep. One sort of pears or apples must be used at once but another sort can be kept over till next year. So there is in Christian work some fruit that does not last. There may be much that pleases and edifies, and yet there is no permanent impression made on the power of the world or the state of the Church. On the other hand, there is work that leaves its mark for generations or for eternity. In it the power of God makes itself lastingly felt. It is the fruit of which Paul speaks when he describes the two styles of ministry: "And my speech and my preaching was not with enticing words of man's wisdom, but in demonstration of the Spirit and of power: That your faith should not stand in the wisdom of men, but in the power of God." (1 Corinthians 2: 4-5). The more of man with his wisdom and power, the less of stability. The more of God's Spirit, the more of a faith standing in God's power.

Fruit reveals the nature of the tree from which it comes. What is the secret of bearing fruit that abides? The answer is simple. It is as our life abides in Christ, as we abide in Him, that the fruit we bear will abide. The more we allow all that is of human will and effort to be cut down short and cleansed away by the divine husbandman, the more intensely our being withdraws itself from the outward that God may work in us by His Spirit. That is, the more wholly we abide in Christ, the more our fruit will abide.

What a blessed thought. He chose you, and appointed you to bear fruit, and that your fruit should abide. He never meant one of His branches to bring forth fruit that should not abide. The deeper I enter into the purpose of His electing grace, the surer my confidence will become that I can bring forth fruit to eternal life, for myself and others. The deeper I enter into this purpose of His electing love, the more I will realize what the link is between the purpose from eternity, and the fruit to eternity: the abiding in Him. The purpose is His, He will carry it out. The fruit is His, He will bring it forth. The abiding is His, He will maintain it. Let everyone who professes to be a Christian worker, pause. Ask whether you are leaving your mark for eternity on those around you. It is not your preaching or teaching, your strength of will or power to influence, that will secure this. All depends on having your life full of God and His power. And that depends upon your living the truly branchlike life of abiding—very close and unbroken fellowship with Christ. It is the branch that abides in Him that brings forth much fruit, fruit that will abide.

Blessed Lord, reveal to my soul that you have chosen me to bear much fruit. Let this be my confidence that your purpose can be realized—you chose me. Let this be my power to forsake everything and give myself to you. You will perfect what you have begun. Draw me to dwell so much in the love and the certainty of that eternal purpose that the power of eternity may posses me, and the fruit I bear may abide. "That ye bear much fruit." Oh my heavenly vine, it is beginning to dawn upon my soul that fruit, more fruit, much fruit, abiding fruit, is the one thing you have to give me, and the one thing as branch I have to give you. Here I am. Blessed Lord, work out your purpose in me. Enable me to bear much fruit, abiding fruit, to your glory.

31

PREVAILING PRAYER

"I appointed you that ye should go and bear fruit, and
that your fruit should abide: that whatsoever ye shall ask
of the Father in my name, He may give it you"
(John 15:16).

In the first verse of our parable, Christ revealed himself
as the true vine, and the Father as the husbandman, and
asked for himself and the Father a place in our hearts. Here,
in the closing verse, He sums up all His teaching concerning
himself and the Father in the twofold purpose for which
He had chosen us. With reference to himself, the vine, the
purpose was, that we should bear fruit. With reference to
the Father, it was, that whatsoever we should ask in His
name, should be done of the Father in Heaven. As fruit is
the great proof of the true relation to Christ, so prayer is of
our relation to the Father. A fruitful abiding in the Son, and
prevailing prayer to the Father, are the two great factors in
the true Christian life.

"That whatsoever ye shall ask of the Father in my name,
he may give it you." These are the closing words of the
parable of the vine. The whole mystery of the vine and its
branches leads up to the other mystery—that whatsoever we
ask in His name the Father gives. See here the reason for
the lack of prayer, and for the lack of power in prayer. It is
because we so little live the true branch life, because we so
little lose ourselves in the vine, abiding in Him entirely, that
we feel so little constrained to much prayer, so little confident
that we shall be heard, and so do not know how to use His
name as the key to God's storehouse. The vine planted on
earth has reached up into heaven. It is only the soul that is
wholly and intensely abiding in it that can reach into Heaven

with power to prevail much. Our faith in the teaching and the truth of the parable, in the truth and the life of the vine, must prove itself by power in prayer. The life of abiding and obedience, of love and joy, of cleansing and fruit-bearing, will surely lead to the power of prevailing prayer.

"Whatsoever ye shall ask." The promise was given to disciples who were ready, in the likeness of the true vine, to give themselves for others. This promise was all their provision for their work. They took it literally, believed it, used it, and found it true. Let us give ourselves, as branches of the true vine, and in His likeness, to the work of saving sinners, of bringing forth fruit to the glory of God, and we shall find a new urgency and power to pray and to claim the "whatsoever ye shall ask." We shall waken to our wonderful responsibility of having in such a promise the keys to the King's storehouses, and we shall not rest till we have received bread and blessing for the perishing. "I have chosen you, and ordained you, that ye should go and bring forth fruit, and that your fruit should remain: that whatsoever ye shall ask of the Father in my name, he may give it you." Beloved disciple, seek above everything to be a person of prayer. Here is the highest exercise of your privilege as a branch of the vine. Here is the full proof of your being renewed in the image of God and His Son. Here is your power to show how you, like Christ, live not for yourself, but for others. Here you enter Heaven to receive gifts for men (Psalm 68:18). Here your abiding in Christ has led to His abiding in you, to use you as the channel and instrument of His grace. The power to bear fruit for men has been crowned by power to prevail with God. "I am the true vine, and my Father is the husbandman" (John 15:1). Christ's work in you is to prepare you for the Father so that His Word may be fulfilled in you: "At that day ye shall ask in my name: and I say not unto you, that I will pray the Father for you: For the Father himself loveth you" (John 16: 26-27).

323

The power of direct access to the Father for others, the liberty of intercession claiming and receiving blessing for them in faith, is the highest exercise of our union with Christ. Let all who would truly and fully be branches give themselves to the work of intercession. It is the one great work of Christ the vine in Heaven, the source of power for all His work. Make it your one great work as the branch. It will be the power of all your work.

"In my name." Yes, Lord, in your name, the new name you have given yourself here, the true vine. As a branch, abiding in you in entire devotion, in full dependence, in perfect conformity, in abiding fruitfulness, I come to the Father, in you, and He will give what I ask. Oh, let my life be one of unceasing and prevailing intercession! Amen!

THE TRUE VINE
STUDY GUIDE

1. THE VINE

1. How can you learn more about Jesus?
2. Jesus said, "I am the true vine." What should your response be to this?

2. THE HUSBANDMAN

1. What is one of the great lacks in most Christian lives?
   a. Is it lacking in yours?
2. Explain the two lessons that are taught in this meditation.
   a. How they should apply to you.

3. THE BRANCH

1. Why are you as a branch essential to the vine?
2. What is your one purpose as a branch?
3. What is absolutely necessary in order for you to perform your purpose as a branch?

4. THE FRUIT

1. What happens to the branch if it doesn't fulfill its purpose?
2. What's the object for which you've been made a member of Christ's body?
   a. Is it to keep you from going to hell?
   b. Is it to give you an abundant, prosperous, life?

5. MORE FRUIT

1. What is God's purpose in cleansing you?
2. In what specific ways has God been cleansing you personally?
3. Have you been cooperating with God's cleansing or resisting it?

6. THE CLEANSING

1. Why must every branch be pruned?
2. What happens to a branch if it isn't pruned?
3. Is pruning only to keep you from sinning?

7. THE PRUNING KNIFE

1. What is God's pruning knife?
2. How does it do its work of pruning?
3. Can God's pruning knife work without your cooperation?
   a. If so, how?
   b. If not, in what ways must you cooperate?

8. ABIDE

1. What happens when a new branch is grafted into a vine?

2. What are some of the things that happened to you when you were first grafted into Christ?

3. Why are both parts of the verse "I in you" and "abide in me" so important?

a. If you're not making the spiritual progress you think you should be making, which part do you think is missing?

9. EXCEPT YE ABIDE

1. Can you bear fruit by yourself that is acceptable to God.

a. If so, how?

b. If not, why not?

2. What essential lesson must you learn about "abiding"?

10. THE VINE

1. What must you do to fully understand what it means for Christ to be the vine?

2. How did Christ come to be the vine?

a. How did you come to be a branch?

11. YE ARE THE BRANCHES

1. What is Christ trying to get you to understand when He says, "Ye are the branches"?

2. Do you need anything more than to be a branch?
    a. If so, what?
    b. If not, why not?

12. MUCH FRUIT

1. What is the difference in Christian life between work and fruit?
    a. Which is most prominent in your Christian life?
2. What is the law of sure and abundant fruitfulness?
3. What does it mean if you're only bearing a little fruit?

13. YOU CAN DO NOTHING

1. How is your life as a branch like the Lord's life as a vine?
2. What is the basic root of a strong spiritual life?
3. Why can you do nothing apart from Christ?
    a. Truthfully, how much do you *think* you can do apart from Christ?

14. WITHERED BRANCHES

1. Are there any withered branches in your church?
    a. How can you tell?
    b. Are you one of them?
2. What do you have to do to be a fresh, green, and vigorous branch?

15. WHATSOEVER YE WILL

1. What constitutes a healthy life of a believer?
2. What are the two things that are connected to the promise of "Whatsoever ye will"?
3. What is essential to fulfill your calling to bear much fruit?

16. IF YE ABIDE

1. Why are the natural vine and branch such a true parable of the Christian life?
2. What is the secret of abiding?
   a. What is the second part of the secret of abiding?

17. THE FATHER GLORIFIED

1. How can you glorify God?
   a. What are some of the ways in which you are presently glorifying Him?
   b. On what basis do people judge a gardener?
   c. On what basis do people judge God as a husbandman?
2. Why is it necessary that you bear fruit for God?

18. TRUE DISCIPLES

1. If you do not bear much fruit, are you a true disciple of Jesus Christ?
2. What are some of the differences between those who bear much fruit and those who do not?

3. If there are two classes of disciples, in which class are you?

    a. Why are you in the class of disciple that you're in?

19. THE WONDERFUL LOVE

1. What is Christ trying to teach you by saying that His love for you is the same as the Father's love for Him?

2. In what ways did God manifest, or show, His love for Jesus?

3. In what ways does Christ show His love for you?

20. ABIDE IN MY LOVE

1. What did Jesus mean when He said, "abide in my love"?

    a. How do you abide in His love?

2. Is the Father's love for His Son a sentiment; i.e., an emotion?

    a. Is Christ's love for you a sentiment; that is, an emotion?

3. How can understanding what Jesus meant by "abide in my love" change your Christian life?

21. OBEY AND ABIDE

1. How do you enter into a life of rest and strength in Christ?

2. What does it fully mean to keep the commandments of God; i.e., does it just mean written commandments?

22. YE, EVEN AS I

1. How is Jesus' life in relation to His Father an exact model of yours in relation to Him?

2. Explain the divine connection between obeying and abiding.

23. JOY

1. What is the only way you can be a joyful Christian?

2. Do you feel that abiding in Christ is a strain or painful effort?

    a. If you do, why do you?

    b. If you don't, why don't you?

3. What is Christ's joy that He promises will be in you?

4. What is religion (Christianity) meant to be in your everyday life?

24. LOVE ONE ANOTHER

1. Why is it unnatural for Christians *not* to love one another?

2. What are some of the ways in which you can demonstrate your love for others; keeping in mind that the love that is commanded is not a sentiment or an emotion?

25. EVEN AS I HAVE LOVED YOU

1. What are some of the ways that Jesus demonstrated His love for His disciples?

a. What is the ultimate way that He demonstrated His love for you?

2. Why do so few Christians seem to understand the kind of life a branch can live?

a. What is the way to start to learn the mystery of the vine and the branch?

26. CHRIST'S FRIENDSHIP: ITS ORIGIN

1. What is the secret root and strength of everything that Christ does for us as the vine?

2. What is the greatest measure of love?

3. How should the greatest measure of love affect our everyday relationships?

a. How should it make us act toward others?

b. How should it make us respond to their faults, weaknesses, and mistakes?

27. CHRIST'S FRIENDSHIP: IT'S EVIDENCE

1. What proof did Jesus give of His love for you?

2. What proof are you to give of your love for Him?

3. Does God command you to do anything that you are not capable of doing? Explain your answer.

28. CHRIST'S FRIENDSHIP: ITS INTIMACY

1. What is the highest proof of true friendship? Explain your answer.

2. What did Jesus mean when He spoke of keeping His Father's commandments?

a. How does that relate to your keeping Christ's commandments.

3. What are some of the things that friendship involves; i.e., some of the effects of friendship, of being true friends?

29. ELECTION

1. What does election mean?
2. Do you believe in election?
  a. If you do, in what way do you believe in it; i.e., what form of election do you believe in?
3. What are some of the ways in which Christ choosing you can give you confidence and assurance?

30. ABIDING FRUIT

1. What does it mean if your fruit does not last?
a. What does fruit reveal about the tree
2. What is the secret of being fruit that abides?
3. What helps to increase your confidence that you can bring forth much fruit to eternal life, for yourself and for others? Explain your answer.

31. PREVAILING PRAYER

1. What is the twofold purpose for which Christ has chosen you as a branch?
2. What is the basic reason for the lack of prayer and the lack of power in prayer?
  a. Do you pray much?
  b. Do you have power in prayer?

    c. What percentage of your prayers are answered?

3. What are the keys to God's storehouse?

4. What should you seek to be above all else?

    a. Why is it the highest exercise of your privilege as a branch of the vine?

    b. Why is it full proof of your being renewed in the image of God and His Son?

5. What are the three parts of the highest exercise of your union with Christ?

BIOGRAPHICAL ENTRIES

Ambrose, Saint (c. 340–397) When the bishop of Milan died, a dispute over his replacement was causing violence. Ambrose intervened to calm both sides. In the process, he impressed everyone so much that while he was still an unbaptized catechumen, he was chosen to fill the position of bishop. He resisted, claiming that he was not worthy, but to prevent further violence, he agreed , and on December 7, 374 he was baptized, ordained as a priest, and consecrated as bishop. Among other things for which he is noted, he counseled Augustine of Hippo in religious matters and baptized him and brought him into the Roman Church. As the Roman Catholic bishop of Milan, he became one of the most eminent bishops of the 4th century. Together with Augustine, Jerome, and Gregory I, he is considered to be one of the four doctors of the West of ancient Roman Church history. He died on April 4, 397.

Augustine, Saint (345-430) Augustine of Hippo was born in North Africa to a devoutly Christian mother and pagan father. He was given Christian instruction but waited until later in life to be baptized. Augustine's sexual appetite drove him to seek pleasure where he could find it, but also plagued his conscience. His hunger for religious things led him to many of the belief systems of the day. Augustine finally turned to God in 386 when he heard a child say, "Take, read" a copy of Paul's letter to the Romans. Upon his conversion to Christianity, Augustine became a prodigious writer, with his writing standing second only to the apostle Paul in their impact on the Church. Augustine was born on November 13, 354, in Tagaste, Algeria. He died on August 28, 430, in Hippo Regius, Algeria.

For more information about St. Augustine, see the Pure Gold Classic *Confessions of Augustine*, published by Bridge-Logos Publishers.

Browne, Sir Thomas Thomas Browne was born in London on October, 19, 1605. He graduated with an M.A. from Broadgates Hall, Oxford (1629). He then studied medicine privately and worked as an assistant to an Oxford doctor. Later he attended the Universities of Montpellier and Padua, and in 1633 he graduated as an M.D. at Leiden. His medical education in Europe also earned him an M.D. from Oxford. In 1637 he moved to Norwich, where he lived and practiced medicine until his death in 1682. As an author of varied material in medicine, science, and religion, Browne first came to the attention of readers with his best known work, *Religio medici*, which is about his personal Christian faith. He wrote it around 1635, and in 1642 it was published without his consent. The next year he approved a new printing, however, and the book became a best-seller, and was translated into several European languages.

Bushnell, Horace (1802–1876) Horace Bushnell was an American Congregational clergyman and theologian. Bushnell was a born on April 14, 1802 in the village of Bantam, township of Litchfield, Connecticut. He graduated from Yale in 1827, was literary editor of the New York Journal of Commerce from 1828–1829, and in 1829 became a tutor at Yale. Here he initially studied law, but in 1831 he entered the theology department of Yale College. In May, 1833 Bushnell was ordained pastor of the North Congregational church in Hartford, Connecticut, where he remained until 1859, when he resigned his pastorate because of continued poor health. He held no official office after that, but he was a prolific author and occasionally preached. He died on February 17, 1876, in Hartford, Connecticut.

Carey, William (1761-1834) Carey was born in a small thatched cottage in Paulerspury, a typical Northamptonshire village in England, August 17, 1761, of a weaver's family. From this humble beginning, and more trained by God than by men, he became a scholar, linguist, and missionary. After pastoring for a short time, he went to India, where he remained for the next 41 years serving the Lord and translating the Scriptures into several languages. In a letter to a friend he wrote, "The work of translation is going on, and I hope the whole New Testament and the five books of Moses may be completed before this reaches you. It is a pleasant work and a rich reward, and I trust, whenever it is published, it will soon prevail, and put down all the Shastras of the Hindus. ... The translation of the Scriptures I look upon to be one of the greatest desiderata in the world, and it has accordingly occupied a considerable part of my time and attention."

One of his biographers wrote this about Carey: "He ... was almost single handed in conquering the prevailing indifference and hostility to missionary effort; Carey developed a plan for missions, and printed his amazing Enquiry; he influenced timid and hesitating men to take steps to the evangelizing of the world." Another wrote of him, "Taking his life as a whole, it is not too much to say that he was the greatest and most versatile Christian missionary sent out in modern times." On his deathbed Carey called out to a missionary friend, "Dr.

Duff! You have been speaking about Dr. Carey; when I am gone, say nothing about Dr. Carey—speak about Dr. Carey's God." He died in Serampore, India, on June 9, 1834.

Chapman, Wilbur Dr. Wilbur Chapman (1859-1918) was an American Presbyterian evangelist, revivalist and pastor. He was also a song writer and wrote the words to the hymns One *Day, Jesus!, What A Friend for Sinners (Our Great Saviour),* and *'Tis Jesus.* He conducted evangelistic campaigns in Canada, Hawaii, the Fiji Islands, Australia, New Zealand, England, Scotland, Japan, Tasmania, and the Philippine Islands. He was born in Richmond, Indiana, on June 17, 1859, and died in New York City, New York, on December 25, 1918.

Coleridge, Samuel Taylor Samuel Taylor Coleridge (1772–1834) was an English poet, critic, and philosopher who, along with his friend William Wordsworth, was one of the founders of the Romantic Movement in England and one of the Lake Poets (so called because they lived in the English Lake District of Cumberland and Westmorland—now Cumbria). Coleridge was born on October 21, 1772 in the rural town of Ottery St Mary, Devonshire, England. He was the youngest of ten children, and his father, the Reverend John Coleridge, was a well respected vicar in the Anglican Church. Coleridge suffered from constant ridicule by his older brother Frank, partially due to jealousy, as Samuel was often praised and favored by his parents. To escape this abuse from critics, he frequently sought refuge at a local library, which led him to discover his passion for poetry. He is probably best known for his long narrative poem, *The Rime of the Ancient Mariner.* He died of heart failure in Highgate, London, England, on July 25, 1834.

Edwards, Jonathan (1703–1758) Jonathan Edwards was a colonial Congregational preacher and theologian. He is known as one of the greatest and most profound of American theologians and revivalists. Although his theological and doctrinal work is varied, he is often associated with his defense of Calvinist theology and the Puritan heritage. He best-known sermon is probably "Sinners in the Hands of Angry God." When he preached this sermon, sinners fainted and strong men hung on to the church pillars, certain that they were about to plunge into a fiery hell. It was these manifestations that got Edwards involved in a controversy over "bodily effects" of the Holy Spirit's presence. In 1734-1735, Edwards oversaw some of the initial stirrings of the First Great Awakening, and ministered often with the great English evangelist, George Whitefield. He gained international fame as a revivalist and "theologian of the heart" after publishing A *Faithful Narrative of the Surprising Work of God* in 1738, which described a spiritual awakening in his church. He was born on October 5, 1703, and died on March 22, 1758.

For more information about Jonathan Edwards, see the Pure Gold Classic *Sinners in the Hands of an Angry God*, published by Bridge-Logos Publishers.

Fry, Caroline (1787-1846), Caroline Fry was a British Christian writer. She was born at Tunbridge Wells in Kent on December 31, 1787—one of ten children born to John and Jane Fry. She married William Wilson at Desford, Leicestershire on 26 May, 1831. Fry's family was affiliated with the High Church in the Church of England. After Fry's conversion experience in 1822, which she wrote about in her autobiography and also in her book. *Christ Our Example*, she produced an impressive list of publications over the remaining years of her life. Fry was an Anglican theologian, writer, poet and Christian educator who wrote from a Reformed perspective on a variety of theological issues. She died in Tunbridge Wells on September 17, 1846.

Gordon, Adoniram Judson (1836 – 1895) A. J. Gordon was born in New Hampshire on April 13, 1836. He was saved when he was fifteen, and expressed a desire to go into the ministry when he was sixteen. In 1856 he attended Brown University and in 1860 entered Newton Theological Seminary. When he graduated in 1863, he accepted a pastorate at a church in Jamaica Plain near Boston. He stayed there for six years, and then went to pastor the Clarendon Street Baptist Church in Boston. The church was in a low spiritual condition for several years, and then Dwight L. Moody came to Boston and set up a temporary tabernacle across the street. Revival came to Boston and to the Clarendon Street Baptist Church, where it never stopped. Under Gordon's leadership, the Clarendon Street Baptist Church became "one of the most spiritual and aggressive in America." For years he was a favorite speaker in Moody's great Northfield conventions. During his ministry, Gordon wrote several hymns and books. One of his most successful books was *The Ministry of the Holy Spirit*. In it, Dr. Gordon wrote, "It seems clear from the Scriptures that it is still the duty and privilege of believers to receive the Holy Spirit by a conscious, definite, act of appropriating faith, just as they received Jesus Christ." He also wrote *The Ministry of Healing*, a highly revered book on physical, mental, and spiritual healing. Dr. Gordon died on February 2, 1895.

Hyde, John (1865-1912) John Hyde was a missionary to India who became known worldwide for his concentrated prayer life and the hundreds of sinners that were brought to Christ by his prayers. His ministry of prayer in India during the next 20 years was such that the natives referred to him as "the man who never sleeps." Some termed him "the apostle of prayer." But more familiarly he was known as "the praying Hyde." He was all these and more, for deep in India's Punjab he envisioned his Master, and face to face with the Eternal he learned lessons of prayer that were amazing. Often he spent 30 days and nights in prayer, and many times was on his knees in deep intercession for 36 hours at a time. His work among the villages was very successful, in that for many years he won four to ten people a day to the Lord Jesus Christ. Because of his prayers, revival sweep through the Punjab region and many other parts of India. Praying Hyde was born on November 9, 1865 in Carrollton, Illinois, and died on February 17, 1912. His last words were "Shout the victory of Jesus Christ!" Before his death, he shared what God had once shown him while he was in prayer.

"On the day of prayer, God gave me a new experience. I seemed to be away above our conflict here in the Punjab and I saw God's great battle in all India, and then away out beyond in China, Japan, and Africa. I saw how we had been thinking in narrow circles of our own countries and in our own denominations, and how God was now rapidly joining force to force and line to line, and all was beginning to be one great struggle. That, to me, means the great triumph of Christ. We must exercise the greatest care to be utterly obedient to Him who sees all the battlefield all the time. It is only He who can put each man in the place where his life can count for the most.

For more information about the praying life of John Hyde, see the book, *Praying Hyde: Apostle of Prayer*, published by Bridge-Logos Publishers.

Knox, John (1514?-1572) John Knox was a Scottish religious reformer who took the lead in reforming the Church in

Scotland along Calvinist lines. He is considered to be the greatest Reformer in the history of Scotland, and is widely regarded as the father of the Protestant Reformation in Scotland and of the Church of Scotland. Knox is generally credited with having prayed, "Give me Scotland or I die." But it was his son-in-law, the godly John Welch—who prayed 5 to 6 hours a day, who actually prayed it. The exact place and date of John Knox's birth is not known with certainty, but it is generally accepted to be Giffordgate, 16 miles east of Edinburgh, in either 1513 or 1514. His father was William Knox, who fought at the Battle of Flodden, and his mother was an educated woman named Sinclair. Knox wrote *The History of the Reformation in Scotland*. He died in Edinburgh on November 24, 1572.

Law, William (1686-1761) In 1711 law became a Fellow of Emmanuel College, Cambridge, and was ordained there. He resided at Cambridge, teaching and preaching, until the accession of George I in 1714, when his conscience prevented him from taking the oaths of allegiance to the new government, which was of the House of Hanover; for it would have required him to give up his allegiance to the House of Stuarts. Because of this he could no longer serve as a university teacher or parish minister. Being thus deprived of his livelihood, he became a private tutor to the children of Edward Gibbon, the grandfather of the historian, Edward Gibbon (*The History of the Decline and Fall of the Roman Empire*). He resided with them for ten years.

Since he was now forbidden the use of the pulpit and the lecture-hall, Law preached through his books. These include *Christian Perfection, the Grounds and Reasons of Christian Regeneration, Spirit of Prayer, the Way to Divine Knowledge, Spirit of Love,* and best-known of all, *A Serious Call To a Devout and Holy Life*, published in 1728. The theme of this book is that God calls us to a life of complete obedience that is centered in Him. In it, Law wrote, "If you will here stop and ask yourself why you are not as pious as the primitive Christians were, your own heart will tell you that it is neither through ignorance nor inability, but because you never thoroughly intended it." Law died in 1761 just a few days after his last book, *An Affectionate Address to the Clergy*, went to the printers.

Lawrence, Brother (1611-1691) Brother Lawrence was born Nicholas Herman in Hériménil, near Lunéville in the region of Lorraine, located in modern day eastern France. When he was 18, he became what was known as a religious person and soon decided that he wanted to enter a religious order. In the meantime he fought in the Thirty Years' War and later served as a valet. When he was 24 he joined the Discalced Carmelite Priory in Paris as a lay brother because he did not have the education necessary to become a cleric. He took the religious name Lawrence of the Resurrection. He spent the rest of his life within the walls of the priory, occasionally traveling outside on errands. He worked in the kitchen for most of his life, and then repaired shoes when he was no longer able to do kitchen work. He is best known, however, for the profound peace that he developed. His fame spread wide and far, so much so that even the Pope is said to have visited him to learn what he did to have such peace. He shared what he learned in conversations and in letters, which later became the basis for the book, *The Practice of the Presence of God*. The book was compiled after he died by one of those whom he inspired, Father Joseph de Beaufort, later vicar general to the Archbishop of Paris. It became popular among Catholics and Protestants alike, with John Wesley and A. W. Tozer being among those who recommended it. Brother Lawrence died on February 12, 1691.

For more information about Brother Lawrence, see the Pure Gold Classic *The Practice of the Presence of God*, published by Bridge-Logos Publishers.

Luther, Martin (1483-1546) Martin Luther was a German monk, priest, professor, theologian, and church reformer. His teachings inspired the Reformation and deeply influenced the doctrines and culture of the Lutheran and Protestant traditions, as well as the course of Western civilization. In the beginning of his religious life, Luther dedicated himself to monastic life, devoting himself to fasts, long hours in prayer, pilgrimage, and frequent confession. He tried to please God through this dedication, but it only increased his awareness of his own sinfulness. He would later remark, "If anyone could have gained heaven as a monk, then I would indeed have been among them." Luther described this period of his life as one of deep spiritual despair. He said, "I lost hold of Christ the Savior and Comforter and made of him a stockmaster and hangman over my poor soul."

Then, in God's providence, Luther lectured on the Psalms, Hebrews, Romans and Galatians from 1510 to 1520. As he studied these books of the Bible, penance and righteousness took on new life. Soon he was teaching that salvation is a gift of God's grace in Christ and is received by faith alone. The first and chief article is this, Luther wrote, "Jesus Christ, our God and Lord, died for our sins and was raised again for our justification. ... therefore, it is clear and certain that this faith alone justifies us. ... nothing of this article can be yielded or surrendered, even though heaven, earth, and everything else falls."

As the Holy Spirit opened his eyes and heart more clearly to the truth in God's word, he began to see the evils that now permeated the Roman Church, especially in relation to the salvation of souls, and in the selling of indulgences to gain their release from a purgatory that Luther now doubted even existed. So on October 31, 1517, he wrote to Albert, Archbishop of Mainz and Magdeburg, protesting the sale of indulgences in his episcopal territories and inviting him to a formal debate on the matter. He enclosed his 95 Theses, a copy of which, according to tradition, he posted the same day on the door of the Castle Church in Wittenberg. This protest was the catalyst of the separation of Luther from the Roman Catholic Church and the start of the Protestant Reformation. Luther was born on November 10, 1483, and died on February 18, 1546.

For more information about Martin Luther, see the Pure Gold Classic *Table Talk*, published by Bridge-Logos Publishers.

Martyn, Henry (1781-1512) Henry Martyn was born on February 18, 1781, in Turro, Cornwall, England. He studied at Cambridge and became the University's best undergraduate mathematician. He also had a considerable ability in learning languages. Under the encouragement of Charles Simeon, his spiritual father, he abandoned his intention of going into law and instead went to India as a chaplain in 1806. In India he translated the New Testament into Hindi and Persian, revised an Arabic translation of the New Testament, and translated the Psalter into Persian and the Prayer Book into Hindi. In 1811 he left India for Persia, hoping to do further translations and to improve his existing ones, there and in Arabia. But travel in those days was extremely hazardous and he was in poor health. He did not survive the trip. There was a plague raging in Tokat, Turkey, and he became ill and died there on October 16, 1812. Whether from the plague or from the difficulties of the trip is not known.

Moody, Dwight Lyman (1837-1899) Dwight Lyman Moody, also known as D.L. Moody, was an American evangelist and publisher who founded the Moody Church, Northfield School, Mount Hermon School in Massachusetts (now the Northfield Mount Hermon School), Moody Bible Institute, and Moody Publishers. He was born in Northfield, Massachusetts, to a large family. His father, a small farmer and stone mason, was an alcoholic and died at the age of 41 when Moody was only four years old. His mother struggled to support her family, but some of her eight children still had to be sent away to work for their room and board. Moody was one of them.

When he was 17, he moved to Boston to work in his uncle's shoe store. One of his uncle's requirements was that Moody attend the Congregational Church of Mount Vernon. In April 1855 he was converted to evangelical Christianity when his teacher talked to him about how much God loved him. When he applied, however, for church membership in May 1855, he was rejected. His Sunday-school teacher, Mr. Edward Kimball, said about him, "I can truly say, and in saying it I magnify the infinite grace of God as bestowed upon him, that I have seen few persons whose minds were spiritually darker than was his when he came into my Sunday-school class; and I think that the committee of the Mount Vernon Church seldom met an applicant for membership more unlikely ever to become a Christian of clear and decided views of Gospel truth, still less to fill any extended sphere of public usefulness. Mr. Moody remained in my class for two years, until he bade me good-bye on leaving Boston for Chicago."

In Chicago, Moody joined the Plymouth Congregational Church, and began to take an active part in the prayer meetings. In the spring of 1857 he began to minister to the welfare of the sailors in Chicago's port, then gamblers and thieves in the saloons. He brought so many into the church that the church's Sunday School became the largest of that time. It became so well known that the just-elected President Lincoln visited and spoke at a Sunday School meeting on November 25, 1860.

It was during a trip to England in Spring 1872 that Moody first gained his reputation as an evangelist. In England, Scotland, and Ireland His preaching had an impact as great as that of George Whitefield and John Wesley. Seldom did his meetings have less than 2000 people, and it's reported that at one gigantic meeting there were nearly 30,000 people. This turnout continued throughout 1874 and 1875, with crowds of thousands at all of his meetings. When he returned to the United States, crowds of 12,000 to 20,000 were just as common as in England. His evangelistic meetings were held from Boston to New York, throughout New England and as far as San Francisco, and other West coast towns from Vancouver to San Diego. Before long, Moody's name and reputation as the world's greatest evangelist of the 19th Century was known throughout the world. Moody was born on February 5, 1837, and died on December 22, 1899.

For more information about Dwight L. Moody, see the Pure Gold Classic books *All of Grace* and *Secret Power*, published by Bridge-Logos Publishers.

Moule, H.C.G. (Handley Carr Glyn) (1841-1920) Bishop Moule was the youngest of eight sons of the vicar of Fordington, Dorchester. He was educated at home with his brothers prior to attending university at Cambridge, where he excelled in his studies. He was ordained in 1867 and was curate at Fordington before being appointed as sub-dean of Trinity College, Cambridge in 1873. He became first principal of Ridley Hall Theological College, Cambridge, in

1881, and Norrisian Professor of Divinity in 1899. In 1901, he succeeded B.F. Westcott as Bishop of Durham. Although an evangelical, he was closely associated with the Keswick Convention, which often featured Hannah Whitall Smith as a speaker. Moule wrote many hymns and poems; and his works include expositions and commentaries on nearly all the Epistles, as well as books on devotion and a down-to-earth work on theology, *Outlines of Christian Doctrine.*

Mueller, George (1805-1898) Born in Prussia on September 27, 1805, George Mueller began running from God early in life. By age ten he had devised a scheme to embezzle government money entrusted to his father. He spent his schooldays in drunken immorality. He even served time in jail at age sixteen for failing to pay his bills. The university he attended had some 900 divinity students, but Mueller said there were not nine of them who truly feared God. He continued his sinful habits during his college days until finally at age 20 the burden of his sins overcame him and he trusted Christ as his Savior.

About this, Mueller wrote the British Christian, of August 14, 1902, "I became a believer in the Lord Jesus in the beginning of November 1825, now sixty-nine years and eight months. For the first four years afterwards, it was for a good part in great weakness; but in July, 1829, now sixty-six years since, it came with me to an entire and full surrender of heart. I gave myself fully to the Lord. Honors, pleasures, money, my physical powers, my mental powers, all were laid down at the feet of Jesus, and I became a great lover of the Word of God. I found my all in God, and thus in all my trials of a temporal and spiritual character, it has remained for sixty-six years. My faith is not merely exercised regarding temporal things, but regarding everything, because I cleave to the Word. My knowledge of God and His Word is that which helps me."

J. Gilchrist Lawson, Mueller's biographer, wrote about him, "Among the greatest monuments of what can be accomplished through simple faith in God are the great orphanages covering thirteen acres of ground on Ashley Downs, Bristol, England. When God put it into the heart of George Muller to build these orphanages, he had only two shillings (50 cents) in his pocket. Without making his wants known to any man, but to God alone, over a million, four hundred thousand pounds were sent to him for the building and maintaining of these orphan homes. When the writer first visited them, near the time of Mr. Muller's death, there were five immense buildings of solid granite, capable of accommodating two thousand orphans. In all the years since the first orphans arrived the Lord had sent food in due time, so that they had never missed a meal for want of food."

All that was accomplished without asking anyone but God for what he needed; even to the extent of withholding publication of annual financial reports if they indicated he needed money. It is said that in his Journals, Mueller recorded specific answers to over 50,000 specific prayers. On the morning of March 10, 1898, he was found dead on the floor of the apartment where he lived in one of the orphanages.

Slessor, Mary (1848-1915) Mary Slessor was born in Aberdeen, Scotland, on December 2, 1848. Her father was a shoemaker who early in their life became addicted to alcohol and abandoned his family and left them in poverty. When Mary was 14, she went to work in a factory to help support her family. She stayed there until she was twenty eight. She then offered her services to the Foreign Missions Board of the Scottish Presbyterian Church. They accepted her and sent her to Calabar in Nigeria, where she ministered for the rest of her life. Although she helped everyone who needed help, her chief ministry was to abused women and children. Though only five-feet tall, she had a forceful personality and stood up to many warriors, chiefs, witch doctors, and murderers. She provided medical treatment for hundreds of people; rescued prisoners, slaves, and wives from being murdered; saved and cared for hundreds of babies and children; settled disputes among people and tribes; and witnessed to murderous and barbaric tribes and individuals wherever she could, telling them about the love of Jesus for them. She died on January 13, 1915 of a jungle disease. Her daughter Janie and dozens of her African *children* were there to comfort her.

Smith, Hannah Whitall (1832-1911) Hannah Whitall Smith was an American evangelist and reformer, a major public speaker and writer in the Holiness movement in the United States and the Higher Life movement in Great Britain and Ireland. She was also active in the Women's Suffrage movement and the Temperance movement. She was born on February 7, 1832 in Philadelphia, and died on May 1, 1911 in Iffley [near Oxford], England. She was married to Robert Pearsall Smith. Both were from prominent and influential Quaker families in the New Jersey and Philadelphia region. She wrote two successful books that are still widely read today: *The Christian's Secret of a Happy Life* and *The God of All Comfort*. Both of these are included in the Pure Gold Classic collection published by Bridge-Logos Publishers.

Spurgeon, Charles Haddon (1834-1892) C. H. Spurgeon, as he is commonly known, was born on June 19, 1834 in Kelvedon, Essex, England. He was converted to Christianity on January 6, 1850 at the age of fifteen. On his way to a scheduled appointment, a snow storm forced him to turn into a Primitive Methodist chapel in Colchester for shelter where, in his own words, "God opened my heart to the salvation message." The text that moved him was Isaiah 45:22—"Look unto me, and be ye saved, all the ends of the earth, for I am

God, and there is none else." On April 4, 1850, Spurgeon was admitted to the church in Newmarket. He was baptized in the river Lark at Isleham on May 3 of that year. Later that same year he moved to Cambridge, where he preached his first sermon in 1851.

In 1854, just four years after his conversion, Spurgeon, then only 20, became pastor of London's famed New Park Street Church (formerly pastored by the famous Baptist theologian John Gill). The congregation quickly outgrew their building, moved to Exeter Hall, then to Surrey Music Hall. On January 8, 1856, he married Susannah, daughter of Robert Thompson of Falcon Square, London, by whom he had twin sons, Charles and Thomas, on September 20, 1856. Spurgeon was England's best-known preacher for most of the second half of the nineteenth century. He died on January 31, 1892.

For more information about C.H. Spurgeon and his ministry, see the Pure Gold Classic books *Morning by Morning* and *Evening by Evening*. Also see *Spurgeon Gold* by Ray Comfort. All published by Bridge-Logos Publishers.

Stanley, Henry Morton (1841-1904) Henry Morton Stanley was born to John Rowlands and Elisabeth Parry on January 28, 1841. His parents were not married, and his mother soon abandoned him. At seventeen, he ran away to sea and landed in New Orleans. There he gave himself a new name. First he was known as "J. Rolling", but eventually he settled on Henry Morton Stanley after the cotton broker Henry Stanley, for whom he worked in New Orleans. After serving in the army during the civil war, he became a free-lance journalist and eventually a reporter for the New York Herald. He became famous for his search for David Livingstone and his exploration of Africa. According to his journal, when he finally found Livingstone, he walked up to him and asked, "Dr. Livingstone, I presume?" Whether Stanley actually said this is disputed, but still often quoted. He became Sir Henry Morton Stanley when he was made a Knight Grand Cross of the Order of the Bath in 1899, in recognition of his service to the British Empire in Africa. He died in London on May 10, 1904.

Torrey, R. A. Reuben Archer Torrey (1856–1928), was an American evangelist, pastor, educator, and writer. He was born in Hoboken, New Jersey, on January 28, 1856. In 1875 he graduated from Yale University, and three years later from Yale Divinity School. Immediately following graduation he became a Congregational minister in Garrettsville, Ohio, where he met and married Clara Smith in October, 1879. From 1881 to 1893, they had five children.

In 1882 and 1883 Torrey took advanced studies of theology at Leipzig University and Erlangen University in Germany. Then in 1889, he joined Dwight L. Moody in his evangelistic work in Chicago, and became superintendent of the Bible Institute of the Chicago Evangelization Society (now Moody Bible Institute). Five years later, he became pastor of the Chicago Avenue Church (now The Moody Church). He served as a chaplain with the YMCA in both the Spanish-American War and World War I. For over twenty years Torrey and his song leader Charles Alexander held highly successful evangelistic services in almost every English-speaking country in the world. During this same period, he wrote over forty books. Because of failing health, he held his last evangelistic meeting in 1927. He died at home in Asheville, North Carolina, on October 26, 1928.

Wesley, John (1703-1791) John Wesley was an Anglican clergyman, evangelist, and cofounder of Methodism. The

15th child of a former nonconformist minister (his father was the rector of Epworth, Lincolnshire, when John was born), he graduated from Oxford University and became a priest in the Church of England in 1728. From 1729 he participated in a religious study group in Oxford organized by his brother Charles (1707-1788). Its members, which included George Whitefield, were dubbed "Methodists" for their emphasis on methodical study and devotion. The group was also known as the Holy Club. His brother Charles wrote over 9000 hymns and poems during his lifetime.

In 1735 John Wesley and his brother Charles became missionaries in America. After three unsuccessful years with the English settlers in Georgia, Wesley returned to England and joined George Whitefield in Bristol. Wesley's passionate sermons upset the local clergy and he found their pulpits closed to him. To overcome this problem in 1739 Wesley built a Methodist Chapel in Bristol. At Whitefield's urgings, Wesley also gave sermons in the open-air. It wasn't long before thousands were flocking to their meetings. Then when Whitefield went to America for evangelistic meetings, and to convert the heathens, both of which were highly successful, Wesley became the leader of the revival in England and brought the converts into his fold. By the end of his life, it is estimated the Methodist movement had over 76,000 members. Wesley was born on June 17, 1703, and died on March 2, 1791.

For more information about John Wesley, see the Pure Gold Classic book *The Holy Spirit & Power*, published by Bridge-Logos Publishers.

Whitefield, George (1714-1770) George Whitefield was born on December 16, 1714 in Gloucester, England. He was educated at Oxford and was a member of the Wesley brothers *Holy Club*. He was the originator of open-air preaching in England, and convinced John Wesley to take his place in the field while he went on a evangelistic mission to America. Wesley resisted at first, believing that ministers should only preach in buildings, but finally gave in and was highly successful at it. So much so, that when Whitefield returned from America he discovered that Wesley had taken over the Evangelical Revival that had originally started under his open-air preaching. Nevertheless, Whitefield was a major contributor to the revival on both sides of the Atlantic—the one attributed to John Wesley in England, and the Great American Awakening that originated with Jonathan Edwards in America.

Whitefield was a better preacher and theologian than Wesley, but did not have Wesley's talent for organizing. Lord Bolingbrook (1678-1751) said about Whitefield, "The most extraordinary man of our times." And Charles H. Spurgeon said about him, "Often as I have read his life, I am conscious of a distinct quickening whenever I turn to it. He lived. Other men seemed to be only half alive; but Whitefield was all life, fire, wind, force. My own model, if I may have such a thing in due subordination to my Lord, is George Whitefield; but with unequal footsteps must I follow in his glorious track." Whitefield died on September 30, 1770 in Newburyport, Massachusetts.

For more information about George Whitefield and his ministry see the book, *Whitefield Gold* by Ray Comfort, published by Bridge-Logos Publishers.

Zinzendorf, Count Nikolaus (1700-1760) Nikolaus Ludwig von Zinzendorf und von Pottendorf, Imperial Count of Zinzendorf and Pottendorf, German religious and social reformer, founder and bishop of the Moravian Church, was born at Dresden on May 26, 1700. The Moravians and Count Zinzendorf were noted for their devotion to Jesus Christ. To them, loving fellowship with Christ was the essential manifestation of the Christian life. Throughout the Count's life, "His blessed presence" was his all consuming theme. His life-motto and constant confession was, "I have one passion; it is Jesus, Jesus only." The Moravians became noted for their zeal for souls and for prayer.

Although the Baptist missionary William Carey is often referred to as the "Father of Modern Missions," the Moravians were on the mission field some fifty years earlier than Carey, and he himself credited Zinzendorf with that role. In 1727, the Moravians had a great revival that swept hundreds into God's kingdom. Out of that revival came constant prayer. Rev. John Greenfield, a Moravian evangelist, wrote, "Was there ever in the whole of Church history such an astonishing prayer meeting as that which was started by the Moravians in 1727? It was known as the *Hourly Intercession*. By relays of brothers and sisters, prayer without ceasing was made to God twenty-four hours a day for all the work and wants of His Church—not just for several days or for a week or month but for 100 years." Zinzendorf was born on May 26, 1700, and died on May 9, 1760.

INDEX

A

A. J. Gordon 340
abiding 264, 269, 276, 277, 278, 279, 280, 281, 284, 285, 287, 288, 289, 292, 293, 295, 297, 300, 301, 303, 305, 306, 307, 310, 321, 322, 323, 324, 327, 329, 331
Ambrose 335
angels 294
assurance 248, 269, 273, 281, 289, 302, 311, 319, 333
Augustine 335, 336

B

blessing 250, 259, 262, 273, 274, 287, 291, 293, 300, 301, 307, 308, 323, 324
Brother Lawrence 343, 344
Browne, Sir Thomas 336
Bushnell, Horace 336

C

Carey, William 355
Chapman, Wilbur 338
China 341
Christ-like love 309
church 247, 309, 328, 337, 339, 340, 344, 346, 347, 351
Church of England 339, 353
cleansing 271, 272, 273, 274, 275, 278, 297, 323, 326
Coleridge, Samuel Taylor 338
compassion 295
confidence 259, 263, 264, 266, 273, 275, 278, 282, 287, 319, 321, 333
consecration 265, 302

counsel
    of God 317
Cross 352

D

David 351
disciples 264, 280, 282, 286, 290, 296, 297, 308, 309, 312,
        316, 317, 323, 330, 331
divine
    life 262, 278, 286, 300, 312
    love 298, 299, 300, 307, 312, 315
    warning 269
doubt 287

E

Edinburgh 342
Edwards, Jonathan 339, 354
eternal security 319
eternity 313, 319, 320, 321
evil 249, 250

F

failure 300, 309, 310, 338
faith
    simple 295, 349
faithfulness 259, 319
fellowship 251, 305, 307, 315, 317, 321, 355
friend 315, 316, 317, 337, 338
friendship 312, 313, 314, 315, 316, 332, 333
fruit
    of the Spirit 284
fruitfulness 245, 259, 285, 287, 297, 324, 328
Fry, Caroline 339

G

glorified 262, 293, 294, 295, 296
glory 243, 261, 263, 267, 269, 271, 273, 280, 287, 291, 294, 295, 297, 298, 304, 311, 312, 321, 323
good works 284, 287
Gordon, A. J. 340

H

heaven 250, 261, 262, 278, 279, 322, 344
helplessness 264, 272, 287
holiness 308
Holy Spirit 248, 249, 262, 263, 272, 274, 279, 280, 282, 285, 290, 299, 308, 312, 313, 316, 317, 339, 340, 344, 353
humility 282, 317, 319
Hyde, John 340, 341

I

infirmities 274
in His name 291, 322
intercession 324, 341
intercessor 293

J

Jesus Christ 248, 251, 294, 329, 340, 341, 344, 355

L

life
    divine 262, 278, 286, 300, 312
love
    Christ-like 309
    divine 298, 299, 300, 307, 312, 315
Luther, Martin 344, 345

M

Martyn, Henry 345
ministry
    of prayer 340
Moody, Dwight L. 340, 346, 347, 352
Muller, George 349

O

obedience 276, 278, 283, 288, 293, 302, 303, 304, 305, 309,
    311, 312, 314, 315, 317, 319, 323, 343

P

Pentecost 317
planting
    of God 263, 281
praise 319
prayer
    for healing 249
    prevailing 322, 323
prayer meeting 355
preacher 339, 351, 354
presence
    of God 249
pride 274
pruning 263, 271, 272, 273, 274, 278, 284, 287, 326

R

resting 277, 282, 289, 298
revival 341, 353, 354, 355

S

salvation 268, 270, 295, 308, 318, 344, 345, 350
Satan 291
self-will 278

Sermon on the Mount 274
sinners 268, 269, 270, 285, 291, 295, 307, 323, 339, 340
Slessor, Mary 349
Spirit
    fruit of the 284
spiritual life 249, 250, 286, 328
Spurgeon, C.H. 350
St. Augustine 336
Stanley, Sir. H. M. 351, 352
storehouse
    of God 322, 334

T

temptation 288
Torrey, R. A. 352

V

victory 250, 341
vineyard 264, 294
vision 280

W

warning
    divine 269
Whitall Smith, Hannah 348, 350
Whitefield, George 339, 347, 353, 354
wisdom of men 288, 320
Word of God 250, 273, 274, 348
worship 259, 262, 283, 299, 301

Z

Zinzendorf, Count Nikolaus 354, 355

Pure Gold Classics

AN
EXPANDING
COLLECTION
OF THE
BEST-LOVED
CHRISTIAN
CLASSICS OF
ALL TIME.

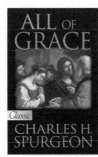

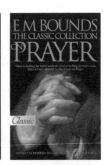

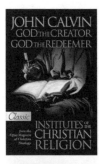

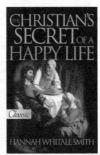

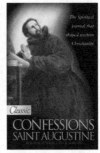

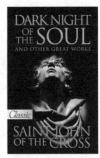

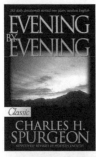

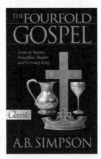

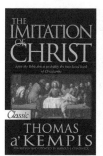
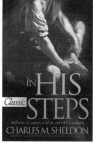
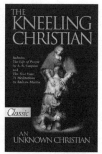

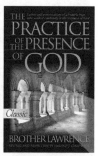
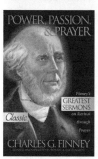
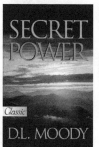
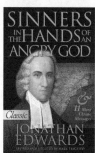

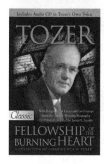

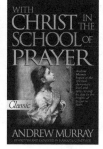
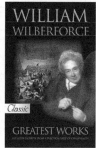

Pure Gold Classics

CHRISTIAN CLASSICS

A classic is a work of enduring excellence; a Christian classic is a work of enduring excellence that is filled with divine wisdom, biblical revelation, and insights that are relevant to living a godly life. Such works are both spiritual and practical. Our Pure Gold Classics contain some of the finest examples of Christian writing that have ever been published, including the works of John Foxe, Charles Spurgeon, D.L. Moody, Martin Luther, John Calvin, Saint John of the Cross, E.M. Bounds, John Wesley, Andrew Murray, Hannah Whitall Smith, and many others.

The timeline on the following pages will help you to understand the context of the times in which these extraordinary books were written and the historical events that must have served to influence these great writers to create works that will always stand the test of time. Inspired by God, many of these authors did their work in difficult times and during periods of history that were not sympathetic to their message. Some even had to endure great persecution, misunderstanding, imprisonment, and martyrdom as a direct result of their writing.

The entries that are printed in green type will give you a good overview of Christian history from the birth of Jesus to modern times.

The entries in red pertain to writers of Christian classics from Saint Augustine, who wrote his *Confessions* and *City of God*, to Charles Sheldon, twentieth-century author of *In His Steps*.

Entries in black provide a clear perspective on the development of secular history from the early days of Buddhism (first century) through the Civil Rights Movement.

Finally, the blue entries highlight secular writers and artists, including Chaucer, Michelangelo, and others.

Our color timeline will provide you with a fresh perspective of history, both secular and Christian, and the classics, both secular and Christian. This perspective will help you to understand each author better and to see the world through his or her eyes.